Readings in

Individualized Educational Programs

Robert Piazza
*Assistant Professor Department of Special Education,
Southern Connecticut State College, New Haven, Connecticut.*

Irving Newman
*Assistant Professor and Coordinator of the Mentally
Retarded and Severely/Profoundly Handicapped Programs, Southern Connecticut State College, New Haven,
Connecticut.*

Special Learning Corporation

42 Boston Post Rd. Guilford, Connecticut 06437

SPECIAL LEARNING CORPORATION

Publisher's Message:

The Special Education Series is the first comprehensive series designed for special education courses of study. It is also the first series to offer such a wide variety of high quality books. In addition, the series will be expanded and up-dated each year. No other publications in the area of special education can equal this. We stress high quality content, a superb advisory and consulting group, and special features that help in understanding the course of study. In addition we believe we must also publish in very small enrollment areas in order to establish the credibility and strength of our series. We realize the enrollments in courses of study such as Autism, Visually Handicapped Education, or Diagnosis and Placement are not large. Nevertheless, we believe there is a need for course books in these areas and books that are kept up-to-date on an annual basis! Special Learning Corporation's goal is to publish the highest quality materials for the college and university courses of study. With your comments and support we will continue to do this.

John P. Quirk

©1978 by Special Learning Corporation, Guilford, Connecticut 06437

First Edition

1 2 3 4 5

ISBN 0-89568-078-5

Manufactured by the Redson Rice Corporation, Chicago, Illinois

CONTENTS

1. Introduction

2. Objectives and Goals

3. Assessment and Evaluation

Focus   122

4. Programs and Services Within The Least Restrictive Educational Environment

GLOSSARY OF TERMS

academic ability Competence in performance of school subjects like language, arts, mathematics, sciences, and social sciences.

affective domain Area of behavior emphasizing the feelings, emotions, attitudes, interest, values, appreciations and adjustments of the individual.

assessment Comprehensive appraisal of strengths and weaknesses of a person's learning. Also, assessment refers to the present educational status of the child.

classification An activity of placing objects or abstract concepts in different categories.

cognitive domain Area of behavior emphasizing the mental or intellectual processes of the individual.

criterion referenced tests The tests which do not have normative data based on standardization. In Criterion Referenced Tests, a student is compared not with other students but with himself or herself.

developmental lag A child not as advanced in physical, intellectual, social, motoric and emotional aspects when compared to other children his age.

diagnostic teaching This instructional approach involves diagnosis, prescription, remediation, and follow-up strategies which are based on individualization of a program.

educational tests One of the categories of tests designed to assess academic learning or achievement.

evaluation A process of arriving at decisions regarding learning abilities or behavioral levels of a subject.

follow-up A process of detecting specific problems which may still exist after, and in spite of, proper diagnosis and remediation.

goal A general statement concerning the performance of a child that is open to interpretation.

Individualized Education Plan (IEP) A formal written program developed by school personnel, a child's parents, and when appropriate the child him/herself, in order to delineate assessment, placement, goal setting, special services, and evaluation procedures.

mainstreaming Process of placing exceptional children in a regular class of a school by withdrawing them from a special education class.

objective A description of specific behaviors with specification of how they will be measured.

observation One of the tools of collecting information on a child by recognizing or noting specific behaviors. Often, but not always, it involves measurements of some magnitude.

performance Tasks involving a child's motor, manual, or manipulative ability.

precision teaching A technique used to chart and evaluate the behavior of an individual in order to check the progress from one time to the other.

psychological tests One of the categories of tests designed to assess one's behavior, academic aptitudes, emotional state, personality traits, and intellectual abilities. Also known as Mental Tests. See Educational Tests for comparison.

remediation Process of correction of learning and behavioral problems.

task analysis The isolating, describing, and sequencing of the subskills of a major objective.

terminal behavior Refers to the behavior you would like the learner to be able to demonstrate at the time your influence over him ends.

TOPIC MATRIX

COURSE OUTLINE:

Readings in Individualized Educational Programs provides the college student a comprehensive overview into the field in preparation for teaching exceptional children. It is designed to correlate with an introductory course in exceptional children.

Introduction to Individualized Educational Programs

I. Legislation and Litigation – Overview
II. Accountability Issues
III. Components of an IEP
IV. Writing Instructional Sequences
V. Testing
VI. Placement and Services
VII. Due Process and Parental Participation

Readings in IEP

I. Introduction – Involvement of a Process called the IEP
II. Goals and Objectives
III. Assessment and Evaluation
IV. Placement and Services in The Least Restrictive Educational Environment
v. Parental Involvement

Related Special Learning Corporation Titles

I. Readings in Learning Disabilities
II. Readings in Mental Retardation
III. Readings in Behavior Modification
IV. Readings in Speech and Hearing
V. Readings in Deaf Education
VI. Readings in Emotional and Behavioral Disorders
VII. Readings in Psychology of Exceptional Children
VIII. Readings in Diagnosis and Placement
IX. Readings in Visually Handicapped Education
X. Readings in Mainstreaming
XI. Readings in Physically Handicapped Education
XII. Readings in Gifted and Talented Education
XIII. Readings in Dyslexia
XIV. Readings in Special Education

PREFACE

    This book of readings is designed for two major audiences: students in undergraduate and graduate programs and personnel interested or involved in the IEP process. Its objective is to provide the reader with a basic understanding and framework for writing individualized programs.

The articles included in the monograph represent current viewpoints from professionals at different levels of education and related professions concerned with the responsibility of individualizing educational programs for handicapped children. The need for such a monograph has become especially acute since the passage of P.L. 94-142, the Education for All Handicapped Children Act of 1975. According to this law, future services for the handicapped must stress educational programs that are designed to meet the individual needs of each handicapped child. An individualized educational plan must be developed jointly for each child by the local school representatives, the parents, the teacher, and, when appropriate, by the child as well.

Most of the information contained in this text is generic, that is, it has relevance across disability areas. Although it is not offered as the definitive text on IEPs, it should resolve some of the complications surrounding implementation, development and evaluation. There has been a conscious attempt by the editors to present the IEP as a process by which responsible, competent individuals have wide discretion in facilitating an adequate program plan for the child.

Irving Newman

Robert Piazza

Introduction –
Involvement of a Process Called The IEP

PL-94-142's feature calling for individualized educational programs for all handicapped children has addressed itself to the accountability issues that have been surrounding the education field during the last 20 years. While educators have been discussing how to make the instructional process meaningful and measureable, legislators have attempted to insure this accountability through legal mandate.

Will educators be able to make the Individualized Educational Plan a beneficial effort for exceptional children? To insure a positive answer to this question the components of an IEP must be adequately developed, implemented, monitored, and/or reviewed. These components are:

1. The assessment of the child's current level of educational functioning.
2. The writing of annual goals and specific instructional objectives.
3. The determination of special education and related services to be provided. Dates for the beginning and endings of these services must also be decided upon.
4. The placement of the child in the least restrictive environment.
5. A written justification which supports the educational placement and the personnel responsible for implementing the IEP.
6. The specification of evaluation procedures to determine if the goals and objectives have been met.

To make the IEP an effective instrument the special educator must work as part of a team. Parents of the handicapped child, experts from many fields, (e.g. social work, psychology, speech and language, reading, physical and occupational therapy, administration, regular education, and medicine, among others) must also be involved in the IEP process. A consortium with shared responsibilities is paramount to successfully determine the IEP aspects previously mentioned. These individuals should be asking themselves the following questions: Which special education methods and procedures really work? How can these methods be adapted and used with individual and/or small groups of children? and What is the most effective way to evaluate the appropriateness of these procedures? The matrix found in the Focus section of this book may assist school systems in ascertaining the responsibilities specific members of their child study teams may have.

Forces in special education which have brought about the IEP process, roles and responsibilities of those developing IEP's, and anticipated problems and pitfalls will be discussed in the following selections.

the who, where and what of IEP's

Tom Lovitt

The author is with the Child Development and Mental Retardation Center, Experimental Education Unit, University of Washington, Seattle.

The enactment of Public Law 94-142 has stimulated considerable activity. Books have been written, and workshops organized, in attempts to explain this legislation. The activity is not without cause, for the new law—also known as The Education for All Handicapped Children Act—is indeed complex.

As welcome as the legislation may be, many teachers and school administrators are deeply concerned about implementing the act. They are, for example, uneasy about setting up procedures which guarantee the many rights of parents and anxious about locating tests which are nondiscriminatory. However, the provision which has probably caused the most apprehension is the one which calls for the maintenance of an Individualized Education Program (IEP) for each handicapped child.

But why be apprehensive? Haven't we all known for years that individualized teaching was the way to go? Haven't we been told that children are unique and that, therefore, programs should be ''fitted to their needs'' so they can perform ''at their own pace''? Such bromides about individualized education have been the bases for countless books and workshops, and have been bandied about the colleges of education for generations. So what's the problem?

Well, part of the problem is that although there's been a lot of talk about individualized instruction, few teachers have been able to bring it off. Because of the numbers of children in their classes, or the lack of varied materials, or whatever reason, most teachers have not programmed individually for their youngsters.

To complicate matters, individualization IEP-style goes far beyond what most teachers think of as constituting individualized instruction. It's not simply assigning children to one group or another for reading or math instruction. Nor is it just anticipating that certain children will accomplish a great deal; others, not as much; and still others, nothing at all.

Under the IEP concept of individualized instruction teachers (and others who design programs for children) must explain in writing the many details of their educational plans. Among other things, they must describe what will be taught and by whom, where instruction will take place and for how long. Furthermore, those plans must be measurable and they must be designed by a group of individuals, many of whom are specialists.

Little wonder then that so much anxiety and confusion exits over IEP's. Not only have most of us managed to avoid specifying individual objectives, but when we did state goals, they defied measurement. What's more, when we wrote down those few nebulous aims, they were invariably our own creations; rarely did we seek the assistance of other professionals or parents.

The intent of this series of workshop articles is to explain the features of IEP's to the extent that teachers and others can develop and implement them in their classrooms. In this first article we'll take a look at some of the who's, where's and what's of IEP's. In subsequent articles, we'll outline the referral process and develop a sample IEP.

Who and Where. In an effort to guarantee that various approaches will be used to assess handicapped youngsters, one of the provisions of 94-142 is that children will be evaluated by a Child Study Team (CST). Depending on the type and extent of the handicap, a CST would include some of the following professionals: regular and special ed teachers, vision and hearing specialists, school psychologist, communication disorder specialist, physician and social worker.

''The Who, Where, and What of IEP's,'' Tom Lovitt, *Early Years*, Vol. 8, No. 1, September 1977. © 1977 Alan Raymond Incorporated.

Following an evaluation, the CST holds a planning conference. The purposes of this meeting are to develop an appropriate IEP and determine where the child should be educated. Each school must insure that the following participants are included in the planning conference: a representative of the local educational agency, other than the child's teacher; the child's teacher, or teachers, who have a direct responsibility for implementing the program; the child's parent(s); the child, when appropriate; and other individuals at the discretion of the parent or the school district.

Based on the evaluation of the CST and the recommendation of the planning committee, a placement for the child is suggested. According to 94-142, the child must be assigned to a facility that is "least restrictive" and the rationale for such a placement must be explained. The following are some of the placement options, ranging from least to most restrictive:

• Regular class with supportive services. The child is assigned to a regular classroom. Special ed and/or other personnel assist the teacher with advice about methods or materials. The child does not receive direct instruction from the support personnel.
• Regular class with support instruction. The child is assigned to a regular classroom and receives some direct instruction in the classroom from a special ed teacher or other specialist.
• Regular class with resource-room instruction. The child is assigned to a regular classroom, but receives some instruction in another location from a specialist.
• Separate class, part-time, regular school. The child is assigned primarily to a special ed classroom, but receives some instruction in a regular classroom. This particular placement is possible only when the school has both kinds of classroom.

• Separate class, full-time, regular school. The child is not integrated in a regular class, but spends full-time in a special ed classroom. Here, too, the school must have both regular and special ed classrooms.
• Special class, part-time, separate facility. The child is assigned to a special class in a separate school on a part-time basis. All of the children in this facility are handicapped. The child receives some instruction, however, in a facility which has classes for regular and special students.
• Special class, full-time, separate facility. The child receives all of his education in a school for special children.
• Homebound. The child receives an educational program in the home from special ed teachers or other specialists.

The wide range of placement options provided by P.L. 94-142 should be reassuring to regular teachers. As you can see, handicapped children are not going to be arbitrarily assigned to regular classrooms, regardless of the nature or extent of their handicaps. However, there's another reason for listing the various placement options here: The conditions of the child's placement figure prominently in the writing of the IEP.

What Is an IEP? In order to develop an appropriate IEP, the CST and others who participated in the planning conference must respond in writing to the following nine components which relate to the handicapped child's program:

1. Statement of current educational level. A report must be written which describes present levels of educational performance. This includes information on the child's academic achievement, social adaptation, prevocational and vocational skills, psychomotor skills and self-help skills.

2. Statement of goals. Written descriptions must be included of the goals to be achieved by the end of the school year under the child's IEP. These goals should be written in terms of the student and should specify clearly the desired behavior. For example, an appropriate goal would be: "The student will increase his reading comprehension skills."

3. Statement of objectives. Written statements must be provided of the short term instructional objectives; in other words, the measurable intermediate steps between the present level of educational performance and the annual goals. The objectives should include the following conditions: descriptive, conditional, evaluative and temporal. An example of an objective might be: "The student will be able to answer, in writing, the comprehension questions which follow stories in *Reading for Concepts,* Book B, with at least an 80 percent accuracy by the end of the quarter."

4. Statement of services. This statement describes specifically the educational services needed by the child. These must be determined without regard to the availability of those services. The statement must include a description of: (a) all special education and related services that are needed to meet the unique needs of the child, including the type of physical education program in which the child will participate; (b) any special instructional media and materials that are needed.

5. Dates of services. Statements must be included about the dates special services will begin and the length of time they'll be in effect. Beginning and ending dates will be entered for each service the child will receive. If he is to be provided assistance from a special ed teacher, a regular teacher and a communication disorders specialist, three sets of dates must be entered in the IEP.

1. INTRODUCTION

6. Time in regular programs. Information must be furnished which details the extent to which a child will participate in regular education programs. Some children will be integrated in regular classes for only a few activities; for example, music, art and physical education.

7. Justification of placement. A written statement must accompany the IEP which supports the type of educational placement recommended for the child. School personnel, of course, must make every effort to educate handicapped youngsters with children who are not handicapped. Handicapped children should be placed in special classes, separate schools, or otherwise removed from their normal peers only when the nature or severity of the handicap is such that education in regular classes with the use of special aids and services cannot be achieved satisfactorily.

8. Responsible individuals. A list must be furnished of the names of individuals who are responsible for implementing the IEP. For some children, this list will contain only one or two names. For other children, several professionals will be included: special and regular teachers, communication disorders specialist, vision specialist and so on.

9. Evaluation plan. The IEP must include statements about the objective criteria, evaluation procedures and schedules for determining whether the short term instructional objectives are being achieved. The objectives must be evaluated at least once a year. For example, if the objective was to increase a child's ability to comprehend, he might be required to answer in writing, each day, the questions following a story from a specific book. His answers would then be checked against a key. This in-formation, along with other facts provided earlier in our example of an objective, would inform the reader about the criteria, procedures and schedule for evaluating the attainment of objectives.

Hopefully, this brief description of the who, where and what of IEP's will help ease your apprehensions over this provision of P.L. 94-142. Writing an acceptable IEP isn't the easiest thing you've ever done, of course, but at the same time there's nothing in an IEP that need scare any teacher.

In a subsequent issue, we will detail the steps which are followed before a child receives special instruction—from the time he becomes a focus of concern to the implementation of an IEP. We'll also show how an IEP might be developed by providing pertinent data on a special child and using that information to design a plan.

Implementing the IEP Concept

In its call for an "individualized education program" (IEP) for each handicapped child, P.L. 94–142 can be credited with having codified what has long been recognized as superior teaching practice. In doing so it may very well speed the use of the approach for all children. In any case, the IEP is for several reasons of particular importance in the education of children with handicaps. Not the least of these reasons is the fact that it provides a natural point of departure from the conventional tendency to see handicapped children primarily in terms of their disabilities rather than as individuals—of viewing them as homogeneous, failing to recognize the wide variations that they, no less than nonhandicapped children, display. Another is lowered expectations, of demanding (and thereby usually getting) far less of the handicapped child than of his or her "normal" peer. These matters are of specific relevance to the preparation of individualized programs, since the attitudes reflected in IEPs cannot help but be of key importance in determining the substance and reality of the activities they call for.

No matter how carefully it may be defined, the term "individualized education program" can be expected to mean different things to different people, depending on the nature of their involvement in it. One particular point of view is represented by those who are in various ways directly concerned with putting the IEP into practice.

Toward exploring the IEP from that approach the Committee asked three representative kinds of "implementers" to join in its deliberations: the mother of a handicapped child—Mrs. Carol Smith of Ballston Lake, New York; an educator at the local level—Robert Gibson, Director of Special Education for the Hartland Area Education Agency in Ankenny, Iowa; and a member of the BEH staff involved in drafting regulations concerning the IEP, Jerry Vlasak of the Aid to States Branch.

Enforcing a view of handicapped children as individuals rather than as faceless members of a category is but one of a number of potential advantages of the IEP. It provides accountability for achieving specific goals in specified periods of time. It serves as a quality control mechanism, requiring the discipline of developing plans that are well-reasoned and well-considered. By calling for the involvement of parents, it fosters closer communication and greater trust between the school and the community. It replaces random instructional activities, based on standardized goals, with particularized activities calculated to achieve goals important to the particular student. By virtue of the requirement that it be a written document that can readily be referred to, it promotes term-to-term continuity and consistency. It can accommodate varying grouping patterns (e.g., one-to-one tutoring, small groups, large groups, hospital or homebound instruction, and special resource activities). By introducing an interdisciplinary, team approach—rather than depending on the vagaries of one individual's decisions—it can be productive of more balanced and comprehensive planning. And such an interdisciplinary approach results in an atmosphere far more supportive of the classroom teacher.

As with other innovations, the IEP concept also presents potential problems, not because of weaknesses inherent in the technique itself but because its application entails the acceptance of some new viewpoints. In some schools it may represent a considerable break with customary practices. Not simply the IEP but P.L. 94–142 in general calls for ending the pervasive feeling in school circles that handicapped children and the teachers who serve them are not really a part of the "regular" school system but have separate needs and interests. To the extent that this feeling persists, it will constitute a significant barrier to progress. Another potential problem is the possibility that some individual staff members may contend that they do not have time to get involved in preparing IEPs, or there may be

"Implementing the Concept," *The Individualized Educational Program: Key to an Appropriate Education for the Handicapped Child,* 1977 Annual Report. National Advisory Committee on the Handicapped, U.S. Government Printing Office, Washington, D.C., 1977.

1. INTRODUCTION

those who prepare them only on a casual, pro forma basis and thereafter pay them no attention.

For the most part, however, the IEP will essentially mean the formalization and perhaps elaboration of what the teachers in many if not most school systems have long accepted as good practice. To a not insignificant extent, of course, the IEP approach may very well entail some rather extensive administrative adjustments, including several that some school officials may not have taken into account. The fact is that preparing IEPs *will* command special amounts of time, not only for the handicapped child's teacher but for other members of the staff who should be included on the planning team, and perhaps for outside professionals whose counsel may be crucially important.

Moreover, the teacher will not only be deeply engaged in developing the content of the IEP but in most cases will probably have to take the lead in carrying out the school's obligation to set up IEP conferences, arrange for the time and place, make sure that the parents and appropriate members of the staff will be there, and in general handle what may in some cases prove to be fairly complex logistical situations. Further, staff allocations are going to have to be made in such a way as not only to accommodate planning conferences and other necessary activities, but to make sure that the children's schooling does not grind to an abrupt halt because the staff is buried in writing IEPs.

In short, for those portions of the school year that henceforth must include allowance for writing and revising IEPs, the classroom teacher is going to need special backup support—clerical and secretarial as well as professional—plus access to special services, facilities, and materials. Further, time will have to be set aside for training teachers and other members of the staff in the IEP's preparation and implementation. While the essence of the individualized program is its content rather than the mechanics of how it is designed and prepared, not just *some* teachers but even the most experienced will need appropriate in-service training and if possible access to model programs.

As for who should be involved in drawing up the IEP, the proposed regulations can be read as requiring only the bare minimum of the child's teacher and another member of the staff qualified as a teacher or supervisor in special education. The child's parents or guardian also are to be present if possible (and in fact the school must otherwise produce persuasive, documented evidence that a substantial effort was made to get a parent to take part), and the student if appropriate. BEH officials responsible for drafting these regulations have sought to make it clear that in practice they would see the presence of a parent as fundamental and the participation of other staff members who deal closely with the child as at least highly desirable and in professional terms requisite.

However, they said, BEH has made every effort not to over-regulate but instead to keep Federal requirements to a minimum, particularly until there has been time to gain experience with the new provisions. By the letter of the law, then, the IEP could theoretically be the product of just two members of the school staff—the child's teacher and one other academically qualified person—provided that the parents steadfastly declined or refused to participate and that the child clearly was unable to contribute. By the spirit of the law, however, not to speak of appropriate professional practice, the IEP's preparation will definitely involve not only one or both parents and probably the child, but other teachers and staff—special and "regular" alike—directly involved in the child's school experience. Only then is the IEP likely to meet the expectations of Congress and to be of optimum scope, content, and effectiveness. Moreover, the process would be strengthened if arrangements were made to involve a kind of ombudsman, a person to serve as advocate and if necessary as mediator, on behalf of the child and of the child's parents.

As in the case of who shall be involved in writing programs, that part of the proposed regulations dealing with the IEP's content seeks only to set forth the minimum. To some degree, however, the regulations do go beyond the law's barebones listing in order to clarify what was intended even if not explicitly stated. Thus the regulations echo the language of P.L. 94–142 in requiring that all IEPs include statements of the child's present levels of educational performance, annual goals, short-term instructional objectives, the extent to which the child will participate in regular programs, the dates during which the

IEP will be applicable, and the criteria and procedures that will be used in evaluating the program's effectiveness.

However, whereas the law calls for a statement of the services the school will seek to provide to the child, the proposed regulations ask for a statement of the specific services the child needs, irrespective of whether those services are actually available—thereby providing parents and administrators with a checkpoint for determining what the school must do to provide handicapped children with the kind of education foreseen in the law. Similarly, while the regulations closely follow the language of the law in asking for a description of the extent to which the child will participate in regular education programs, the proposed regulations go a step further and ask for "a justification for the type of educational environment which the child will have." Also, the proposed regulations ask for "a list of the individuals who are responsible for implementation of the individualized program," thereby signalling an expectation that the school's representation in preparing IEPs will consist not just of the child's teacher and one other member of the staff, but that the process will be a team approach involving all school personnel who could make a useful contribution.

The National Advisory Committee would in general approve the list of required IEP contents as set forth in the regulations, and judges from the comments of people from whom it invited testimony that this feeling is widespread. In practice the various elements of the list would presumably be fleshed out and expanded upon by the teachers and other members of local school staffs. The possibilities of such expansion are indicated by what the mother of a handicapped child said she would like to see in an IEP. She proposed that it include the following: "(1) A statement of my child's present development level in all areas relating to physical, emotional, and intellectual development; (2) a statement of my child's learning strengths; (3) a statement of any medical, environmental, or cultural consideration particular to my child; (4) a statement of my child's education needs and their relationship to the total sequence of developmental skills; (5) a statement of specific goals and timetables; (6) a statement of instructional alternatives; (7) a listing of appropriate educational materials relevant to my child's learning characteristics; (8) a clear delineation of the responsibilities of the entire planning team; (9) established time frames for daily programming, periodic review, and evaluation; and (10) a description of program procedures."

Looking at the IEP from the point of view of the teaching staff of a district that is already employing the IEP approach (Ankenny, Iowa), the basic educational component of an individualized program is seen in terms of "Sequence Skills Development," with the sequence consisting of specific objectives involving activities that can readily be changed (daily if need be) in accordance with a system of continuing evaluation of how well or poorly the objectives are being achieved. The model can be described, the staff says, as being a cyclic process characterised by "pre- and post-testing, observations, evaluation, and establishment of new objectives." They note that the program review component reaches beyond the progress of the child to analyze the effectiveness of methods and materials, activities, objectives, and the chosen criteria, with the ultimate purpose of the program being "the child's absorption into regular educational channels or vocational endeavors."

Whatever the format of the IEP, there seems to be little question that the strength and viability of the approach will depend in large measure on the breadth and quality of information gathered prior to writing it, and that this information should among other things reflect the contributions of an interdisciplinary team competent to measure the child's physical, emotional, and intellectual status and needs.

Equally important, of course, it should reflect the observations and opinions of the parent. That point was made time and again in the Senate and House debates concerning the bill, and was one of the reasons for a provision in the Senate version which would have required that IEP planning conferences for each child be held three times a year. This requirement was ultimately dropped in favor of "at least annually," chiefly on grounds that the frequency of conferences should not be rigidly fixed in Federal law but rather should be determined by the individual IEP planning group in accordance with the individual student's needs.

In agreeing to this compromise, however, many of the IEP's proponents emphasized that

1. INTRODUCTION

the law obviously did not preclude more frequent meetings and that in fact additional sessions would serve such valuable purposes that a once-yearly schedule would probably be the rare exception. Beyond the benefits of infusing the parent's insights and observations into the discussion, it was pointed out, their frequent involvement would function as an extension of the procedural protections now being guaranteed to the parents of handicapped children, offering them not only an opportunity to check on their children's progress but putting them in a position to monitor such possible problems as labeling and misclassification.

Equally important, frequent conferences were seen as enabling the parents to get a better understanding of their children's needs and problems, to receive professional counseling, and to learn how to bolster the child's school experiences by providing supplementary educational experiences in the home.

So, although the law and the regulations prescribe only that IEP conferences shall be held "at least annually," a more frequent schedule clearly was envisaged by the law's designers, on grounds that additional meetings would produce important additional results.

Nonetheless, the National Advisory Committee would commend BEH for avoiding any temptation to over-regulate in this or any other aspect of the individualized education program. Good sense suggests minimum intervention until the IEP and other provisions of P.L. 94–142 have been tested in the schools. The Committee feels a similar restraint about recommending any changes in these regulations as they now stand, or in the law itself.

At the same time the Committee is aware that individualized education programs have been the subject of considerable study during recent years; and that under this designation or some other, the basic concept is already being used with handicapped children in 23 States. It would seem clear that teachers and school officials elsewhere would benefit from the knowledge and experience that has thus been gained. The Committee would therefore recommend that the Bureau of Education for the Handicapped consider possible ways of making model IEPs (and the thinking and experimentation and testing behind them) readily available to interested school districts and teacher training institutions. In advancing that suggestion the Committee would also note its support of the following propositions:

1. That the individualized education program is an invaluable education tool which should be fully and unreservedly used by every school in the Nation, with every handicapped child;

2. That the IEP should be seen as concerning the whole child, in all aspects of his or her life—outside of school as well as in it, and bearing on physical and emotional as well as intellectual needs;

3. That the preparation of each IEP should be an interdisciplinary effort, with appropriate participation by every member of the staff who can make a substantial contribution;

4. That every effort should be made to involve parents both in the development of IEPs and in their implementation; and

5. That school officials should demonstrate their understanding of the importance of IEPs by establishing priorities, special in-service training programs, teacher schedules, and resource allocation procedures that recognize the needs involved and assure optimum results.

The Intent of Congress

The importance attached by the Congress to the individualized education program called for in Public Law 94–142 is suggested by the emphasis placed on it in the Act itself, in the Senate and House colloquy prior to the law's enactment, and in special congressional reports.

What the law says

Quoting first from the law itself, section 4(a) (3) provides the following definition:

The term "individualized education program" means a written statement for each handicapped child developed in any meeting by a representative of the local educational agency or an intermediate educational unit who shall be qualified to provide, or supervise the provision of, specially designed instruction to meet the unique needs of handicapped children, the teacher, the parents or guardian of such child, and, whenever appropriate, such child, which statement shall include (A) a statement of the present levels of educational performance of such child, (B) a statement of annual goals, including short-term instructional objectives, (C) a statement of the specific educational services to be provided to such child, and the extent to which such child will be able to participate in regular educational programs, (D) the projected date for initiation and anticipated duration of such services, and (E) appropriate objective criteria and evaluation procedures and schedules for determining, on at least an annual basis, whether instructional objectives are being achieved.

Under the heading "Eligibility," section 612 provides that "In order to qualify for assistance under this part in any year, a State shall demonstrate to the Commissioner that the following conditions are met," and in citing those conditions goes on to say—under section 612(4)—that "Each local educational agency in the State will maintain records of the individualized education program for each handicapped child, and such programs shall be established, reviewed, and revised as provided in section 614(a)(5)."

Under section 613, dealing with "State Plans," section 613(a)(11) declares that these plans shall, among other things, "provide for procedures for evaluation at least annually of the effectiveness of programs in meeting the educational needs of handicapped children (including evaluation of individualized education programs), in accordance with such criteria that the Commissioner shall prescribe. . ."

Regarding the review alluded to above in connection with section 612, section 614(a)(5) states that any local education agency or intermediate educational unit that wants to receive funds under the law shall "provide assurances that the local educational agency or intermediate educational unit will establish, or revise, whichever is appropriate, an individualized education program for each handicapped child at the beginning of each school year and will then review and, if appropriate revise, its provisions periodically, but not less than annually."

Comments in the Senate

As reflected in the *Congressional Record*, the debate in the Senate regarding the proposed Education for All Handicapped Children Act was launched with the issuance on June 2, 1975, of Senate Report No. 94–168, prepared by the Senate Committee on Labor and Public Welfare. On page 4 the report noted that:

"The bill provides for an individualized planning conference, to be held at least three times a year, involving the parents or guardian, an individual representing the local educational agency qualified to provide special education, the child's teacher and the child when appropriate who will meet jointly to develop and review a written statement describing the educational services to be provided and, when ap-

"The Intent of Congress," *The Individualized Educational Program: Key to an Appropriate Education for the Handicapped Child*, 1977 Annual Report. National Advisory Committee on the Handicapped, U.S. Government Printing Office, Washington, D.C., 1977.

1. INTRODUCTION

propriate, to revise such statement with the agreement of the parents."

Then on pages 10 and 11 the report goes into the subject of the IEP more deeply, as follows:

"The Committee bill defines individualized planning conference as a meeting or meetings to be held at least three times a year for the purpose of developing, reviewing, and when appropriate and with the agreement of the parents or guardian, revising a written statement of appropriate educational services to be provided for each handicapped child. The planning conference shall be conducted with the joint participation of the parents or guardian, the child (when appropriate), the child's teacher and a representative of the local educational agency who is qualified to provide or supervise the provision of special education.

"In reviewing the testimony on this bill and after consultation with professionals in the field, the Committee recognizes that in order to derive any benefit to the child, parent, and teacher an individualized planning conference must be held a minimum of three times per year. The frequent monitoring of a handicapped child's progress throughout the year is the most useful tool in designing an educational program for not only the child but those who are responsible for his management in school and at home.

"There is evidence that an individualized planning conference on an annual basis is insufficient. It is the Committee's intent in requiring that individualized planning conferences be provided for each handicapped child that these conferences be utilized as an extension of the procedural protections guaranteed under existing law to parents of handicapped children, and that they be the logical extension and the final step of the evaluation and placement process.

"They are not intended to be the evaluation process itself. Thus, it is the intent of this provision that local educational agencies involve the parent at the beginning of and at other times during the year regarding the provision of specific services and short-term instructional objectives for the special education of the handicapped child, which services are specifically designed to meet the child's individual

needs and problems. The Committee views this process as a method of involving the parent and the handicapped child in the provision of appropriate services, providing parent counseling as to ways to bolster the educational process at home, and providing parents with a written statement of what the school intends to do for the handicapped child.

"It is not the Committee's intention that the written statement developed at the individual planning conferences be construed as creating a contractual relationship. Rather, the Committee intends to ensure adequate involvement of the parents or guardian of the handicapped child, and the child (when appropriate) in both the statement and its subsequent review and revision. The Committee has included a requirement that any revision of the statement be done only with the agreement of the parents or guardian in order to ensure that services to the child are not arbitrarily curtailed or modified.

"During the hearings on this bill, the Committee received testimony that the individualized written educational plan (as contained in the bill introduced in January) would require school systems to develop an expertise and ability to provide services guaranteed to assure educational progress. The Committee recognizes that in many instances the process of providing special education and related services to handicapped children is not guaranteed to produce any particular outcome. By changing the language of this provision to emphasize the process of parent and child involvement and to provide a written record of reasonable expectations, the Committee intends to clarify that such individualized planning conferences are a way to provide parent involvement and protection to assure that appropriate services are provided to a handicapped child. The Committee has deleted the language of the bill as introduced which required objective criteria and evaluation procedures by which to assure that the short term instructional goals were met. Instead it has required the Commissioner of Education to conduct a comprehensive study of objective criteria and evaluation procedures which may be utilized at a later date in conjunction with individualized data available through the individualized planning conference to determine the effectiveness of special education and related services being provided.

"The Committee further points out that it intends that a copy of the statement thus developed be retained on file within the school district with copies provided to parents and others involved subject to strict procedures for protection of confidentiality. While it believes that such statements may be useful to a State educational agency for purposes of audit and evaluation, it does not intend that such records be forwarded to the State agency, but be available for inspection."

Several pages later the report added that the law

". . .requires that the State assure that local educational agencies provide and maintain records of the individualized planning conference for each handicapped child including the written statement developed from the conferences, and that such conferences will be conducted at least three times a year to develop, review and, with the agreement of the parents or guardian, revise the statement. Fifth, the bill requires that the State educational agency be responsible for insuring the implementation of and compliance with provisions of the Act, and for the general supervision of educational programs for handicapped children within the State, including all such education programs administered by any other State or local agency. Finally, to assure orderly due process with regard to carrying out the provisions of the Act and to assure compliance with provisions of the Act, the Committee bill provides that the State shall establish policies and procedures to provide consultation with persons involved in or concerned with the education of handicapped children including handicapped individuals and parents of handicapped children. Further, in this regard, the State shall establish an entity to assure compliance with the provisions of the Act which shall conduct periodic evaluation and be empowered to receive, and take such necessary steps as are required, to resolve complaints of violations of the requirements of the Act."

In its final reference to the IEP the report notes that

"The Committee has designed the individualized planning conferences as one method to prevent labelling or misclassification. Furthermore, the Committee points out that due process requirements in existing law were designed specifically to protect against this abuse, and should be examined by the Commissioner and the State educational agency to assure that they are effective in this regard."

Subsequent to the issuance of this report, on June 8, the debate got underway with remarks by Senator Jennings Randolph of West Virginia, Chairman of the Senate Subcommittee on the Handicapped. In analyzing the various provisions of the proposed Act—at that time referred to as S. 6—Senator Randolph noted that

"A feature of the measure that will promote the educational development of handicapped children is the individualized planning conference. It has long been recognized by educators that individualized attention to a child brings rich rewards to the child, his teachers, and family. Handicapped children have been a neglected minority in our school system; individualized planning conferences are a way of targeting the resources of our school systems on handicapped children. These conferences are to be held at least three times a year and will represent a cooperative effort on the part of the school, the parents, and the child himself, when appropriate, to meet the unique educational needs of the child. Frequent monitoring of a handicapped child's progress throughout the school year is a vital component of the individualized planning conference. Preliminary evidence on annual planning conferences indicates that the usefulness of the individualized planning conference would be nullified if held only on an annual basis."

Senator Robert T. Stafford of Vermont then spoke about the makeup of the planning conferences, noting that

"The participants will include the parents, the teacher, and a qualified supervisor or provider of special education services. This provision is extremely important if the child's progress is to be adequately monitored and if appropriate

1. INTRODUCTION

steps are to be taken to assure that the problems with the educational process that the child is having are met in a timely and consistent way. An additional benefit that will result from these conferences is one that is too often overlooked. Not only will the child be better served, and the parents better informed of the limitations their child has due to a particular handicap, but the teacher will learn from this experience as well.

"As we look more and more toward children with handicaps being educated with their normal peers, we must realize, and try to alleviate, the burden put upon the teacher who must cope with that child and all the others in the class as well. The teacher needs reinforcement and a better understanding of the child's abilities and disabilities.

"It is hoped that participation in these conferences will have a positive effect on the attitude of the teacher toward the child, and an understanding of the child's problems in relating to his or her peers because of a handicapping condition."

Commented Senator Randolph:

"Mr. President, the Senator from Vermont explained one feature of this bill, and I will try to emphasize his point. We will promote the educational development of handicapped children through the process of individualized planning conferences.

"What the Senator has stated is very important. Educators generally have begun to realize that some personal attention must be given to a child. I am sure that the child is the better for it. Individual attention is one of the benefits of a good education in institutions of learning for all the people of the United States, not only the handicapped.

"Throughout this country, our schools, colleges, and universities long have stressed the need for individual attention to students. It is the heart of our educational process and it has stood the test of time.

"Perhaps this is not the occasion to mention it, but I do so. I look back upon my school days, and I say to the Senator from Vermont that I recall those teachers who not only were informed, but also were inspiring. They were those men and women who gave of their time a little after the class actually had closed. They gave one the opportunity to come and talk with them. They were there to counsel the students. In a sense, that can be carried over into the specific that the Senator mentioned here—the individual attention to children.

"The individual planning conference is a cooperative effort. It is an effort that must include the teacher, the representative of the local educational agency, the parents, and, when appropriate, the boy or girl who is handicapped. When we do this, we have the opportunity to keep in touch with that child. We monitor the child's progress, as one might say, and that frequent monitoring is a vital component of this training planning conference process. It helps the child, it helps the parents or guardian, and it helps the teachers.

"For these reasons, I comment on what the Senator has said."

Subsequently, following a discussion regarding other provisions of the bill, Senator Williams had this further comment about the IEP:

"In order to involve the parent and the child—when appropriate—in the educational process so that they may fully participate in making decisions regarding their child's education, S. 6 provides for an individualized planning conference, to be held at least three times a year, involving the parents or guardian, a person representing the local educational agency qualified to provide special education, the child's teacher and the child, when appropriate. These persons will meet jointly to develop and review a written statement describing the educational services to be provided for the particular child and, when appropriate, the statement will be revised with the agreement of the parents.

"This conference is intended also to serve as a method of providing additional parent counseling and training so that the parent may bolster the educational process at home. This involvement is particularly important in order to assure that the educational services are meeting the child's needs and so that both parents and child may be part of the process from which they are so often far removed. The conference is not a contractual relationship, but rather a cooperative effort. It serves to fully extend the procedural protections and parent involvement which was initiated last year in the Education Amendments of 1974."

In a query addressed to Senator Randolph, Senator Richard B. Stone of Florida said:

"There is a question which has been raised by some of my constituents concerning the individualized planning conferences.

"Was it the committee's intent that these planning conferences be held three times a year and attended by a small group of persons for the purpose of developing a plan for each child, or was the intent to hold a large meeting three times a year to draw plans for many children?"

Responded Senator Randolph:

"In answer to my colleague, it was the intent, and I believe I can speak for the subcommittee and the committee in this matter, that these meetings to which the Senator makes reference be small meetings; that is, confined to those persons who have, naturally, an intense interest in a particular child, i.e., the parent or parents of the child, and in some cases, the guardian of the child. Certainly, the teacher involved or even more than one teacher would be included. In addition, there should be a representative of the local educational agency who is qualified to provide, or supervise the provision of, specially designed instruction to meet the unique needs of handicapped children.

"These are the persons that we thought might well be included. That is why we have called them individualized planning conferences. We believe that they are worthwhile, and we discussed this very much as we drafted the legislation.

"We thought they should be held three times a year because we have the belief that a lesser number of such conferences would not be productive.

"If the child is not progressing as he or she should, it would be best to identify the problem as quickly as possible. Then we would have the opportunity of correcting the difficulty before a long period of time goes by. Sometimes we bring into focus the needs of a child simply by discussion of his problems.

"We believe, as I said in my opening statement, that frequent monitoring of the child's educational development is certainly valid."

Regarding the burden that might arise from the IEP requirement, Senator Jacob Javits of New York expressed reservation about

"...the dynamics by which the local educational agencies handle a three-times-a-year planning conference for each handicapped child, and a written record. I do not think there can be any objection against maintaining a written record. We do that for every student anyhow.

"As to the three-times-a-year conference, I believe we ought to think about that. That is a lot. It is 21 million conferences. . . . If there is any amendment addressing this issue, we will deal with it, and if there is not, we will probably deal with it anyhow in the House-Senate conference.

"As to the general requirements of the State entity, the amendment which Senator Dole will introduce, in which I very much wish to join, will deal with that situation, so I hope it should obviate reasonable objection to that proposition."

The observations by Senator Javits led to the following colloquy involving him and Senators Randolph, Stafford, Williams, and Robert J. Dole of Kansas:

Mr. DOLE. It was the intent of the Senator from Kansas to offer an amendment which would either delete the planning conference or at least to make it discretionary, because it just seems to me, as I have indicated earlier, if we are going to hold at least 3 times a year an individualized planning conference for everyone who is handicapped, according to the definitions of this act, that is going to be about 24 million conferences and 24 million pieces of paper. That could be an administrative nightmare.

Now the Senator from Kansas understands the problem of the handicapped to some degree. There may be some who need 10 conferences or more per year, there may be some who need one. It would seem to the Senator from Kansas that one thing that we could do between now and October 1976 would be to conduct a pilot program, that has been suggested, in the States of Texas, Florida, and Wisconsin, where they have ongoing programs or at least could have a pilot program to see if a nationwide program were appropriate.

1. INTRODUCTION

Mr. RANDOLPH. Mr. President, will the Senator yield?

Mr. DOLE. Yes.

Mr. RANDOLPH. What is being done in the State of Kansas on this matter?

Mr. DOLE. We allow the State agency to have as many conferences as they want. I do not believe we require any certain number of conferences. As this Senator understands, the purpose is to sit down with parent or guardian and if appropriate, the handicapped individual and establish a clear and meaningful plan.

Mr. RANDOLPH. The only reason I come back to Kansas is because that is the State represented by the Senator and sometimes if we look at our own situation we assess it in view of the national needs. As I understand, these conferences for handicapped persons are held about once a month at the medical center.

Mr. DOLE. But I do not think the number of meetings—whether it be an individual conference once a month or once a year—is set by law or otherwise made inflexible.

Mr. RANDOLPH. There is a file on every handicapped child, starting with an evaluation following right through diagnosis and service. I think this is correct.

Mr. DOLE. This may be technically correct but as far as the conferences, I do not think we have been discussing this but have been discussing whether the number of conferences should be set in law by the Federal Government.

Mr. RANDOLPH. What is being done in some Kansas programs is what we want to do in other States.

Mr. DOLE. Right.

Mr. RANDOLPH. The Senator can understand that. I would hope in this instance that the Senator would not press for this amendment, but let it be a part of the discussion here today. We shall give very careful study to this in the future.

Mr. DOLE. The Senator from Kansas does not quarrel with the conference. This Senator does not quarrel with whether it is 3 or 6 or 9 or 12, but again it is a Federal dictation to a State agency that they must comply; they must have at least three individual conferences. And later on in the bill there are other sections where the States must have statistically valid data based on these individual conferences.

Mr. RANDOLPH. I add further to the Senator, this is only if they desire to participate.

Mr. DOLE. If they do not want to participate in the program, they would not be so constrained.

Mr. RANDOLPH. That is correct.

Mr. DOLE. But the Senator from Kansas is trying to figure out some way that, before we launch into this massive effort, we have some history. And since the Senator from Washington has delayed the effective date until October 1976, it would seem to me that we should make some legislative history that HEW should conduct a pilot program in at least three States, and maybe Kansas would be a good State.

Mr. RANDOLPH. That is presently being done by DHEW. There are projects in Florida and in Texas. Let us remember that we have adequate time until October 1, 1976 to see the results of these studies, which I feel will prove that this provision will be beneficial.

Mr. JAVITS. Exactly. Mr. President, if the Senator will yield, I commend that, too. I was going to modify an amendment to make it annual so that we do not start out quite so tough.

Also Senator Randolph has now defined in the Stone amendment the matter of the conference and that, therefore, somewhat relieves the strains. Somewhere between one and three we ought to be able to let the matter move from here and strike a fair balance. My suggestion, because I know how strongly Senator Randolph feels about it, to Senator Dole would be to make it twice. In other words, instead of three times, make it twice with the understanding that the pilot work is being done and that seasonably, before the operative date, we will review the figure of two. Then at least you have a mandate which is one-third less, and we have committed ourselves to reducing even further depending upon the actual work of the HEW. I think that is probably the best way.

Mr. RANDOLPH. Will the Senator from Kansas permit me to comment on the words of the Senator from New York.

Mr. DOLE. Yes.

I yield.

Mr. RANDOLPH. I would rather not have it

twice, for the reason that the Senate works with. . .

Mr. DOLE. The House has one conference in their bill.

Mr. JAVITS. I will agree. I will be a conferee, Senator Randolph will be a conferee, and Senator Stafford will be a conferee. I think the Senator should leave it to us, with the legislative record, and he has our feet to the fire. He has agreed to listen to the House and give attention to the findings where the words are being experimented with.

Mr. DOLE. I have no quarrel with that. If all these studies should prove that there is really no benefit from the individualized conferences, whether they are 2 or 10 or whatever number.

Mr. RANDOLPH. I would be ready to amend it.

Mr. DOLE. That is what I am seeking.

Mr. JAVITS. I make the same commitment.

Mr. DOLE. The Senator does not wish to impose any burden on educators, or parents, or handicapped children that does not benefit the handicapped.

Mr. RANDOLPH. No Member of the Senate is more concerned about the handicapped than is the Senator from Kansas. He has been a leader in this field. All of us working on these matters want to do one job, and that is to benefit the handicapped—in this particular instance, the education of the handicapped.

Mr. DOLE. That satisfies me. My concern is that we make every resource, or as much as possible, available to the direct activities and the direct programs that are going to benefit the handicapped.

Mr. WILLIAMS. Mr. President, if the Senator will yield, I think that one of the greatest benefits that can come to the handicapped child is to have the parents brought into this conference, because the education of the child continues after the school doors close and that child is at home. This is part of the educational process. That is one of the reasons why we have developed the idea of the mandatory conference, to make sure that the parent is part of the education of the child. We have to have more than one, it seems to me. That is almost a "get acquainted" meeting, and a followup meeting is essential. I support the three meetings that Senator Randolph put into this bill, and I hope we can keep it at that, at this point.

Mr. JAVITS. Mr. President, if the Senator will yield, as the ranking member, I pledge to Senator Dole to pay the most serious attention to the findings of the work which will be done in the interim until the new operative date. As will Senator Randolph, I will be perfectly willing to advocate even its entire omission, if we are convinced that it is a drag instead of an aid to everything that is being done.

Mr. WILLIAMS. It is an absolute promise to do that, because the ends are what we are interested in here. We want to see the best possible approach to education. We will be watching very closely during this period to see how it develops, particularly in the area that the Senator from Kansas has brought forth.

Mr. DOLE. I appreciate the assurances from the Senators from New York, West Virginia, and New Jersey. Their concern for the handicapped is genuine, as is that of the Senator from Kansas. But hopefully we do not want to burden some State agency with a requirement that may prove to be counterproductive. Based on the assurances, the Senator from Kansas will withdraw the amendment.

Mr. STAFFORD. Mr. President, while assurances are being given, I would like to join my three colleagues in offering the same assurance on that.

Mr. DOLE. I appreciate that. It means a great deal to the Senator from Kansas.

Mr. President, I withdraw the amendment.

The PRESIDING OFFICER. The amendment is withdrawn.

The final comments on the IEP during this phase of the debate were offered by Senators Alan Cranston of California and Walter F. Mondale of Minnesota.

Said Senator Cranston:

"S. 6 as reported also would add a new provision that establishes procedures to insure that handicapped children and their parents or guardians are given an opportunity to participate in the planning and development of the educational program, including the assessment of the handicapped child's present educational performance, the specification of instructional objectives, and identification of the specific educational services to be provided.

1. INTRODUCTION

"Mr. President, there are many other significant provisions in S. 6. I am particularly pleased with the specific guarantees of due process of law provided for handicapped children and their parents in all matters relevant to identification, evaluation, and placement, and the prohibition against the classification of children in a manner which promotes racial or cultural discrimination."

Added Senator Mondale:

"This bill represents a major step toward the identification and education of all handicapped youngsters in the near future. In the past, many children have been simply placed in institutions or segregated in schools and classes with little emphasis on adequate education and training. Under S. 6, an individual planning conference, will provide a tailored program for each handicapped youngster to meet his special educational needs.

"In the past, many children have been left to sit at home, providing little opportunity for adequate training and development. Under S. 6, priority is given to provision of a free appropriate public education to children not currently receiving any, as well as those currently receiving inadequate assistance.

"In the long run our whole society will benefit by timely, effective identification and treatment of the needs of those individuals and their families."

Comments from the House of Representatives

Meanwhile the House Education and Labor Committee was busy preparing a report on its companion bill, H.R. 7217. Issued on June 26 and labeled No. 94–332, the report says the following (on page 13) about the individualized education program:

Why does the bill provide for prescription of an individualized education program?

The movement toward the individualization of instruction, involving the participation of the child and the parent, as well as all relevant educational professionals, is a trend gaining ever wider support in educational, parental, and political groups throughout the Nation.

Therefore, this legislation would require each local educational agency to develop with a child's teacher in consultation with the parents of the child (and in appropriate instances the child) an individualized education program. Such a prescription responds to 3 fundamental tenets:

(a) each child requires an educational plan that is tailored to achieve his or her maximum potential;

(b) all principals in the child's educational environment, including the child, should have the opportunity for input in the development of an individualized program of instruction;

(c) individualization means specifics and timetables for those specifics, and the need for periodic review of those specifics—all of which produce greatly enhanced fiscal and educational accountability.

Parenthetically, it may be noted that the 93rd Congress, and, more specifically, this Committee, have already expressed their concern about the need for increased individualization in at least 2 public laws: Public Law 93–112, the Rehabilitation Act Amendments of 1973, and Public Law 93–380, the Education Amendments of 1974 (Title I).

Then five pages later the report adds this:

H.R. 7217 defines "individualized education program" as an educational plan for each handicapped child developed jointly by the local educational agency and an appropriate teacher, in consultation with the parents. This plan would contain a statement of the present levels of educational performance of the child, desired instructional objectives, a statement of the specific educational services provided the child, and the extent to which the child will be able to participate in regular educational programs, a projected date for initiation and anticipated duration of such services, and an annual evaluation of the procedures and objectives.

Agreeing on the bill's IEP provisions

In the subsequent debate on the House floor, as recorded in the *Congressional Record*, Representative John Brademas of Indiana commented as follows regarding the IEP:

"Mr. Chairman, we also provide that an individualized plan of instruction must be provided for each handicapped child and evaluated at least annually. Individualized plans are of great importance in the education of handicapped children in order to help them develop their full potential."

Representative Albert H. Quie of Minnesota also discussed the IEP, noting that the bill

". . .includes a requirement for the development of individualized education programs for each handicapped child. This would be an educational plan which is developed jointly by the local education agencies, a teacher involved with the specific education of the handicapped child, and his parents or guardian. The plan would include a statement of the child's present level of educational performance, a statement of the goals to be achieved, a statement of the specific services which will have to be provided, a projected date for initiation and duration of the services, and criteria and evaluation procedures for determining whether the objectives are being met. Because handicapped children are unique, setting up plans for each one makes good sense and by involving the parents in the development of such plans, the benefits begun in school hopefully would be continued at home. It is important to point out that it is an educational plan developed jointly, but it is not intended as a binding contract by the schools, children, and parents."

Conference Report

Although the two measures subsequently passed by the Senate and the House were alike in their broad outlines, they differed in detail. Thus it was necessary to appoint a conference committee, composed of representatives of each branch of the Congress, to work out the differences. Out of those deliberations came House of Representatives Conference Report No. 94–664, which says on pages 30 and 31:

The Senate bill and the House amendments add to the definitions in the Education of the Handicapped Act a definition of individualized instructional planning for each handicapped child which includes a statement of the child's present level of educational performance, statement of the instructional objectives to be achieved, statement of the specific educational services to be provided to the child, the extent to which the child will participate in the regular educational program, and the projected date

for initiation and anticipated duration of such services.

The Senate bill designates this individualized instructional planning as an "individualized planning conference"; the House amendments designate the planning as an "individualized education program." The Senate recedes.

The Senate bill provides that the individualized planning conference is a meeting or meetings for the purpose of developing a written statement; the House amendments provide that the individualized education program is an educational plan. The House recedes.

The Senate bill provides that the written statement shall be developed by a representative of the local educational agency, the teacher, the parents or guardian of the handicapped child and the child when appropriate; the House amendments provide that the educational plan shall be developed jointly by the local educational agency and an appropriate teacher *in consultation with* the parents or guardian of the child, and the child, whenever appropriate. The House recedes.

The Senate bill, but not the House amendments, provides that the representatives of the local educational agency shall be qualified to provide, or supervise the provision of, specially designed instruction to meet the unique needs of the child. The House recedes.

The Senate bill provides for a statement of *short-term* instructional objectives; the House amendments provide for a statement of *desired* objectives.

The conference substitute provides that the individualized educational program shall include a statement of the annual goals and short-term objectives to be achieved by the child. It is intended that each individual handicapped child will have an educational program which states the annual goals as well as including short-term instructional objectives to be achieved within shorter time perods.

The House amendments, but not the Senate bill, provide that the individualized instructional planning shall include objective criteria and evaluation procedures and schedules for

1. INTRODUCTION

determining, on at least an annual basis, whether instructional objectives are being met.

The Senate recedes with an amendment specifying that such objective criteria and evaluation procedures shall be "appropriate." The conferees intend that this amendment clarify that any criteria and evaluation procedures used are to be consistent with the requirements regarding testing and evaluation procedures in existing law.

The conferees further clarify that it is not intended that the individualized educational programs be forwarded to the U.S. Office of Education or the State educational agency. The individualized educational programs are intended to be retained in the local educational agency. Where inspection or review of such programs may be useful to the Office of Education or State educational agency for purposes of audit or evaluation, it is intended that such activities take place within the local agency, subject to strict procedures for the protection of confidentiality.

The House amendments, but not the Senate bill, add to the Education of the Handicapped Act, a definition of *public educational agency* defining such agency as any State educational agency or any other public agency approved by a State educational agency to provide special education and related services to handicapped children within the State involved. The conference substitute includes a definition of intermediate educational unit, defining such term as any public authority established by State law for the purpose of providing free public education on a regional level within the State which provides special education and related services to handicapped children within that State and which is not a local educational authority but which is under the general supervision of the State educational agency. The conferees include this definition in order to cover certain unique situations in States where public bodies established by State law provide special education and related services for handicapped children, but where the definition of local educational agency does not necessarily apply, e.g., intermediate units in the Commonwealth of Pennsylvania. Generally, the term "intermediate educational unit" is used throughout the conference report wherever the term "local educational agency" is also used.

Requirements for individualized planning conference. The Senate bill requires that the State give assurances to the Commissioner that each local educational agency in the State will maintain records of the individualized planning conference, including the written statement developed pursuant to such conference, and that such conference shall be held at least three times each year to develop, review, and, when appropriate, and with the agreement of the parents, revise such statements. The House amendments require the local educational agency in its application to provide satisfactory assurance that it will maintain the individualized program for each child, and will review the program at least annually, and revise its provisions in consultation with the parents or guardians.

The conference substitute requires that the State give assurances as a condition of eligibility that each local educational agency will maintain records of the individualized education program for each handicapped child, and to provide assurances that each local educational agency within the State shall establish, review and revise such program consistent with requirements on local educational agencies under the local application provisions of the Act.

The conference substitute also requires each local educational agency to provide assurances that it will establish, or revise, whichever is appropriate, an individualized education program for each handicapped child at the beginning of each school year and will then review and, if appropriate revise, the provisions of such program periodically, but not less than annually. In the initial year of a handicapped child's participation in a program of free appropriate public education the individualized education program shall be established at the beginning of the school year and reviewed at least once during that year. Thereafter, the conferees intend that this provision requires at least one annual review of the child's individualized education program.

The conferees have defined the individualized education program as a written statement (including the educational status of the child, the annual goals and short-term instructional objectives, and specific educational services to be provided) for each handicapped child which is jointly developed by the local educational agency, the teacher, the parents, and the child, whenever appropriate. It is intended that *all* parties (the local educational agency, the teacher, the parents, and the child, whenever appropriate) will be involved throughout the process of establishment, review and revision of this program.

Concluding debate—House

In the House following the issue of the conference report, the remarks of Representative Brademas included the following:

"Mr. Speaker, the conference bill, as did the House version, requires the development of an individualized written education program for every handicapped child served, to be designed initially in consultation with parents or guardian, and to be reviewed and revised as necessary at least annually."

To which Representative Quie added the following:

"Not only have we guaranteed (handicapped children) a right to an education, but I think we have written adequate provisions which will protect those rights and guarantee that a child will not be improperly labeled or improperly placed in an educational setting which will not suit his or her unique educational needs. The bill further guarantees that each handicapped child will have an individualized program which is designed to meet his or her special needs. As you know, not every handicapped child is the same; and by designing educational programs which specifically address specific needs and problems, I believe that handicapped children will benefit more from our educational programs. One of the reasons why I feel so strongly that the individualized education program will be so beneficial is that we require that it be developed with the involvement of a child's parent or guardian. By having a child, the parent, and his or her teacher involved in planning, it is my belief that the end result has to be positive."

Concluding debate—Senate

In the Senate following the issuance of the conference report, Senator Harrison A. Williams, Jr., of New Jersey, said the proposed law "assures the individualization of the educational process by requiring an individualized education program tailored to the unique needs of each handicapped child," and subsequently added:

"The provisions requiring an individualized education program for each handicapped child are extremely important protections to the parents and child, and highly necessary to proper planning and programming for the school district. Under the conference agreement, a local educational agency or intermediate unit receiving assistance must assure that this provision is carried out for the handicapped children within their jurisdictions, and the State is required to provide assurances that the program is carried out for all other handicapped children within the State. The Senate bill required a conference to be held at least three times a year for developing, reviewing and revising the plan, in order to assure that changes were made in the plan as appropriate to the child throughout the school year, while the House bill required that this occur on an annual basis. Once again, the conference substitute represents the essence of compromise. For under the conference agreement, this program must be established or revised, whichever is appropriate, for each handicapped child at the beginning of the school year, and must then be reviewed, and if appropriate, revised periodically during the school year, but not less than annually.

"The conferees have further defined the individualized education program as a written statement—including the educational status of the child, the annual goals and short-term instructional objectives, and specific educational services to be provided—for each handicapped child which is jointly developed by the local educational agency, the teacher, the parents, and the child. It is intended that all parties will be involved throughout the process of establishment, review and revision of this program."

Said Senator Stafford:
"The Senate passed bill contained a provision for three individualized planning conferences for each child each year. These conferences were to include, but not necessarily be limited to the teacher, the parent or guardian, a representative of the educational agency responsible

for the child's education, and the child when appropriate.

"The conference agreement changes the name of such conferences to an individualized educational program, but retains in the definitional sense much of the Senate language. The difference is the way in which it will operate. The agreement clearly specifies that there will be two conferences in the first year of the handicapped child's schooling and provides that it will be reviewed at least annually. I wish to point out, however, that the conference clearly did not wish to preclude more than one conference per year.

"The conferees recognize that each child is affected in a different way by a handicap. Some may be more severe for some children than they would be for others. We want to encourage as many conferences a year as any one child may need. It is felt that in some cases numerous conferences would be desired. We did not preclude that possibility."

Concluding the debate, on November 19 Senator Randolph again emphasized that the agreed-upon version of the law

". . .calls for the development of an individualized educational program for each handicapped child, in which there is participation by the parents or guardian of the child, the teacher, a representative of the local educational agency qualified to provide or supervise the provision of special education and related services, and the child when appropriate. Individualized attention to educational needs has and will continue to be one of the most important elements to a child's success in school. By monitoring a child's progress, a teacher can aid the child in achieving educational goals as well as determining where a potential educational problem may arise."

Changing Public Policies in the Individualization of Instruction: Roots and Forces

Thomas K. Gilhool

In 1923, in *Meyer v. Nebraska*, the U.S. Supreme Court held that despite the war hysteria and the Nebraska statute bred by that hysteria, students and parents had a right to have German taught in the public schools and teachers the right to teach it — a right that is part of the liberty guaranteed by the Fifth and Fourteenth Amendments (262 U.S. 390). Writing for the Court, Mr. Justice McReynolds sounded a central theme in the American constitutional experience. The theme has been expressed again in the flood of recent decisions secured from the courts by handicapped citizens. These decisions, whch influence so very much the present agenda in schooling and which frame the inquiry of this conference, mandate the accomodation — I should say, the celebration — of exceptionality in regular classrooms.

For the Court, in *Meyer v. Nebraska*, Mr. Justice McReynolds took Plato's ideal commonwealth as his counterpoint and he wrote,

For the welfare of his Ideal Commonwealth, Plato suggested a law which would provide: "That the wives of our guardians are to be common, and their children are to be common, and no parent is to know his own child, nor any child his parent...The proper officers will take the offspring of the good parents to the pen or fold, and...will deposit them with certain nurses (for nurture and education)... but the offspring of the inferior, or of the better when they chance to be deformed, will be put away in some mysterious, unknown place, as they should be."

Although such measures have been deliberately approved by men of great genius, their ideas touching the relation between individual and State were wholly different from those upon which our institutions rest; and it hardly will be affirmed that any Legislature could impose such restrictions upon the people of a State without doing violence to both the letter and spirit of the Constitution [262 U.S. 390, 401-402].

"Changing Public Policies in the Individualization of Instruction: Roots and Forces," Thomas K. Gilhool, *Education and Training of the Mentally Retarded,* Vol. 11, No. 2, April 1976. ©1976 The Division on Mental Retardation, Council for Exceptional Children.

1. INTRODUCTION

Stereotyping and its consequence — enforced separation — are repugnant to our constitutional tradition. Integration is a central constitutional value and not integration that denies difference but, rather, integration that accomodates difference, that appreciates it and celebrates it. Thus, more fully stated, integration and individuation are among the central constitutional values; integration, most often, taking as its label at the law, equal protection, and individuation, most often taking as its label, due process.

The promise of the Constitution to each citizen, the Supreme Court wrote in 1972 in *Papachristou v. City of Jacksonville*, is "Independence and self-confidence, the feeling of creativity...lives in high spirits rather than hushed suffocating silence (405 U.S. 156, 164)." The function of the law, whether in the name of due process or equal protection, is to purge from the relation between government and citizens, and discourage in relations among the citizens themselves, what Judge Skelly Wright has called the "arbitrary quality of thoughtlessness (Hobson v. Hansen)." Between the values of integration and individuation, there is in the everyday world, and especially in the everyday world of large, official organizations such as the schools, considerable tension. It is to the working out of that tension between integration and individuation and to the realization of arrangements that satisfy both values that the discussions in this conference are meant to contribute. However blunt an instrument for social change the courts may be, as James Coleman has recently charged, correctly or incorrectly, the courts are not likely to cease insisting that other institutions act to serve these constitutional values.

On June 26, 1975, in *O'Connor v. Donaldson*, the first of the right to treatment cases to reach the U.S. Supreme Court, that Court unanimously upheld a damage award against a superintendent of a Florida mental institution who had failed to return to the community a man separated out to that mental institution who was dangerous neither to himself nor others (95 S Ct. 2486). The courts, in our scheme of things, have a special role, as Mr. Justice Stone put it several decades ago, in protecting members of discreet and insular minorities against whom there is prejudice that tends seriously to curtail the operation of those political processes that are ordinarily to be relied upon to protect the rights of citizens (U.S. v. Carolene Products Co.). Blacks, women, and the poor have claimed that special protection from the courts and, in recent years, so have the handicapped.

In this paper, I would like (a) to review with you the recent court cases centering on classification, the so-called right to education, and the right to treatment, and the statutes, especially the federal statutes, which have followed in their wake; (b) to explore the roots of these cases in *Brown v. Board of Education*, the integration imperative, and in such due process cases as *Wisconsin v. Constantineau*, the individuation imperative; and (c) to annotate throughout the implications of these developments for the schools in the present and in the near future.

Let me be clear about where I am going. I see in the developing law the propositions that every child is special, each must be appreciated in a common setting and with common regard, and each is entitled to the recognition of his needs and wishes and to the realization of his capacity and wishes. I believe we will see, in the months ahead, straightforward, pure integration suits of the traditional variety by handicapped students; in Los Angeles, for example, as in most cities across the country, there are some 22 schools enrolling only handicapped students. The fruits of those suits, of course, will be poisoned if they yield merely integration into a mutual sameness; they will be enriched only if each child in all of general education is seen as special and is provided an education tailored to her/him.

I believe that the litigation to date has been less about special education than the uniformity of general education and the necessity of individualizing the education delivered to each and every student. Or, to put it another way, my prediction is that the course of litigation will take us in the direction of values sought in the alternative school movement, voucher plans and schooling fitted to the needs and wishes of each student. With choice of educational program lodged in each student and her/his parents there will be altered patterns of influence in the design of educational programs and techniques. The cases teach us, I think, that these values will be realized, not so much in extensive alternative schools but internally in the public schools proper.

Recent Court Cases

The Classification Cases

The cases of Larry P. [343 F. Supp. 1306 (N.D. Cal. 1972)], Diana (unreported California case), and their cousins across the country have arisen from the overrepresentation by three and four times of racial and national origin groups in EMR (Educable Mentally Retarded) classes. In California, for example, according to State Board of Education Reports, whereas 6% of school-age children were black, some 24% of the children in the EMR classes were black; and whereas 9% of school-age children were Chicano, some 27% of the children in EMR classes were Chicano. The thorough overrepresentation of boys in EMR classes is notorious in the present and, I am told by our historian, was equally notorious 30, 50, and 70 years ago.

The judicial and legislative remedies fashioned in these classification cases have been, I think, largely beside the point. Test instruments standardized to cultural subgroups, despite the legislative mandates, have not been invented. The veto power over placement in EMR classes accorded parents has not been exercised. In the first year in California, fewer than 1% of the parents exercised their veto; in the second year it crept above 1%, but thereafter it slid away again, almost to nothing. And while reporting and justification requirements have significantly cut the gross numbers of children in EMR classes in California, the racial and ethnic group proportions remain about the same. Therein lies the tale. Racial, ethnic, and sex overrepresentation, discrimination, segregation — call it what you will — will disappear only when segregated EMR classes disappear. That is, I predict that integration suits to banish segregated education for the mildly handicapped altogether and order mainstreaming will be filed shortly and will succeed.

The Right to Education Cases

Three cases give the flavor of right to education developments and the sense of their implications: Pennsylvania, Washington, and New Orleans.

1. The federal court in Pennsylvania ordered zero-reject education — access to free public schools for all retarded children, whatever the degree of retardation or associated handicaps (PARC v. Pa.). It may surprise you to know that of the 15,000 previously out-of-school children admitted to the public schools as a consequence of the decree, the greater proportion, some 52%, were only mildly or moderately retarded.

2. The federal court in Pennsylvania ordered that the education provided to all children must be based on programs of education and training appropriate to the needs and capacities of the child. The language of appropriateness and the duty to provide an appropriate program to each child were borrowed from Pennsylvania's education code, which purported to guarantee a proper program of education and training to all of Pennsylvania's exceptional children.

It is interesting that in an as yet incomplete survey of the 50 states, statutes in 19 have been found to declare similar rights to a proper, suitable, or fit program for not only exceptional students but, and most often, each and every student. Parenthetically, as best as my investigations reveal, that language — proper, appropriate, suitable, and fit — seems to have originated in the period of 1910-1930 during the struggle to authorize vocational programs in the schools. The court in Pennsylvania and successor courts were persuaded to borrow the "appropriate" language on testimony that for many retarded children the provision of an inappropriate program was tantamount to providing no education at all. The same theory is embodied in the Department of Health, Education, and Welfare's regulations under Title VI of the Civil Rights Acts of 1964 and was adopted by the U.S. Supreme Court in *Lau v. Nichols* (414 U.S. 563, 1974). In that decision, the Court held that the provision of schooling in the English language alone to children from non-English speaking Chinese families was tantamount to the denial of schooling altogether and, hence, was illegal.

3. The Pennsylvania federal court ordered that the appropriateness of the program for each child be determined within the confines of a presumption in favor of the most integrated, most normalized program; that is, a regular class, including a regular class with resource room instruction, be preferred to a special class in a segregated school, and so on down the list of less integrated, less normal programs and settings. This order for integration was the response to the problem of stigmatic labeling and classification before the court.

1. INTRODUCTION

The trial record displayed the racial, ethnic, sex overrepresentation, and arbitrary and uncertain nature of the classification and assignment process. The court had before it the Garrison and Hammill study indicating that at least 26% and as many as 78% of the children assigned to EMR classes in five-county metropolitan Philadelphia belonged in regular classes (Garrison & Hammill, 1971). The court also had the testimony of Ignacy Goldberg of Columbia Teachers College, James Gallagher and Don Steadman of the University of North Carolina, and Burton Blatt of Syracuse University, expressing the grounds for the professional preference for mainstreaming: the absence of any proof, and significant indications to the contrary, that segregated placements yield better learning outcomes, and thus, the certainty of insufficient advantageous outcomes to override the cost of stigma.

The rather speedy admission of 15,000 children to the public schools in one state, by way of illustration, putting aside for the moment the question of the quality of the school programs to which the children were admitted, was eased considerably by the significant teacher surplus of 1972 and the years since, the vacant classrooms left over from the baby-boom generations, and the release in that and succeeding years of significant revenue-sharing monies. In the year after the decree, Pennsylvania state expenditures for special education increased some $25 million. Between 1971 and the upcoming fiscal year, state expenditures in Pennsylvania will have doubled from $65 million to $140 million. Ironically, a significant number of new teacher positions in special education were created (most of the new pupils, even the mildly retarded were placed in segregated, special classrooms) and some of those positions were filled with retrained or untrained general education teachers at the same time that the court delivered a rather clear hint that it was mainstream teachers who would be required, a hint, whose implications are very clear now. This event is more than an irony; it is an inhibition on the transition to mainstreaming, the strength of which is measured, I suppose, by the increased monies and personnel presently committed to segregated special education stemming from the early implementation of the court decrees.

The Washington and New Orleans cases added two important further dimensions to the right to education: the Washington court extended the zero-reject imperative to all handicaps (Mill v. D.C. Board of Education); and the New Orleans court added to the appropriateness requirement and to the presumption for integrated appropriate programming, the requirement of a written, individualized plan for the education and training of each exceptional child (LeBank v. Spears).

Implications of the Court Cases

Since those three cases, further developments have largely been in the hands of legislatures and state departments of education. Today, some 36 states are under judicial or legislative injunction to provide zero-reject education and appropriate programming in the most integrated setting. Most notably, the Mathias Amendment to the Education of the Handicapped Act of August 1974 and Section 504 of the Vocational Rehabilitation Act of September 1973 generalize those three requirements to all the states. The federal enactments and their implications are discussed in a later section.

It was, as you can appreciate, a necessary condition of security for these orders from the courts that in the last 20 years the invention of operant conditioning and other such techniques, and the reasonably widespread dissemination of teachers, made it possible to say now, as it was not possible to say 25 or 30 years earlier, that every child can benefit from an education. For, as Mr. Justice Stone said in *United States v. Carolene Products*, the constitutionality of a statute which is predicated upon the existence of a particular state of facts — in our case, exclusionary statutes based on the uneducability of certain children — may be challenged by showing that those facts have ceased to exist (304 U.S. 144, 1938). And it was important, in establishing the changed facts before the court, that special educators loudly and clearly said that they had changed, expressing the opinion of the profession encompassed, for example, in the CEC (Council for Exceptional Children) Policy Statement (1971).

Similarly, a current necessary condition of translating the court orders in the right to education cases into reality is the widespread sharing among professionals on the firing line of the knowledge and skill to do what the orders require. It is my observation that the first reaction of professionals on the line to a court or legislative injunction is fear and dread: "My lord! They're mad! We can't do it!" But the second reaction sets in rather quickly: It is the liberation of enormous creative energy and a profound sense of possibility — "Ah, at last! I can do what I've always wanted to do, what my professors taught me I should want to do. And they (the state and superintendent's offices) have been told by the courts and legislature that they must give me the resources to do it!" However, the energy and renewed sense of the possible so released have a limited life. Unless they are put successfully to work and reinforced within a short period of time (unhappily, no one has looked closely enough to determine how short the period is), they die. Too often, I suspect, in community after community and state after state, today, the energy and renewed sense of the possible are dying or are dead because the package of skill and knowledge has not been put in the hands of the persons on the front line.

In implementing the ordered and appropriate education for each child in the most integrated setting possible, the question that arises is, "How is what is appropriate for a particular child to be determined?" All of the cases, most state statutes, and the Mathias Amendment, borrowing from the CEC model statute, have opted for one of a range of due process hearing devices. If a child or parents regards a particular program as inappropriate, he is entitled to a hearing. Typically, the hearing is before a hearing examiner, an impartial professional, usually, who is appointed by and acting for the state Secretary of Education. The parent is entitled to access to all school records and to an independent evaluation of the child and her/his program before the hearing. At the hearing, the parent may be represented by any person of his choice, may present evidence, and may cross-examine any school district and school pesonnel. Theoretically, at least, the only question before the hearing examiner is, "What program is appropriate for this child?" Questions of money and whether the district currently has the appropriate program are irrelevant. The hearing examiner's duty is to decide on the record what the appropriate program is and to order that it be provided.

We have a lot to learn about the structure of the hearing, who the hearing officer should be, what resources must be available to parents, and

so on, and whether the hearing or some other procedure can best yield individually appropriate programs. Some preliminary observations on experience with due process hearings to date, however, are in order.

1. Of the first 70 hearing decisions in Pennsylvania, nearly a score resulted in orders requiring the creation of a program that had not previously existed in the school district in question.

2. On the question of integration, two nearly identical hearings resulted in opposite decisions. In both, the question was an appropriate placement for a third-grade boy, heretofore in a usual third-grade classroom. Both boys had been assigned an IQ in the mid-60's. In one case, the hearing examiner ordered regular classroom placement with resource room assistance. In the other, the child was ordered into an EMR class and the school district was ordered to persuade the parents, who had had one bitterly unsuccessful experience with another EMR child, that their son would indeed prosper and thrive in the EMR class. (That order was rather difficult to implement, I suspect.)

3. A preliminary analysis of the Pennsylvania hearings to date, by Kuriloff, Kirp, and Buss (1974) suggests, as one would suspect, that parents and children win depending on their resources: lawyers, trained lay advocates, and other experts who can be marshaled in the presentation of their side of the case.

A bill introduced this spring in the California legislature by a member of the Assembly Ways and Means Committee, would appropriate state funds and assign Mathias Amendment monies to parent organizations and coalitions of parent organizations to engage such resources for complaints in the hearings. But, just as the availability of hearings on Public Assistance eligibility determinations, in the 30 years that the Social Security Act has provided for such, has had the effect on caseworkers of resolving doubts in favor of recipients, so, if parents are provided properly with resources, one may expect the very existence of a hearing opportunity to lend influence and weight to a parent and child's perception of what is the appropriate program.

Apart from functioning to establish authoritatively defined, individually appropriate programs and to apportion greater influence in school decisions to students' and parents' views of children's needs and their wishes, the hearings may have other uses. For example, the

hearings may function to allow a school professional on the line, who is blocked by the
hierarchy or a shortage of resources from providing what (s)he regards as a proper program,
to press the question in an authoritative and
relatively protected form.

Clearly, the advent of education to such
hearing opportunities presents new role demands and possibilities for teachers and other
school professionals; and the education of
teachers and school professionals, generally, for
these roles, becomes very important. Questions,
for example, of school professionals' ability and
willingness to validate professional judgments in
a contest...to see professional wisdom derived
dialectically rather than hierarchically...to put
their opinions and judgments on the record for
scrutiny...to accept decisions, not arm-in-arm,
but with some grace and not with defensive,
destructive bitterness. It is a new set of goals to
which educators will have to be educated.

The third set of cases — the right to treatment
cases — recapitulates the same theme. Apart
from defining certain minimum quantitative
standards of staffing which must be met by
mental institutions. Wyatt and Stickney and its
progeny declare the right of each resident to a
program of habilitation — and that expressly
includes education — that is reasonably calculated to realize the resident's capabilities (1972).
Also, each resident must be provided a written,
individualized plan of treatment. Further, resort
must be available for each resident to an impartial forum, most often committees, rather
than hearing examination-based decisions, to
determine if that treatment plan is appropriate.
And the treatment must be provided in the least
restrictive setting possible. Thus, the order in
the Willowbrook case just a few weeks ago,
requiring that within six years all but a handful
of residents be provided treatment in com-
munity-based programs (1973).

Roots of the New Rules

Zero-reject and Integration

Zero-reject and integration imperatives have
their modern source in *Brown v. Board of
Education*. In *Brown*, the Court wrote,

Today, education is perhaps the most important function of state and local governments. "It is required in the performance of
our most basic public responsibilities." It is
the very foundation of good citizenship. Today it is the principal instrument in awaken-
ing the child to cultural values, in preparing
him for later professional training, and in
helping him to adjust normally to his environment. In these days, it is doubtful that
any child may reasonably be expected to
succeed in life if he is denied the opportunity
of an education. Such an opportunity, where
the state has undertaken to provide it, is a
right which must be made available to all on
equal terms. [347 U.S. 483,493, 1542]

Clearly, if schooling is provided to children
generally and, indeed to most handicapped
children, it must be provided to all handicapped
children; hence, zero-reject education.

But *Brown*, after all, is primarily an integration decision: Separate educational facilities required by law are inherently unequal.

John W. Davis, the Democratic candidate for
the presidency in 1924 who twice declined appointment to the U.S. Supreme Court, was, in
his day, the most highly regarded appellate
lawyer in the nation. In 1954, he represented the
state of South Carolina, a defendant, in *Brown v.
Board of Education*. He opened his argument to
the U.S. Supreme Court as follows:

Mr. Davis: May it please the Court, I think if
the appellants' construction of the Fourteenth
Amendment should prevail here, there is no
doubt in my mind that it would catch the
Indian within its grasp just as much as the
Negro. If it should prevail, I am unable to see
why a state would have any further right to
segregate its pupils on the ground of sex or on
the ground of age or on the ground of mental
capacity . . . [Friedman, 1969]

Well, John Davis was right. *Brown* has been
extended to the Indian and to the Chicano and
to women and it will, in my opinion, be extended
to mental capacity and physical and mental
handicap generally. The analogies between the
black and the handicapped and their respective
experiences in our society are startlingly exact,
and thus their legal posture is startlingly similar.
Both have been subjected to a history of pur-
poseful discrimination and segregation, and
relegated to a position of political powerlessness.
The classifying criterion in each case — race and
handicapped — is visited accidentally and im-
mutably upon them and the injury suffered from

separation, even if all other things were equal, is the same. As the Court put it in *Brown*,

> To separate them . . . generates a feeling of inferiority . . . that may affect their hearts and minds in a way unlikely ever to be undone. "Segregation" has a detrimental effect upon the . . . children." The policy of separating (them) is usually interpreted as denoting . . . inferiority." (In) the field of public education, the doctrine of 'separate but equal' has no place. [347 U.S. 483,494-5]

The prehistory of *Brown*, perhaps, makes the point most clearly. In *Sweatt v. Painter*, a case that preceded *Brown* by four years, Texas defended the exclusion of the plaintiff from the "white" law school in Texas and his assignment to the exclusively "black" law school in the state on the ground, among others, that the "black" law school had a lower student-teacher ratio. The Court noted that the plaintiff was "excluded from (school) contact with the racial group which numbered 85% of the population and with whom he would eventually be dealing," and held that "excluded from such a substantial and significant segment of society, we cannot conclude that the education offered plaintiff is substantially equal (Sweatt v. Painter)."

As with the law schools, so also for primary and secondary education: the constitutional point, with respect to integration, is now also the statutory law of the land, enforceable in court in its own right.

The Mathias Amendment, borrowing from the constitutional theme sounded by the courts and CEC's model statute, requires as a condition of federal funds that each state adopt

> procedures to insure that to the maximum extent appropriate, handicapped children, including children in public or private institutions or other care facilities are educated with children who are not handicapped, and that special classes, separate schooling, or other removal of handicapped children from the regular education environment occurs only when . . . education . . . cannot (otherwise) be achieved satisfactorily [P.L. 93-380].

From the language of the statute, I would add the empirical observation that this is not being done. Parenthetically, Section 504 of the Vocational Rehabilitation Act of 1973 adopts precisely and verbatim the language of Title VI of the Civil Rights Act of 1964 and prohibits discrimination against the mentally and physi-

cally handicapped in any program funded with federal monies.

Acting on these imperatives of a constitutional and statutory variety, it is interesting to note that the Arkansas State Board of Education, 17 years after Little Rock, recently has called an end to what it terms "another form of separate but equal education," and has directed that the integration of handicapped children occur in Arkansas by the 1979-80 school year: in regular classes, where possible; in special classes located in regular schools where necessary. Such action, the Arkansas Board of Education said, was necessary to teach all children "human dignity." Note that the Mathias Amendment enjoins that handicapped children be educated *with* children who are not handicapped, not that they be educated in the same way. Thus, we return to individuation and its roots and to some thoughts about its implications.

There is a long-standing due process doctrine that once a state has extended a benefit to one of its citizens, whether it is a driver's license, unemployment compensation, public assistance, or whatever, it may not take that benefit away without notice and the opportunity of a hearing. So, too, for education. Similarly, the state may not impose stigma upon a citizen without notice and the opportunity to be heard. The case is *Wisconsin v. Constantineau* (400 U.S. 433, 1971).

Wisconsin had a statute authorizing the local sheriff or other official, if he judged a person publicly drunk too often, to post the person's name in the town square and outside the taverns in the town. Mrs. Constantineau found her name posted. She sued and won, and the U.S. Supreme Court said as follows

> . . . the only issue present here is whether the label or characterization given a person in posting, though a mark of illness to some, is to others such a stigma or badge of disgrace that the procedural due process requires notice and the opportunity to be heard. Here, the private interest is such that those requirements must be met. Only when the whole proceedings leading to the pinning of an unsavory label on a person are aired, can oppressive results be presented [400 U.S. 433, 436].

Thus, hallowed doctrine in the law: due process — individual look and scrutiny, individual record, and individual judgment — is required before the state may deprive a citizen of a hard-won benefit and before the state may attach stigma to that citizen.

The integration imperative is welcome. If, however, it yields integration into, say, undifferentiated sameness, then, as I suggested earlier, there is little gain. Thus, if the directions take by the special education cases are to be fully realized, general education to which special students shall be integrated, must itself take on characteristics of individuation. There are, I suggest to you, two sources in the law that make such a result likely. (a) As exceptional students are integrated in regular classes, by due process, individuation mechanisms created in the cases will travel to general education with them. (b) The same conditions that make due process hearings in individuation necessary as a matter of law in special education are present as well in general education. Consider tracking. To find oneself in the wrong track, or in the track one wishes not to be in, is to suffer the loss of a benefit extended by the state. And often, to find oneself in a particular track, is to find oneself assigned stigma. It is, I believe, perfectly predictable that treating the special education cases as precedent, the courts, very shortly, putting aside for the moment the question of the continued existence of tracking, will order individuation devices, due process hearings, notice, and the opportunity to be heard before and in the course of tracking systems. Thus, coupled with attention by the courts to those phrases — suitability, appropriateness, proper fit — in state education codes that extend to general education, it is my belief that individuation will, in the months not very far ahead, be brought home to general education itself.

Thus, special education may become general and general education special. We are approaching the day when for each child, handicapped or not, the law will require that the schooling fit the child, his needs, his capacities, and his wishes; not that the child fit the school. That, I believe, is the purport of the so-called special education cases.

Discussion

Gilhool: As against two . . . and . . . 100 years, I would predict that the process of individuation, of making general education special, will occur in 30 years, and that we ought to continue our work and get it together again then

to see. Perhaps I have used 30 years not because it is an objectively based prediction but because in 30 years, maybe we can get it together and see.

Question: How do you define equality of rights? Is it equality of dollar treatment? Equality of time? Equality of achievement at the end of the treatment? Do you see yourself as operating with any particular explicit definition of equality?

Gilhool: Yes, I reject equality of output. I am an adherent, I suppose, of the position that equality should be measured in input terms. More to the point, as I think my remark suggests, I am concerned about equality in process, that is to say, equality of choice.

Question: I want to raise a question out of the Philadelphia experience and the court order. How much flexibility do you, from a legal standpoint, see that there can be in implementation? In Philadelphia, we started with a problem of economics; we did not have the money or the time needed to assemble staff, facilities, and so on. Yet there was a very real problem of response to the court order. As we have moved ahead in implementation we have accomplished a great deal of attitudinal change and we have made many steps toward responding to the new population. But there are some specifics, such as the problem of including in classes pupils who had previously not been contained because of the threat to other children their behavior presented. How much flexibility is there within the limits the law has described?

Gilhool: There is no possible general answer. When the Pennsylvania court said, a year, give or take a few months, to find all the children and bring them into the school, I think that the court said "reasonably." Indeed, I think that the experience in Philadelphia, Pennsylvania, Michigan, and other places indicates that a year is a reasonable period of time. When discourse goes to other more qualitative questions, the equality of program and the fit between program and child, I think it is very clear now as, I think, it was clear in the beginning, that we are talking about a lengthy struggle — a struggle over time. One has to speak to particulars in order to make predictions about what time or what particulars courts or hearing officers or associations for retarded children, legislators, lawyers, or anyone else will allow. Delay is constitutionally suspect, as the Court has said, but once that is said, it still does not tell us very much. One would have to deal, I think, in particulars.

References

Friedman, L. (Ed.) *Argument: The oral argument before the supreme court in Brown v. Board of Education of Topeka, 1952-55.* New York, Chelsea House, 1969, 51.

Garrison, M. Jr. & Hammill, D. Who are the retarded? *Exceptional Children*, 1971.

Hobson v. Hansen, 269 F. Supp. 401, 497 (D.D.C. 1967).

Kuriloff, Kirp, & Buss. Legal reform of special education: Empirical studies and procedural propsoals. California Law Review, 1974, *40*.

Lebank v. Spears, 60 F.R.D. 135 (E.D. La. 1973).

Mill v. D.C. Board of Education, 348 F. Supp. 866 (D.D.C. 1972).

New York State Association for Retarded Children, Inc. v. Rockefeller, 357 F. Supp. 752 (1973).

Pennsylvania Association for Retarded Children v. Pennsylvania, 343 F. Supp. 279 (E.D. Pa. 1972).

P.L. 93-380; U.S. Code Section 1413 (13).

Sweatt v. Painter, 339 U.S. 629, 634 (1950).

United States v. Carolene Products Co., 304 U.S. 144, 152-53 n. 4 (1938).

Wyatt v. Stickney, 344 F. Supp. 387 (M.D. Ala. 1972) affirmed sub. nom.

Wyatt v. Aderholt, 503 F 2d. 1305 (5th Cir. 1974).

Issues Regarding the IEP: Teachers on the Front Line

JOSEPHINE HAYES
SCOTTIE TORRES HIGGINS

JOSEPHINE HAYES *is a Specialist for Policy Research and* SCOTTIE TORRES HIGGINS *is Assistant Director for Policy Research, Governmental Relations Unit, The Council for Exceptional Children.*

Each school year brings with it significant dates to be placed on the calendar by professionals. This school year and next, two dates emerge as being critical for any professional who provides special education or related services to handicapped children. The first significant date, last October 1, 1977, has come and gone. On that date an individualized education program (IEP) had to be developed for each eligible handicapped child in order to be counted for purposes of funding in compliance with the Education for All Handicapped Children Act of 1975, Public Law 94-142. The forthcoming date to remember will be September 1, 1978. On that date each local, intermediate, and state education agency must provide a free, appropriate public education to each handicapped child or stand in violation of the rights and protections set forth under federal law, the Education for All Handicapped Children Act and Section 504 of the Vocational Rehabilitation Act of 1973, Public Law 93-112.

The October date has passed. As the new year begins, it is critical to look to September and identify what changes have been made for handicapped children and what changes yet remain so that they will be afforded the rights guaranteed in federal law. Professionals on the front line must respond in order to fulfill their responsibilities.

Since the passage of Public Law 94-142 in late November 1975, education agencies have undergone numerous policy and procedural changes. These changes have in turn generated considerable dialogue, both positive and negative, in communities and in faculty lounges across the country. The key elements of Public Law 94-142 are often misunderstood or little attempt is made to relate those key elements to the IEP. This article addresses this concern and explores how Public Law 94-142 makes teachers responsible and accountable for assuring that each handicapped child receive the required special education and related services set forth in the IEP.

Federal IEP Requirements

Public Law 94-142 requires that each eligible handicapped child receive an education designed to meet that child's unique learning needs. This specially designed instruction must be provided at no cost to the parents. In fact, the statute specifically requires the development of the IEP in order that the handicapped child receive an appropriate education. Therefore, the IEP becomes the cornerstone of the law and the management tool that parents, teachers, and other professionals, as well as the eligible student, can refer to when questions arise concerning resources or educational goals.

Section 504 of the Vocational Rehabilitation Act of 1973 states that the IEP, as required in Public Law 94-142, is one way to document assurance of an appropriate education. While we know that a written document must be produced according to federal requirements for every handicapped child, this requirement is not necessarily new. Many states have had some requirements to provide an individualized and appropriate or suitable education for a number of years. However, for teachers no doubt experiences have occurred over the past year where many procedures have changed for identifying and placing handicapped students. Teachers can get discouraged as an administration changes procedures that result in new or revised reports from new teaching staff. Therefore, teachers must be cognizant of the critical requirements of federal law and understand how those impact on their professional behavior. For that reason, several significant components of Public Law 94-142 have been selected for discussion here.

Least Restrictive Environment

One provision of Public Law 94-142 is the concept of placement of a child in the *least restrictive environment*. Too often educators interchange this new term with an old one— *mainstreaming*. Public Law 94-142 is not a mainstreaming law. The term mainstreaming does not appear in the law. Yet, this term has often evoked confusion in the profession and overreaction from the education community as a whole. If the term mainstreaming is phased out because of the different interpretations for everyone hearing and using it, regular educators may have a clearer understanding of what appropriate education for handicapped children in the least restrictive environment means. A word change alone is not enough.

Teachers must consciously change their thinking on how handicapped children receive special education and related services. Historically, children who required special education were pulled out of the regular program and put into self contained classes. This was too often an all or nothing

approach since children either fit the program or they did not qualify for services. As early as 1961, Deno's (1974) cascade of services showed us that the continuum concept must be in effect in order to assure a range of appropriate options. The least restrictive environment provision requires that placement decisions be made on the basis of the individual's needs. No child can be removed from regular class participation any more than is appropriate for that child and Public Law 94-142 requires documentation in the IEP of the extent to which the child can participate in the regular program.

For many years, handicapped children were denied participation in regular physical education or vocational education programs. Annually, many teachers would negotiate with their colleagues to permit access for their handicapped students to these programs. The federal laws now guarantee that a handicapped student can not be discriminated against and must have access, where appropriate for the child, to physical education and vocational education programs, specially designed if necessary. In addition, the least restrictive environment provision means that handicapped children have access to the variety of educational programs and services available to nonhandicapped children such as art, music, industrial arts, and consumer and homemaking education. For teachers, this expands the programing options for their handicapped student on a systematic rather than random basis.

Procedural Safeguards

Due Process. A second requirement of federal provisions regards the necessary procedural safeguards established to ensure that handicapped students receive a free, appropriate public education. Reinforcing Constitutional guarantees, Public Law 94-142 sets forth procedures to ensure that due process is afforded each handicapped child at every point educational decisions are made. As soon as a child is referred for potential special education and related services, parents and teachers must be involved. Teachers who either initiate the referral and/or currently teach the child must document what interventions in learning have occurred for that child and identify the child's education strengths and weaknesses. As new assessments are

1. INTRODUCTION

conducted, the parents must be informed as to what information will be collected and how that information will be used. School district personnel have, over the past few years, made significant progress in informing parents of what is being done "to" their child. Emphasis needs to be placed on the "whys." When parents and teachers work together from the point of referral, few surprises occur as the IEP is developed.

Due process affords parents the right to a hearing if they disagree with the written IEP. When this occurs, and the procedures vary from state to state, the appeals process begins. The child shall remain in the current placement until a decision is rendered as to the appropriate program for the child. Just as teachers must be involved as the IEP is developed, they may also be involved when that IEP is being appealed. Minimally, the educational assessment information and reports that teachers have written become part of the evidence used at the hearing. In some instances, teachers will be requested to appear in support of the professional reports made. Occasionally this request to appear comes from the parents rather than the administration. A teacher's role has been and must continue to be to make sound professional decisions and professional judgments for each handicapped child. If these recommendations are judicious, then no teacher should have cause to worry about the hearing process. It is important to retain the child-advocate perspective rather than engage in adversarial relationships.

Confidentiality. Another procedural safeguard ensures the confidentiality of all the reports and records pertinent to the education of each handicapped child. While the IEP and all of the documents used to develop the IEP are confidential, parents and the child of majority age must be informed of their right to request access to all such records. This has implications for how each teacher will record, store and retrieve all personal and professional records.

Personnel Development

A third provision of Public Law 94-142 has direct implications for every regular and special educator working with handicapped children. Each local education agency must spec-ify in writing the procedures to be used in the local implementation of the comprehensive system of personnel development established by the state education agency. Essentially, the federal law requires that inservice training be provided to both regular and special educators "and that activities sufficient to carry out this personnel development plan are scheduled" (Public Law 94-142, Final Regulations, Sec. 121a.380, 1977). Teachers must have input into the planning and designing of the personnel development activities so that the inservice training will be relevant to teacher needs. The entire process of developing IEP's requires some expanded roles and responsibilities of teachers. Competencies and skills required by teachers to successfully develop and implement each IEP may be a major area identified for purposes of professional development.

The policy areas of Public Law 94-142 presented here were selected to identify teacher issues that are peripheral to but necessary requirements of individualized education programs. Many changes regarding IEP's have occurred in schools to date. Teachers must review the basic IEP requirements to ascertain who must meet to develop the IEP and determine what constitutes a written document.

Meeting to Develop the IEP

The purpose of developing the IEP is to set forth in writing a commitment of resources that indicates what special education and related services will be provided to meet each handicapped child's unique needs. The IEP is a management tool that allows parents, teachers, and administrators to know what educational services have been committed. The purpose of an IEP is not to plan the total instruction of the handicapped child. Good instructional planning on a day to day and week to week basis is not a new phenomenon to competent teachers. Caution must be exercised that teachers and other support personnel recognize the distinction between instructional planning and the requirements as set forth in federal law that become the individualized education program (Torres, 1977 a, b, c). Otherwise, teachers may be trapped into documenting too much information in the meeting to develop the IEP. Public Law 94-142 (1975) requires that the IEP be developed in any meeting by a representative of the local educational agency or an intermediate educational unit who shall be qualified to provide, or supervise the provision of, specially designed instruction to meet the unique needs of handicapped children, the teacher, the parents or guardian of such child, and whenever appropriate, such child. (Sec. 4(a)(4)(19))

Translating this federal requirement into practice requires decisions to be made at the local level regarding teacher participation in the IEP meeting. Difficulty in teacher participation in the development of an IEP frequently comes about in two ways. First, many state and local education agencies have tacked the IEP meeting on top of an already existing system of evaluating and placing handicapped children. The results too frequently find a cadre of people assembled including health care personnel, psychologists, social workers, administrators, perhaps each teacher that works with the child, and the parents.

The second difficulty regarding teacher participation occurs more often at the secondary level. Typically, a student may have four or five regular education teachers as well as at least one special educator. Which teacher(s) should be designated to participate in the IEP development? The authors would insist that those decisions must be made on a per child basis, with priority given to the teacher(s) who has the primary responsibility for implementation of the IEP. Recognizing that often the logistics of release time during school hours is a complex problem, particularly at the secondary level, the federal law does not require that all of the child's teachers develop the IEP. Clearly, some mechanism must exist for two way communication involving all IEP implementers to guarantee an exchange of relevant information. It is critical for teachers to have input into and understand the policy and procedures used in their district governing appropriate teacher participation.

The Written IEP

As each teacher knows by now, the content requirements of the IEP as set forth in Section 4(a)(4)(19)(A-E) of Public Law 94–142 (1975) are straightforward. Each IEP must be written and must contain statements regarding the following information:

1. Child's present levels of educational peformance.
2. Annual goals, including short term instructional objectives.
3. Specific special education and related services to be provided to the child and the extent to which the child will be able to participate in regular educational programs.
4. Projected dates for initiation and duration of services.
5. Appropriate objective criteria and evaluation procedures and schedules for determining, on at least an annual basis, whether the short term instructional objectives are being achieved.

The responsibility for accomplishing the actual writing task itself is not federally legislated. Alternative arrangements may be made for recording the information. This task is not necessarily a teacher responsibility. Teacher input into district procedures regarding this responsibility is desirable. It is critical to remember that the IEP document is not totally new as a result of Public Law 94–142. In fact, 27 states have had for several years some sort of requirements for a written document for each handicapped child. (CEC Policy Research Center, 1977.)

Accountability and Teacher Advocacy

Much anxiety arises as teachers frequently perceive the IEP as an accountability measure that can be used against them if the student does not attain the specified annual goals or short term objectives.

It is imperative in viewing the IEP as a management tool that teachers, parents, and administrators realize that specific resources (i.e., time, personnel, money) are being committed by the education agency to the handicapped child vis-a-vis the IEP. But what about teacher liability for student mastery of skills? Public Law 94–142 does not require that any teacher, agency, or other person be held accountable if a child does not achieve the growth projected in the IEP. Clarification in the commentary that accompanies the regulations of Public Law 94–142 states that the intent is

to relieve concerns that the individualized program constitutes a guarantee by the public

1. INTRODUCTION

agency and the teacher that a child will progress at a specified rate. However, this section does not relieve agencies and teachers from making good faith efforts to assist the child in achieving the objectives and goals listed in the individualized education program. Further, the section does not limit a parent's right to complain and ask for revisions of the child's program, or to invoke due process procedures, if the parent feels that these efforts are not being made. (Public Law 94-142, Final Regulations, Sec. 121a.349 (Comments), 1977)

While teachers may not be held responsible for pupil attainment of the annual goals and short term objectives, teachers are now, more than ever, in a situation where they can positively advocate for those services they need as required and specified in the child's IEP. However, as child advocates, teachers must be cognizant of the potential conflict they are placed in when having to confront the system. When evidence of program weaknesses or lack of services promised exists, the teacher, who is on the front line, is usually the first person to recognize the breakdowns in the system. It is at this point that teachers must place their responsibility to the children they serve ahead of all other concerns by responsibly advocating for the necessary remedies. Perhaps the most appropriate style of advocacy can be termed cooperative advocacy whereby all parties (i.e., teachers, administrators, support personnel, parents) contribute to make the system responsive to the child and ensure that the resources committed in the IEP are provided.

The quality of educational services for handicapped children resides in the abilities, qualifications, and competencies of the personnel who provide those services. Professionally trained and competent personnel engaging in positive public relations with parents, with other educators, and in the community at large are a force not to be dismissed lightly.

In the months to come, many opportunities for the exercise of teachers' most persuasive efforts to protect children's best interests will undoubtedly present themselves. Special educators will have the responsibility to share their specialized knowledge concerning handicapped children. They must be responsive as regular educators struggle with the implications that the least restrictive environment has on their class. Special educators

must be able to explain why the child does not have to be removed from the regular class unless there are compelling reasons for doing so. Teachers must advocate for appropriate resources needed as a result of IEP requirements for special education and related services rather than being forced to make recommendations based on existing categorical programs. Finally, teachers must work toward changing attitudes about special education by focusing on the educational and developmental needs of handicapped children (CEC, 1976). These issues must be positively integrated into all aspects of professional activities in order to protect each handicapped child's right to a free, appropriate public education. Unless these rights are protected now, then potentially much may be lost later at the collective bargaining table.

Changing Roles and Responsibilities

With the changing times, modern technology, and the age of accountability, it is particularly important that teachers understand how their roles have changed and their responsibilities have increased. It is no longer enough to know how to competently work with students and guide their learning. Teachers must be informed, knowledgeable, and responsible to assure that they are contributing to the free, appropriate public education that each handicapped child is now guaranteed.

Consequently, teachers must be informed regarding the child rights and protections that exist. They have the right to be kept informed on relevant interpretations made by the courts or by policymakers at the federal, state, or local level that impact on a teacher's role in developing and implementing the IEP. They have the right to inservice training to prepare themselves for IEP participation. Teachers have the right to know current administrative procedures employed in their education agency and they need to understand how to impact on that system to effect positive and appropriate educational services through the IEP for each handicapped child. To that end, teachers also have the responsibility to seek out accurate and reliable information from a variety of sources regarding their professional rights and responsibilities in the development and implementation of the IEP. Because second hand information can sometimes be incomplete, misleading, or even faulty, teachers have a responsibility to collect accurate information. Nothing serves to erode a professional's credibility faster than inaccurate information.

Resources

There exists today a myriad of information regarding federal, state, and local policy requirements for the appropriate education of handicapped students. It is recommended that teachers make use of a variety of sources to obtain information that is most relevant to them. Their professional organization, The Council for Exceptional Children, has and will continue to make available to professionals and parents accurate information and policy interpretations. The authors have identified several policy documents that every teacher should have and should be familiar with. Minimally, these are as follows:

1. Public Law 94-142 and Section 504 of Public Law 93-112. Copies of both the federal statutes and regulations may be obtained from a local congressperson. Teachers should read firsthand what others are interpreting for them.
2. A copy of the state's special education laws and regulations.
3. A copy of the local application, which may be obtained from a special education administrator. Public Law 94-142 requires that each education agency assure to the state that a free, appropriate public education is provided every eligible handicapped child. A description of the policy methods and procedures must be described. Teachers may want to pay particular attention to the following sections: facilities, personnel, and services; personnel development (inservice training); parent involvement; IEP; procedural safeguards; and participation in cegular education programs.
4. The state plan, which may be obtained from the state department of education. Each state education agency certifies to the federal government the assurances that every handicapped child in the state is receiving appropriate special education and related services. Teachers may want to review the following sections to determine where their district stands in relation to the rest of the state: comprehensive system

of personnel development; IEP; procedural safeguards; least restrictive environment; and identification, location, and evaluation of handicapped children. Teachers may request permission to Xerox these sections or write to their state consultant for these portions.

A comparison of the above policy documents will enable teachers to better understand the background behind administrative decisions; the intent of school policy; and the distinction between federal, state, and local requirements in order to better advocate for policy change or better implementation as needed.

Conclusion

In the final analysis, it must be remembered that professionals themselves, both directly and through professional organizations, have largely influenced landmark federal legislation. While selected issues relating to the individualized education program have been discussed, others have yet to be identified. What remains to be known as September approaches is how teachers on the front line will continue to respond to the IEP mandates of Public Law 94-142.

References

The Council for Exceptional Children (CEC). Policy statements of The Council for Exceptional Children as established by the delegate assembly. Reston VA: CEC, 1976.

The Council for Exceptional Children (CEC) Policy Research Center. Unpublished analysis. Reston VA: CEC, 1977.

Deno, E. Special education as developmental capital. In G. J. Warfield (Ed.), Mainstream currents: Reprints from Exceptional Children 1968-1974. Reston VA: CEC, 1974.

Public Law 93-112, Vocational Rehabilitation Act of 1973, 93rd Congress, 1973.

Public Law 94-142, Education for All Handicapped Children Act of 1975, 94th Congress, 1st Session, 1975.

Public Law 94-142, Education for All Handicapped Children Act of 1975, Final Regulations US Office of Education, 1977.

Torres, S. (Ed.). A Primer on individualized education programs for handicapped children. Reston VA: The Foundation for Exceptional Children, 1977. (a)

Torres, S. The individual education program

Accountability: An Overview of the Impact of Litigation on Professionals

H. RUTHERFORD TURNBULL, III

□ It is now common to hear discussions about governmental accountability, its theoretical basis, the rights of consumers and clients in enforcing it, the strategies for securing it, and the consequences of abiding by it. In part, these discussions have been provoked by and are a response to frontier opening judicial acknowledgments of rights to education and treatment. They also are a response to court decisions (a) holding professionals personally liable in damages for treating patients in mental health and mental retardation institutions in professionally unacceptable ways or for refusing to treat them at all and (b) establishing and enforcing the right to treatment and education. To the extent that litigation has been the catalyst for imposing a principle of accountability to consumers and the public at large on professionals involved with the handicapped, it has been and will continue to be welcome, desirable, and even necessary.

THE ISSUES

To know what accountability means is far from a difficult task. To make a person accountable is to challenge or contest him, or to hold him answerable; that which is accountable is capable of being explained; he who is accountable is held answerable.

To appreciate what accountability means, however, is a far more difficult task. Accountability raises a myriad of principal issues: Who holds whom responsible, for what action, according to what standards, under what theories of law, how, and for what reasons of policy. And there are a host of ancillary questions: What types of accountability are now required and are likely to be required in the future? What types of accountability should the law require? How far does or should accountability extend to

a claimant of it? What interests in accountability are asserted by various claimants? How are the claimants' sometimes conflicting claims to be balanced against each other? Finally, how is accountability to be extended to various aspects of the client-provider relationship?

Viewed from the perspective of the law, none of these issues is free from immense complexity, although the answers to the principal issues seem simple. Who holds whom accountable? The client consumer holds the professional service provider accountable, responsible, and liable. For what action? For the manner in which the professional deals with, or fails to deal with, the client. According to what standards? According to standards developed in law for protecting the rights of other disabled persons, such as prisoners and minors, and also according to standards developed by professionals working with the handicapped. Under what theories of law? Primarily under the constitutional principles of due process and equal protection, as embodied in the 5th and 14th Amendments, and under a new application of the doctrine of cruel and unusual punishment under the 8th Amendment. How? By guaranteeing due process, by ordering remedies of violations of legal rights, and by requiring the professionals (and thus governments and the body politic) to treat disabled persons as equals and on equal terms. For what reason of policy? For the reason that, although humans are divisible into groups, human and constitutional rights are not.

UNDERLYING PRINCIPLES

Behind these complex judicial responses lie two major themes: First, human and constitutional rights are not divisible and may not legally be parceled out according to the mental, emo-

"Accountability: An Overview of the Impact of Litigation on Professionals," H. Rutherford Turnbull, III, *Public Policy and the Education of Exceptional Children*, 1976. © 1976 The Council for Exceptional Children.

tional, or physical attributes of a person; and, second, the unequal person is entitled to equal treatment under the law.

Also behind these complex judicial responses lies the engrained belief of society, enforced at law, that persons should be answerable to each other for what they do to each other. In the law of trusts, the "prudent man" rule requires the caretaker of another's property to account to its owner for his actions. In the law of torts, the "reasonable man" rule requires that one person answer in damages to another for acting in an unreasonable way toward him and thereby injuring him. In the law of crimes, the right of the public to apply sanctions requires that persons who commit crimes against the public be punished, rehabilitated, and prevented from doing so again.

Although the concept of accountability is not new to the law, its present application to the providers of service to the handicapped is of recent origin, thus prompting the question, why? The reasons, of course, are manifold. Professionals recently have made such significant advances in understanding and treating disabled persons that they are thereby enabled and thus required to deal in new ways with respect to their clients. The public is newly aware of the needs of the disabled. Law reformers are engaged in the continuation of old civil rights battles on new battle grounds. Finally, this is an age of egalitarianism, an age that is capable of adopting as its tenets the indivisibility of human and constitutional rights and the essential equality of all persons.

THE RIGHT TO TREATMENT

The court decisions establishing the right to treatment have two principal goals: the improvement of the condition of the handicapped person himself, and the improvement of the conditions in which the person is treated or confined. The unstated predicate of these decisions is that an improvement in the person will result from an improvement in his environment. The unstated implication is that neither type of improvement can occur unless professionals can be held to account for at least the environmental conditions and their professional relationships to their clients.

Three Legal Theories

To hold the professionals accountable, the courts have resorted to three well known legal theories. The first is procedural due process, which guarantees a person the right and a meaningful opportunity to protest and to be heard before government may take action with respect to him. This is the rule that the government must proceed fairly before it acts (usually applied to commitment of the mentally ill or retarded). Second is substantive due process, which signifies that there are certain rights and privileges that a state may not arbitrarily take from a citizen (such as the deprivation of liberty through confinement) and that the state may not act unreasonably, arbitrarily, or capriciously in dealing with a citizen. Third is equal protection, which guarantees to the handicapped person the same rights and benefits all other citizens have with respect to their government (including all of the constitutional rights of procedural and substantive due process) unless the withholding of the rights or benefits by the state is for a valid reason that justifies the state in singling out the handicapped person for differential treatment.

These theories are applied solely by reason of the fact that the handicapped person is confined by the state and is in its custody. It is the creative application of these theories that is the vehicle for insuring the state's and professionals' accountability.

Procedural due process, for example, has been applied to prevent unjustified civil commitments to mental institutions (*Baxtrom v. Herald*, 1966; *Specht v. Robinson*, 1967; *McNeil v. Director, Patient Institution*, 1972). It is also beginning to be applied to prevent unjustified transfers from one type of an institution to another (*Kesselbrenner v. Anonymous*, 1973). Both applications advance the principle of accountability—that professionals be required to justify the action they propose to take before being allowed to take it.

Substantive due process, for example, has been applied to civil confinement, the nature and duration of which bears no reasonable relation to the purposes for which the person was confined (*Jackson v. Indiana*, 1972; *Wyatt v. Stickney*, 1971). If the purpose of confinement is habilitation or treatment, confinement may not partake of merely custodial care or, worse, punishment. Substantive due process thus advances accountability by requiring the state and its professionals to provide habilitation and treatment.

Finally, equal protection requires that a person's civil confinement be justified by a rational reason or compelling state interest (since confinement affects the fundamental right of personal liberty). This requirement can be satisfied only if treatment and rehabilitation are furnished, since the person is classified as needing confinement on the basis of his need for treatment. In the absence of confinement with treatment, there is no rationality or compelling state interest in the classification or confinement, and the person's equal protection guarantee is violated (*Baxtrom v. Herald*, 1966). In the same manner as substantive due process, equal protection advances a principle of accountability.

Other Judicial Responses

The exact nature of the state's duty to treat those

1. INTRODUCTION

it has confined has not been agreed upon, and it is misleading to suggest that judicial responses to claimed accountability are unanimous. Indeed, some courts have rejected the federal constitutional basis for the duty (*Burham v. Georgia*, 1972), while others have held that the state's duty is only to prevent deterioration or harm (*NYARC v. Rockefeller*, 1973). Some, however, have held that the state's duty is to habilitate (*Wyatt v. Stickney*, 1972; *Welsch v. Likens*, 1974), and those courts have had no problem in devising the standards of that obligation and the methods for overseeing its implementation.

The Standards

The new standards for insuring accountability are those recently created by the mental health and mental retardation professionals themselves. They are the standards of the Joint Council on Accreditation of Hospitals, American Association on Mental Deficiency, Accreditation Council for Facilities for the Mentally Retarded, and Department of Health, Education, and Welfare (*Rockefeller*, 1973; *Wyatt*, 1972; and *Donaldson v. O'Connor*, 1974).

The courts have been reluctant to impose all of the professionally created standards at one time and have instead required compliance with minimum standards (*Wyatt*, 1972; *Rockefeller*, 1973; *Welsch*, 1974; and *Donaldson*, 1974), for the stated reason that the state had insufficient fiscal ability to implement all of the professional standards at one time (*Rockefeller*, 1973; *Wyatt*, 1972).

In what ways are minimum standards applied? They are applied principally by requirements that staff personnel be increased in quantity and upgraded in quality (*Wyatt*, 1972; *Welsch*, 1974), and by prohibitions or restrictions on certain types of treatment (*Welsch*, 1974; *Rockefeller*, 1973; *Wyatt*, 1972). Curiously, the *Welsch* court recently found that the 8th Amendment's prohibition of cruel and unusual punishment had been violated by forms of seclusion, physical restraint, and chemotherapy, as practiced. Previous courts had found violations of 5th and 14th Amendment due process or equal protection but not of the 8th Amendment. Standards have also been applied by the requirement (*Wyatt*, 1972; *Welsch*, 1974) that individualized treatment plans be developed for the residents of state institutions. These requirements have serious implications for educators of the handicapped, as discussed later.

The courts may also have hesitated to require full and immediate compliance with the new standards for other reasons (e.g., a belief that such a requirement would be mocked because of the obvious impossibility of compliance, a sense that their decisions will be acceptable only if they can be complied with). They may also have realized that a substantial restructuring of the institutional care system would be

required and that they are not in a good position to monitor the details of the change or to oversee the implementation of massive court ordered change. Nevertheless, by requiring minimum standards of treatment to be furnished, the courts have moved out boldly to assure accountability. Whether their actions will prove to have unwanted or unexpected consequences is a different matter.

In the right to treatment litigation, the courts are assuring accountability by applying principles emanating from a constitution that itself derives from the people as their statement of limitations on the power of government and of the duties of the government to them. Other governmental responses to the needs for accountability having been inadequate (i.e., legislative and executive avenues), the courts have been the only remaining governmental source for requiring accountability. Although they have taken this role by default, in the end this may prove to be the most successful way to insure public and professional accountability. Surely the courts can do no worse than a self serving bureaucracy or an inattentive legislature.

THE RIGHT TO EDUCATION

A nationwide attack is under way against public school practices that deny equal educational opportunities to handicapped persons.

These practices include totally excluding handicapped persons from the public school (*PARC v. Commonwealth*, 1972; *Mills v. D.C.*, 1972; *MARC v. Maryland*, 1974), unjustifiably classifying persons as retarded (*Larry P. v. Riles*, 1972; *LeBanks v. Spears*, 1973; *Diana v. State Board of Education*, 1973; *Guadalupe Org. v. Tempe*, 1972), funding special education as special services at lower levels than regular education services (*Mills*, 1972; *MARC*, 1974), establishing separate criteria for admission of handicapped persons to the school systems (*PARC*, 1972; *Mills*, 1972), limiting the size of special education classes and the capacity of special educational programs (*David P. v. State Dept. of Education*, 1973), and failing to provide education to homebound or institutionalized persons (*MARC*, 1974). Collectively, these practices demonstrate the lack of accountability by the state to the handicapped where accountability means fulfilling a duty to educate both the handicapped and the normal pupil.

Defined by the Courts

The court-ordered remedies address each of the discriminatory practices, thus attempting to assure accountability. Statutes and practices that permit exclusion have been held unconstitutional (*PARC*, 1972; *Mills*, 1972; *MARC*, 1974). Zero reject policies have been established

(*PARC*, 1972; *Mills*, 1972; *MARC*, 1974). The implementation of mandatory education for the handicapped legislation has been judicially supervised (*Rainey v. Watkins*, 1973; *Panitch v. Wisconsin*, 1972; contra, *Harrison v. Michigan*, 1972). Compensatory educational opportunities for the handicapped have been ordered (*Mills*, 1972; *LeBanks*, 1973). Alternatives to in classroom education have been decreed (*MARC*, 1974). School budgets have been ordered to be increased or amended to provide for education for the handicapped (*Mills*, 1972; *MARC*, 1974). Classification criteria have been ordered to be revised (*LeBanks*, 1972). IQ tests have been temporarily suspended (*Larry P. v. Riles*, 1972). Finally, procedural due process has been imposed on school exclusion and classification decisions (*PARC*, 1972; *Mills*, 1972).

In the right to education litigation, then, accountability means adhering to compulsory school attendance laws, extinguishing exclusionary and unjustifiable classification practices, affirming the principle that all persons are capable of learning and developing (*PARC*, 1972; *Mills*, 1972; *MARC*, 1974). It also means affirming the opportunity of the handicapped to receive appropriate education (*Lau v. Nichols*, 1974; *Guadalupe v. Tempe*, 1972; *Serna v. Portales*, 1972), and affirming the responsibility of the state to deal fairly (through procedural due process) with the handicapped. Additionally, erasing and compensating for long standing deprivations and discrimination, providing a free education, furnishing an education to all handicapped persons, whether they are in their communities or in state institutions (*MARC*, 1974), and redefining the traditional 3 R's concept of education (*MARC*, 1974) all come under the definition of accountability.

The Right to Access

The increasing willingness of courts to permit consumers to have access to educational records concerning them also serves to advance the principle of accountability. Access is granted under the safeguards of procedural due process (*PARC*, 1972; *Mills*, 1972; *LeBanks*, 1973) as well as under federal statutes (P.L. 93–380, Sec. 513) and state statutes (e.g., General Assembly of North Carolina, Ch. 1293, 1973 S.L., 2nd Sess.) for reasons of accountability.

It is appropriate for educators to collect information so that they can better know what a pupil's needs are and can make better judgments about what is in his best interest. However, the pupil also has an interest in the information and is entitled to access to it to insure that it is correct and that decisions based on it are justified by it. Without access he is unable to hold the professional accountable, and professional efforts at denying access may often be correctly seen as resistance to accountability.

In light of such resistance it may be salutory to provide a statutory remedy that grants not merely the right of access, copying, clarification, and expunction but also grounds for the civil action of mandamus (court ordered access) and a misdemeanor level criminal sanction. By the same token, the disclosure of information, without the justification of necessity for treatment or placement decisions, for example, likewise is hard to tolerate on grounds of acceptable professional conduct. A technique for assuring professionalism and accountability for unjustified disclosure has been a lawsuit for invasion of privacy, breach of contract, breach of fiduciary relationship, or defamation. However, since damages are usually difficult to prove in such cases and since the legal elements of any of these actions are sometimes hard to satisfy, a misdemeanor level crime might be a more effective technique.

The Rights of the Individual

Accountability as imposed by the courts in right to education litigation minimally means requiring the state to do what it has undertaken to do—provide an appropriate education to all pupils, including the handicapped. It means more than this, however. The requirements that procedural due process must be satisfied before placement and classification decisions are made tend to focus attention on the individual student's needs, rights and interests. As the requirement that individualized treatment plans be developed for the institutionalized person brings the person, not his environment, to stage center, so too the procedural due process guarantee forces educators to do what they have been reluctant or unable to do before—to individualize education. Moreover, the *PARC* and *Mills* requirements of appropriate educational placement likewise carry the implication of individualized education. It hardly overstates the case to assert that right to education litigation will revolutionize the educational practice of treating students as members of a group or as components in an aggregated consumer group.

The Goal

There is a unifying theme to these judicial efforts. The new theme is that education must be child centered rather than system centered. To assert this is one thing; to insure it is altogether another. School systems are intractable. There is no consensus on what is the proper or sound educational practice to be followed in the case of handicapped persons, and the bureaucratic structure of the schools tends to thwart the child centered changes that the courts require. Moreover, change by the judicial route is particularly incremental, usually taking up one case at a time and, even in the class action litigation, being without power to

1. INTRODUCTION

insure the effective and meaningful implementation of judicial decrees. What educators, legislatures, and consumers have been unable to do over many years—insure equal educational opportunity to the disabled and individualize education—one cannot expect the courts to accomplish overnight. Accountability in the sense of equal educational opportunities for all exceptional children is still a distant goal.

PERSONAL LIABILITY

In the right to treatment and the right to education litigation, courts have attempted to insure accountability by imposing rules of conduct on whole institutions (for the mentally ill and the mentally retarded) and systems (of public education). Their efforts are directed at assuring accountability on a grand scale; they attempt to make the professionals in the institutions or systems accountable by requiring that the institutions and systems themselves become accountable. Yet there is a great difference between court orders directed at institutions and systems, on the one hand, and orders directed at individuals themselves, on the other. The former rarely carry personal liability (except sometimes for contempt of court for noncompliance or dismissal from employment for noncompliance or incompetence), while the latter always do (by personal liability for damages).

Two Examples

Two prominent illustrations serve to emphasize the accountability mileage that can be gained through actions for personal liability. Doctors at a state institution for the mentally ill have been held personally liable to a patient for their bad faith refusal and inexcusable failure to provide him with even the most minimal and rudimentary psychiatric treatment (*Donaldson v. O'Connor*, 1974). In addition, personal damages have been sought against a doctor who performed and state officials who authorized an unnecessary or unjustified involuntary sterilization (*Cox v. Stanton*, 1974). Accountability can often be most expeditiously accomplished through the pocketbook device of personal liability. Indeed, personal liability may effect more system changes than all the minimum standards' requirements of a host of cases. It has the power to personalize the obligation of accountability in a far more direct, understandable, and significant way than the more usual litigation against institutions and systems. It carries power over money.

Other Appropriate Applications

To date, physicians have been the most likely persons against whom the principle of accountability has been applied, through money damages for bad faith, malpractice and deprivation of constitutional rights of liberty and treatment (*Donaldson v. O'Connor*, 1974). Yet there is no reason to think that the same principle should not be asserted against other professionals. Thus, bad faith action that fails to comply with generally recognized standards of acceptable professional conduct may become actionable in cases involving educators (e.g., for unjustified classification), nonmedical administrators of institutions (e.g., for illegal confinement), and psychologists (e.g., for deprivation of certain basic needs, such as clothing, food, or bedding, as part of behavior shaping token economics).

Surely the standards of competence and accountability that the law applies to the medical profession will be appropriately applied to other professions as well, especially where the medical professionals frequently jointly participate with other professionals in making interdisciplinary judgments concerning such important matters as confinement, treatment, habilitation, and educational placement and classification. These professionals should be held accountable in personal liability for their bad faith failure to give advice or engage in conduct that measures up to and is consistent with the generally recognized standards of acceptable conduct in their respective professions.

It may be the task of the courts to set those standards in advancing the interests of accountability. Surely consumers will not ignore the effect that such standard setting may have in improving the quality of the services they receive.

To the end that the principle of accountability is made applicable to the many affected professions, the state's shield of sovereign immunity and the provision of statutory exculpability or immunity for professionals should be seriously reconsidered. If the shield protects the individual whose bad faith actions fail to measure up to the standards of appropriate professional conduct, it serves only the questionable state purpose of protecting those who should not be protected. That surely is not a legitimate use of the shield. Moreover, it thwarts the consumer interests of accountability. The interests of immunity and exculpability on the one hand, and accountability on the other, can best be served by immunity or exculpability from good faith actions only.

CONCLUSION

The courts predictably will be asked to handle many more cases directed at professional accountability and the subject matter of those cases will become increasingly diverse and complex. For professionals who have acted as though they are above rules of accountability, this prospect must be alarming and disarming.

For those who have traditionally recognized that they are subject to the rules of accountability, the prospect may be managerially annoying, but not much worse. For all persons the prospect should be welcomed, for it ultimately will result in improving the social conditions of the handicapped. If their social conditions are improved, one may hope that their capacities likewise will be improved.

REFERENCES

Baxstrom v. Herald, 383 U.S. 107 (1966).

Burham v. Georgia, 349 F. Supp. 1335 (N.D.Ga. 1972) app. filed No. 72-3110 (5th Cir. Oct. 5, 1972).

Cox v. Stanton, Cir. Act. No. 800 (U.S.D.C., E.D.N.C., filed July 12, 1973) app. filed (by plaintiff upon grant of defendants' motion for dismissal of proceedings upon pleadings on grounds of statute of limitations) (4th Cir., filed Sept. 23, 1974).

David P. v. State Dept. of Education, Cir. Act. No. 658–826 (S.F. Super Ct., filed April 9, 1973).

Diana v. St. Board of Education, C-70-37 R.F.P. (N.D. Cal. Jan. 7, 1970 and June 18, 1973).

Donaldson v. O'Connor, 493 F.2d 507 (5th Cir. 1974).

Guadalupe Org. v. Tempe Elementary School Dist. No. 3, Cir. Act. No. 71-435 (D. Ariz. 1972).

Harrison v. Michigan, 350 F. Supp. 846 (E.D. Mich. 1972).

Jackson v. Indiana, 406 U.S. 715 (1972).

Kesselbrenner v. Anonymous, 33 N.Y.2d 161, 305 N.E.2d 903, 350 N.Y.S. 889(1973).

Larry P. v. Riles, 343 F. Supp. 1306 (N.D. Cal. 1972).

Lau v. Nichols, 94 S.Ct. 786 (1974), *dicta* on appropriateness of education.

LeBanks v. Spears, 60 F.R.D. 135 (E.D.La. 1973).

Maryland Association for Retarded Children (MARC) v. Maryland, Cir. Ct., Baltimore County, Equity No. 100/182/77676 (May 3, 1974).

McNeil v. Director, Patuxent Institution, 407 U.S. 245 (1972).

Mills v. Board of Education of District of Columbia, 348 F. Supp. 866, 968, 875 (D.D.C. 1972).

NYARC v. Rockefeller, 357 F. Supp. 752, 755-6, 758, 768 (E.D.N.Y. 1973).

Panitch v. State of Wisconsin, No. 72-C-461 (E.D. Wisc., filed Aug. 14, 1972).

Pennsylvania Association for Retarded Citizens (PARC) v. Commonwealth, 334 F. Supp. 1257 (E.D.Pa. 1971) and 343 F. Supp. 279, 282, 296 (E.D.Pa. 1972).

Rainey v. Watkins, Civil No. 77620-2 (Chancery Ct. Shelby County, Tenn., filed April 5, 1973).

The Individualized Education Program — Part 1: Procedural Guidelines

Ann P. Turnbull, EdD, Bonnie Strickland, MEd,
and Susan E. Hammer, MEd

This two-part article gives a concise description of the PL 94-142 regulations. Part 1 has suggestions for implementing the regulations and Part 2 regards the components of an Individualized Education Program (IEP). The legal requirements are reviewed and step-by-step procedures described for legal compliance, for developing useful IEPs, and for effective administration. No official government endorsement was sought or is implied though the overview is believed to be accurate and authoritative. — G.M.S.

This paper examines the procedural guidelines for developing and implementing individualized education programs (IEPs). Guidelines are discussed in two areas: the development of an IEP for a handicapped student and the initial introduction of the IEP to the school faculty. The procedures set forth in these guidelines offer a clarification of how the IEP requirement might be implemented in local education agencies.

Requirements of the individualized education program (IEP) exist only as one aspect of a much broader set of requirements dealing with nondiscriminatory evaluation, placement in least restrictive appropriate settings, and due process. Thus, in preparing IEPs, it must be insured that all other requirements are met so the IEP development, rather than an isolated entity, becomes an integral part of the entire process of providing an appropriate education. An explanation of each of these steps will be included to clarify this procedure.

DEVELOPING AN IEP FOR AN LD STUDENT

The first step in this procedure is referring the student for evaluation in order to pinpoint educational handicaps and provide special education services. It is important to note the date of referral on the IEP since a completed IEP is required within 30 days of the initial diagnosis. Indicating the name of the referring individual provides a contact person for further information.

Informing Parents
Prior to any formal testing for learning disabilities services/special education placement, parents must be informed of the purpose of testing and the nature of the tests to be administered according to the due process regulations of PL 94-142. Written parental permission must be obtained

"The Individualized Education Program – Part I, Procedural Guidelines," Ann P. Turnbull, *Journal of Learning Disabilities*, Vol. II, No. 1, January 1978. © 1978 The Professional Press Incorporated.

before evaluation can begin. At the same time, parents must also be informed of their right to examine educational records; to obtain an independent evaluation of their child by a professional examiner outside the school system and to have this evaluation information considered when educational decisions are made; and to present complaints to officials of the school system during an impartial hearing regarding issues related to identification, evaluation, and placement (*Federal Register* 1977). The National Association of State Directors in Special Education has published a manual entitled *Functions of the Placement Committee in Special Education* (1976) which provides sample letters to parents including required due process information.

Evaluation

The specific tests used to decide whether a student has a learning disability is a controversial topic. Questions continue to be posed regarding the most appropriate evaluation tools (Lloyd, Sabatino, Miller, & Miller 1977). The tests used during the identification process may or may not be the same ones used to document level of performance and to serve as a basis for specifying goals and objectives for the IEP. It certainly would be a timesaver to be able to use evaluation information collected at this point in the procedure for writing the IEP goals and objectives, if the evaluation data finds the student handicapped, thus requiring an IEP. In this case, instruments with instructional relevance and identifying the child's abilities and skills yet to be learned must be used.

The proposed regulations do state that a team must evaluate the student during the identification process. Members of this team must include a regular classroom teacher, a teacher trained in the area of learning disabilities, and one individual licensed to administer individual diagnostic examinations (*Federal Register* 1976). The composition of this evaluation committee is different to some degree from the composition of the IEP committee. For example, parents are not required to be members of this evaluation committee while an individual licensed to administer

diagnostic examinations is not a required member of the IEP committee.

Compiling Evaluation Results

After the evaluation has been completed, the committee should compile and analyze the results. When the basis for determining learning disabilities is finally established by the federal rules and regulations, the committee will have criteria and guidelines for interpreting evaluation data. If the student is identified as having a learning disability, the IEP would then be written. The IEP is required only for those students formally identified as handicapped. The committee should at this point consider a tentative recommended placement for the student so that the teachers likely to be responsible for teaching the student can be involved in the IEP development. The tentative nature of the placement decision should be stressed. After the next several steps of the developmental procedure, more precise information will be available on exactly what will constitute an appropriate education for the student with a learning disability. The placement decision should not become final until the IEP is officially approved.

Contacting Parents

Parents must be informed of the evaluation results, the decisions, and recommendations of the evaluation committee. Again, they should clearly understand their right to challenge these decisions and recommendations (*Federal Register* 1977).

If the student has been identified as having a learning disability, the parents should be informed of the school's responsibility to develop an IEP. This explanation should include the purpose, content, and educational utility of the IEP, as well as outline the importance of parental involvement in its development. Traditionally, many parents have had little involvement in helping to specify curriculum goals and objectives for their child, and many parents believe they have little to contribute to this process. The manner in which parents are initially contacted and informed about the IEP is crucial in developing shared responsibility

1. INTRODUCTION

for this task. Parents need to know they are vital members of the team.

The date and time of the initial meeting to develop the IEP should be set at the mutual convenience of all parties including a teacher, a representative from a local educational agency (LEA) responsible for provision or supervision of special educational services, the parents, possibly the student, and others designated by the committee members. If parents cannot attend a conference due to work schedules, transportation problems, or other reasons, a home visit or telephone conference is an alternative strategy for getting parental support and contribution.

Meeting of IEP Committee

Major issues to be discussed by the total committee to formulate the IEP include:

(1) student's current level of performance, both strengths and weaknesses,

(2) the curriculum areas to be included in the student's educational program (e.g., reading, math, physical education),

(3) priorities for the important skills and concepts he needs to learn from the perspective of all committee members,

(4) learning rate,

(5) an examination of placement alternatives with specification made of the extent of time in the regular educational program and the type of resource services to be provided,

(6) identification of the portions of the regular education curriculum which will require "specially designed instruction" in order to identify the curriculum areas around which the IEP must be written,

(7) any special concerns or management (e.g, behavior, emotional status, health factors) which must be considered in developing the IEP,

(8) deciding which individual or individuals will form a subcommittee to write the IEP,

(9) a timeline for writing the IEP, and

(10) a schedule for obtaining approval of all committee members for the completed IEP.

Records of the decisions made at this meeting should be kept to serve as a guideline for the individual(s) responsible for IEP development and to be included in the student's permanent folder.

Developing the IEP by Subcommitteee

The heart of the IEP is the goals and objectives which will provide a blueprint for instruction. Since developing goals and specifying objectives in a sequential fashion is tedious and time-consuming, a small group or groups can more efficiently accomplish these tasks. The persons on the subcommittee should probably include those who will have primary responsibility for implementing the IEP, e.g., the resource and regular teacher who have been tentatively identified as the responsible agents of the student's instructional program. Although the subcommittee might be vested with the full authority to write the IEP with careful consideration to all recommendations of the full committee, the IEP must go back to the full committee for final approval. Before the subcommittee can start writing goals and objectives, they must decide if evaluation data on the level of performance in curriculum areas to be included in the IEP is available and adequate. If not, the subcommittee must gather these necessary data.

Approving IEP by Total Committee

After the subcommittee has completed the IEP, it should be presented to the full committee, which is responsible for ensuring that the IEP includes all essential components as specified in the federal regulations. The IEP should be judged by the committee to be a relevant and meaningful educational program for the students, i.e., it starts with the present level of performance and systematically moves the student forward in the sequence of skill development. Another important consideration for the committee is the final decision regarding the particular educational placement best suiting the student's needs. If the committee is satisfied that the IEP truly represents a blueprint for an appropriate education for the student under consideration, all members, including the parents, should sign the front page of the IEP as a sign of their approval. Additionally, the date of initial approval is recorded.

INTRODUCING THE IEP TO THE SCHOOL FACULTY

When procedures for developing IEPs are initially established by LEAs, a coordinated and systematic process is essential to ensure careful introduction to the school faculty. In this respect, staff needs must be addressed. The IEP requires more in-depth curriculum planning than many teachers have previously experienced. Additionally, skills in conducting effective parent conferences and establishing positive working relationships based on shared responsibility are critical components of the IEP process. For the IEP to be an effective vehicle for defining appropriate education, the LEA has the responsibility to develop a sound organizational plan for IEP introduction and development. A step-by-step plan is outlined as a guide in this process.

Initial Planning Session

The initial planning session for IEP introduction and development in the LEA might begin with a meeting of curriculum coordinators, administrators responsible for special education, members of the special services team (resource teachers, school psychologists, counselors) from each school, one or two regular classroom teachers, and one or both parents of handicapped students. Because of group size and because writing elementary and secondary level IEPs can be quite different, separate meetings with the elementary and secondary staff are recommended.

The purpose of this initial planning session is to share information on federal and state requirements and guidelines for IEP development. In addition, an assessment of needs is required to identify the major tasks to be accomplished so that systematic procedures and training may be developed. Setting priorities can help the group identify the most pressing concerns so they can immediately be addressed. When discussion has identified needs, the group should pinpoint factors within the system that will contribute positively to meeting the need (carefully sequenced curriculum, availability of resources for staff training, supportive administration) and the factors that will present obstacles (availability of time, amount of paperwork, anticipated unwillingness of parents to participate in conferences). Each school system will differ in the resources already in place and in the potential problem areas. By pinpointing these factors, the group can begin to build on strengths and to de-emphasize or eliminate the obstacles. This meeting, which could require three to four hours, should produce a working draft of needs, resources already in place, and constraints. Tasks could be assigned to individuals to respond immediately to the assessment of needs and to involve more school faculty in this process.

Simulation and Discussion

The same individuals who participated in the initial planning session should also attend the second. During the interval between these meetings, a variety of new ideas, both pro and con, relating to all aspects of the IEP will likely occur to each participant. The first part of the meeting might be devoted to testing these ideas in small groups by simulating the development of an IEP for a handicapped student. Groups could address the different needs of various handicapping conditions by using students with a range of educational handicaps (learning disabilities, blindness, loss of hearing, mental retardation, emotional problems). Before the meeting, group facilitators should have identified a handicapped student and brought materials such as evaulation data for a particular student, curriculum guides for the school system, lists of skill sequences for the content areas to be taught, textbooks used in the student's class, and actual objectives or course outlines provided by the student's teachers.

Before the working session, a variety of examples of how the IEP might be organized can be presented. Since LEAs can use their discretion, as long as requirements are met, trying different formats in the various small groups might be a meaningful way to select a format which best adheres to the preferences of the group. Formats could be collected from a variety of sources including state departments, regional resource centers, and other LEAs. After this initial introduction, the groups should work

1. INTRODUCTION

an hour and a half on the simulated task. Special note can be made of questions and concerns to be raised in the second part of the session following the simulation.

The second part should focus on the IEP development. The needs assessment data pulled together in the initial planning session will also be helpful in this discussion. To facilitate the problem solving session, it may be worthwhile to categorize issues and decide who can deal with the solutions. Some questions can be answered only by administrative personnel (policy decisions). Other questions can be answered by recommendations of the planning group (group recommendations), and some issues must be placed on hold until further clarifications or refinements are made (hold). Examples of questions and their probable solution are:

Policy Decisions. Who is the person responsible for coordinating all procedures related to PL 94-142 and the IEP? LEAs should consider designating one central administrator with overall responsibility specified in his job description for IEP development and implementation.

Group Recommendations. Who will decide on the final format for IEPs? Are all schools going to use the same format? This group might decide on the most effective format and make recommendations to the IEP coordinator.

Hold. What changes are likely to occur in the regulations over the next couple of years? This information is still unavailable from the Office of Education.

Introduction to School Principals

The third meeting aimed at school principals could be organized and presented by a representative group of special service people, regular class teachers, and administrative personnel (the participants of the first two sessions). Topics to be presented to the elementary and secondary principals should again begin with a clear presentation of the legal requirements of PL 94-142 and the state guidelines.

Needs assessment data and recommendations from the prior two meetings should be presented. These recommendations could include a timeline and

procedure for presentation to the entire school faculty and to parents, responsible persons within each school, release time for teachers, financial considerations, needs for clerical support, and in-service teacher training. From the issues discussed, a number of ad hoc committees may be formed to recommend in writing policies and implementation guidelines for the LEA.

Official Adoption of Policies

After the ad hoc committees have recommended policies and implementation guidelines, the IEP coordinator for the LEA should carry these recommendations through the proper channels in order to gain official adoption, these channels varying depending upon the particular organizational structure of the schools. The important aspect is that agreement is reached on specific IEP procedures.

Presentation to Each Member of School Faculty

This step is extremely critical in the introductory process. The manner in which the IEP is initially introduced to the total school faculty is likely to influence greatly the faculty's attitude toward this new requirement. The IEP should have the endorsement of the key leaders in the system, such as the principal, central administrators, and curriculum coordinators. The bulk of IEP development falls mainly to the special and regular classroom teachers, and they need support from the very beginning in recognizing how the task of IEP development can become manageable. However, the shared responsibility of all faculty members should be strongly emphasized. It is important for regular classroom teachers not to feel that the IEP requirement is being imposed by the special educators, a feeling which could build up resentment toward the special services faculty. For this reason, it might be beneficial to have the principal, a curriculum coordinator, or the IEP coordinator rather than a special educator, initially introduce the IEP to the faculty.

At this faculty meeting, the presenter should have copies of system policies, procedural guidelines, and an example of the recommended IEP format. The faculty may appreciate a structured introduction, rather than having the impression that decisions made are still very ambiguous. Faculty members should react by helping make the process more workable, rather than dwelling on the potential problems. Writing IEPs for handicapped students is not a negotiable matter — IEPs must be written. Energy needs to be channeled into constructive problem solving.

Individual faculty members will want to know what will be expected from them, what are the timelines, and what kind of back-up support they can expect. These questions require clear and honest responses based on the adopted policies and guidelines of the system.

Getting Started on the IEP
Informing the school faculty of their responsibilities in developing and implementing IEPs may cause some anxiety. For this reason, a sound strategy may be to begin immediately the process of IEP development on a manageable level.

A good starting point may be in-service training sessions in which teachers are guided through the process of IEP development. Participants can work in small groups made up of both regular classroom and special education teachers in developing an IEP for a particular student. This task could be structured in a similar fashion as the simulated task described above. At this session, group members could be introduced to relevant resource material such as sequenced curriculum guides and skill checklists. As teachers begin to collect these resources, the task of specifying objectives for the IEP can be greatly simplified. After the participants have had the opportunity of working in groups, they will perhaps be more confident in their individual ability to develop IEPs.

Rather than expecting a teacher at once to write IEPs on all handicapped students in his class, the task can be broken down into a series of small steps. Start with one student in one curriculum area. After that task is accomplished, the student's needs in another area can be addressed. Sometimes teachers become overwhelmed by the magnitude of a task. Just as learning disabled students learn skills and concepts best in a step-by-step, sequential fashion, so teachers can best approach many of their responsibilities. Since IEPs have the potential of creating havoc with teachers wondering how they will ever be able to fulfill their responsibilities, school faculties are well advised to work one step at a time within the timelines of PL 94-142. In order to be able to do this, schools must start the process immediately.

Monitoring
Particularly in the initial stages of developing and implementing IEPs, it is very important for the central IEP coordinator in the system to spot-check IEPs to ensure that the individuals writing them are getting started on a strong basis. If teachers are writing objectives which are too specific or if they are too sketchy in their planning, immediate changes can be made before bad habits are established. One should not assume that all procedures and guidelines are interpreted in the same manner by all faculty members. Clarification and reclarification will be needed. Monitoring is important at all times, but special attention in the initial stages of IEP development can be an excellent strategy for preventing future problems.

SUMMARY

The IEP has the potential of being the catalyst for a more individualized and specified approach to education, increased accountability of educators, and shared decision-making between teachers and parents. It can be viewed as a burden of more paperwork or as an opportunity to improve the quality of education for handicapped students and the diagnostic-prescriptive skills of teachers. A great challenge of educators is to make sure that the IEP is not interpreted as the Impossible Education Program rather than the Individualized Education Program. The IEP will significantly assist educators in making sound judgments on the appropriateness of educational placements, if development and implementation are soundly based.

AN APPROACH TO OPERATIONALIZING THE I.E.P.

Floyd G. Hudson and Steve Graham

FLOYD G. HUDSON, Ed.D., is Associate Professor and Coordinator of Learning Disabilities in the Department of Special Education, University of Kansas.
STEVE GRAHAM, MS., is a Doctoral Candidate in Special Education at the University of Kansas.

PL 94-142 specifies that schools are required to develop an Individual Educational Program (I.E.P.) for every handicapped child before services are provided. PL 94-142 does *not*, however specify *how* the I.E.P. is to be developed and implemented. This paper presents a comprehensive, step-by-step procedure for the I.E.P. The authors provide sample forms for all development and implementatin phases of the I.E.P. as well as suggestions for using the I.E.P. as an effective educational management tool for learning disabled youth.   —D.D.D

On November 28, 1975, President Ford signed into law the Education for All Handicapped Children Act, PL 94-142. As a result, schools in every part of the nation will feel the impact of this legislation. It establishes the right of the handicapped to a free and appropriate education.

Within the law, the critical link between the handicapped student and the free and appropriate education he or she is entitled to is the Individual Educational Program (I.E.P.). As a management tool designed to facilitate the process of instructional delivery, the I.E.P. is a written document developed jointly by school personnel, the student's parents or guardians, and, where appropriate, the student himself/herself.

Due to the complexity and practical importance of the I.E.P., a systematic planning model is necessary. The purpose of this paper is to present a guide for the development and implementation of the I.E.P. First, an overview of the process involved in providing services to handicapped children will be reviewed. This overview, which specifies the steps preceding the writing of the I.E.P., will be followed by an indepth, step-by-step presentation of the development and implementation of the I.E.P.

OVERVIEW OF SERVICES FOR HANDICAPPED STUDENTS

Since no set pattern has been followed by state or local school districts in identifying, assessing, and providing services to handicapped students, service arrangements have varied greatly from one locale to the next. However, with the enactment of PL 94-142 specific service arrangement guidelines were established providing each state and

"An Approach to Operationalizing the IEP," Hudson and Graham, *Learning Disability Quarterly,* Vol. 1, No. 1, Winter 1978.
© 1978 The Council for Exceptional Children.

local school district with a set of procedural policies which must be followed from the initial step of identification through service delivery. Although variance will continue to exist between the service arrangements of different school districts, the outline presented in Figure 1 illustrates a common format.

The initial step in providing special education services is to determine who is eligible. A student may become a concern when he or she does not conform to academic and/or behavioral expectations and is consequently brought to the attention of the school by a referral from a teacher, parent, or other interested persons (Step 1).

Upon receiving a referral, a representative of the school district (i.e., school principal) records the date, the reason, and the initiator of the referral. The special services department is then informed of the referral and a school representative notifies the parents of the school's concern (Step 2).

Next, school personnel (i.e., screening team) collect information on the student's current and previous learning history (Step 3) which is then reviewed by a screening team who decides whether or not additional information is warranted. Should the team decide that a comprehensive assessment is indicated, permission to do so is requested from the parents via a signed written consent letter (Step 4). The consent letter explains why additional information is needed, who will gather it, whose decision it was, and when the assessment will be completed.

If the parents refuse to grant permission for the comprehensive assessment, that decision is forwarded to a representative of the superintendent (Step 5). The school can now appeal the parents' decision in which case the screening team becomes the advocate for the student. On the other hand, if the parents grant permission, a multidisciplinary team (Step 6) will conduct a comprehensive assessment in all areas related to the suspected disability. Assessment instruments, which are to be administered by trained personnel, must be appropriate, validated, and without cultural or racial bias.

Once the comprehensive assessment is completed and the data analyzed, a summary is written which includes the student's present level of functioning (Step 7). This summary must be signed by a representative of the school and the responsible team members as an indication that the report is accurate and reflects their own conclusions. In case of dissentors, separate statements should be submitted.

Upon completion of the summary statement, the parents are contacted to set a mutually agreed upon time and place for the staffing conference (Step 8). Staffing participants include those persons who conducted the assessment, representatives of the school district, the student's teacher (regular and/or special), parent or parents, and, when appropriate, the student. The

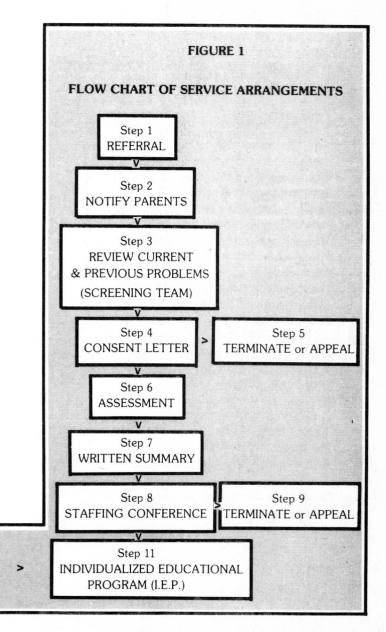

1. INTRODUCTION

information previously gathered is reviewed and a decision rendered on whether or not the student will receive special education services. If the parents disagree with the assessment summary or the proposed special service recommendation, they are informed of their rights to appeal the decision (Step 9).

The final step in the process is the development and implementation of the I.E.P. (Step 11). For those students already receiving special education services (Step 10), an I.E.P. must be developed prior to October 1 of the new school year. For newly identified handicapped students, a meeting or series of meetings to develop the I.E.P. are scheduled (time samples indicate that it takes approximately ten hours per student to develop a written I.E.P.). Once the I.E.P. is operationalized, additional sessions will be necessary to develop implementation strategies and to monitor the I.E.P.

THE INDIVIDUALIZED EDUCATION PROGRAM

The guidelines of PL 94-142 requires that an I.E.P. be in effect for each handicapped student before he or she receives special education and/or related services. If a student is scheduled for special education services before the school year begins, the I.E.P. must be developed by October 1st. However, if a determination is made that a student needs special education and/or related services following the start of the school year, an I.E.P. must be developed within thirty calendar days of that decision.

As mentioned earlier, the I.E.P. is a management tool designed to assure that a handicapped student receives an education appropriate to his or her needs and that this education is actually delivered and monitored. As required by law, an appropriate education is one which can reasonably be expected to achieve the agreed upon annual goals and short-term objectives stated in the I.E.P.

Development of the I.E.P.

The first part of the I.E.P. is the development of the individualized education program. Each school district is responsible for initiating and conducting meetings for the purpose of developing, reviewing, and revising a handicapped student's I.E.P. After a determination has been made that a student is to receive special education and/or related services, a representative of the school district is responsible for setting up a meeting or series of meetings to develop the I.E.P.

To insure that they will have an opportunity to attend the staffing conference, the student's parents must receive advance notice of the purpose, time, and location of the meeting as well as who will attend. The school district is also responsible for insuring that the parents understand the proceedings of the meeting, including an interpreter for parents who are deaf or whose native language is other than English. Furthermore, the meeting must be held at a mutually agreed on time and place and if neither parent can attend, the school district is to use other methods to insure parent participation (e.g., individual or conference telephone calls). A meeting may be conducted without parent participation if the school representative is unable to convince the parents to attend. If this is the case, the district must have a record of its attempts to arrange the meetings, including accounts and results of telephone calls made or attempted, copies and responses of correspondence sent to parents, a list of the results of home and employment visits, and an I.E.P. parent attendance waiver form. The waiver, which is to be signed by one or both parents if they cannot attend the I.E.P. meetings, indicates that the parents have been informed of their rights, that systematic attempts were made to arrange a mutually agreed upon time and place for the meeting, and that the school will inform the parents of their recommendations as a result of the I.E.P. meeting.

Besides the parents, each I.E.P. meeting should include a school representative qualified to provide or supervise special education provisions, the student's teacher or teachers (general, special, or both) the student (when appropriate), and other individuals at the discretion of the parent or the agency (i.e., speech therapist, physician, etc.). For the handicapped student who is being evaluated for the first time, a member of the assessment team or one who is familiar with the assessment and its results should be present.

The development of the I.E.P. consists of the following stages: (a) statement of the student's present level of performance, (b) establishment of priorities, (c) a determination of services to be delivered, and (d) specification of evaluation procedures. First the student is identified as not meeting academic and/or behavioral expectations and the areas of concern are delineated and investigated. An indepth assessment of all areas related to the student's suspected disabilities is conducted resulting in a summary document which includes the student's present level of functioning, strengths and weaknesses, and unique learning needs. These assessment data and the student's individual needs form the basis for a determination of educational and related priorities. Once the student's needs are determined, a means of meeting them is agreed upon. It should be noted that it is in-efficient to have the complete staffing team write the annual goals, short-term objectives, and evaluation procedures. Ideally, the teachers implementing the plan should be charged with this responsibility. Furthermore, to insure that these services are being delivered appropriately, a monitoring system is established. Information from the monitoring process is fed back into the system. If necessary, suitable adjustments are made in the student's educational program.

Implementing the I.E.P.

After priorities, services, and evaluation criteria are established, the plan becomes operational and implementation of the I.E.P. begins to take place. The I.E.P. committee is primarily responsible for the development and monitoring of each handicapped student's educational program, whereas individual implementers (i.e., teachers and specialists) must specify daily activities and strategies necessary for the plan to be functional. At the implementation level, objectives are derived directly from the annual goals and short-term objectives in the I.E.P. The written program cannot be thought of as a static one-time contrivance but must be viewed as a flexible response to the changing needs of the student. As implementers note needed additions, deletions, and changes in the I.E.P., this

information should directly influence the committee's monitoring activities and planned adjustment.

Before the I.E.P. can become fully operational, administrators, educators, and parents must comprehend each component of the process and its relationship to the whole. Therefore, the following sections of this paper will discuss in detail the nature and ramifications of each stage in the development of the I.E.P.: present level of performance, establishment of priorities, delivery of services, evaluation procedures, and implementation.

ESTABLISHING PRESENT LEVEL OF PERFORMANCE

The procedure through which the present level of performance is established will vary from one school district to another. However, an appropriate, systematic procedure would take into consideration the following essential elements: student, referral, instructional history, assessment, and summary document.

Student. To insure that every student is indeed provided an appropriate education, it is important that as many professionals as possible within the school have adequate knowledge of what constitutes a handicapping condition and what steps must be taken to refer such a student for special services. Most often regular teachers and/or parents identify students suspected of being handicapped, but it is obvious that the referral process will be strengthened and thus better services extended to a student if all professionals coming into contact with the student have an adequate knowledge of handicapping conditions and criteria for referring students for special services.

Referral. Traditionally, referrals have been diagnostically nonmeaningful; thus, their importance in the assessment process has been overlooked. Often verbal referrals were made as teachers and principals pass in the hall, while written referrals frequently were simplified to the point that only the name, age, grade level, school and teacher's name were given. While such referrals are of little value in the diagnostic evaluation of any student, it is quite obvious that comprehensive diagnostic referrals are

1. INTRODUCTION

particularly crucial when dealing with students experiencing difficulty in learning.

Ideally, the diagnostic referral documents, the student's instructional history, previous instructional problems, curriculum-related strengths and weaknesses, and non-academic behaviors as viewed by the referring teacher. This form of diagnostic information tends to give direction to the screening team by focusing on important or suspect areas of performance. Following an analysis of a comprehensive referral, the screening team can prepare a strategy for completing necessary and essential assessments.

Instructional History. Information about the instructional history of the referred student can be obtained through the referral form, student's cumulative folder, and interviews with teachers, parents and significant others with knowledge of the student. Basic to such a review is information reflecting:

1. assessment data (formal)
    psychological
    educational
    emotional
    social
2. academic skills (strengths and weaknesses)
3. behavior observations
4. previous learning history
5. relationships of behavior to learning
6. previous instructional methods used
7. previous instructional techniques used
8. previous instructional materials used
9. learning style
10. interpersonal relationships (peers, teachers, and others)
11. unique learning needs
12. related, physical-sensory conditions

Once the instructional history has been completed, a summary document should be prepared to assist the screening team in making decisions related to the selection of appropriate assessment strategies.

Assessment. After having completed an analysis of the referral and a review of the student's prior learning experiences, the screening team either accepts or rejects the referral. If the referral is accepted, a specific assessment plan is designed for the student.

No attempt is made to administer a "set" battery of tests. However, assessment instruments and techniques are selected based on the information related to the specific learning and instructional needs of the student. Generally, the instruments used must be: (1) reliable and valid, (2) appropriate to the specific areas of assessment and (3) appropriate to the individual student's cultural and language background. Assessment techniques used should be documented through research and/or other professional sources.

At this point, the team must request permission from the student's parents or guardians to obtain additional information about their child, determine who is to conduct the assessment, establish criteria for performance, and determine how the information is to be communicated. In addition, the parents are to be given the reason for this request and notified who initiated it.

After reviewing all relevant presenting data, the team determines the specific areas to be assessed. Generally, an analysis of the learner constitutes the major assessment process; however, this oversimplified approach has led to limited success in program planning for children. Therefore, it is obvious that consideration of other variables is essential to successful implementation and maintenance of the I.E.P. Thus, in addition to an analysis of the *learner* using formal and informal techniques, the team must be equally concerned with an analysis of the *instructional environment* and the *instructional variables* which may inhibit or enhance the learning behavior of the student. Chief among these are: the classroom environment (physical-emotional), teacher's attitudes, curricular organization, instructional materials, reinforcement strategies, methods of matching student needs to instruction, and interpersonal relationships with teachers, peers, and others.

Although the regulations in PL 94-142 stipulate initial and annual evaluation, this is considered a minimal standard. Most special educators advocate continuous assessment in order better to monitor the student's progress and the effects of the I.E.P. in maintaining appropriate behavior.

Summary Document. The final step in determining the present level of performance is the development of a comprehensive document integrating all known data relative to the student's present level of performance. In order to secure functional application in developing the I.E.P., criteria for developing this document must be established. The major criterion is a statement integrating complete, concise, objective data easily translatable into annual goals and short-term objectives. Additional criteria will deal with the following topics: Will the document facilitate the staffing process? Does it coordinate information from multiple disciplines? Does it serve the communication among staffing participants?

ESTABLISHMENT OF PRIORITIES

Once the present level of functioning, unique learning needs, strengths and weaknesses, etc., have been determined, the next task in developing the I.E.P. is to establish priorities, i.e., determine which skills are most in need of educational attention. Because it will not be possible to work simultaneously on all the strengths and weaknesses identified during the assessment, the team must decide which instructional skills to include in the I.E.P. and state these in terms of annual goals and short-term objectives. Such specification is advantageous for the following reasons:

Written goals and objectives direct the teaching process by establishing which critical skills are to receive educational attention, thus, better enabling the teacher who implements the I.E.P. to prepare lessons geared to the student's needs. In addition, each instructional activity can be planned to strengthen a specific goal or objective. The result is intentional learning.

Written goals and objectives can motivate both the teacher and the student. Since the purpose of the instructional activities is shared with the student, the relevancy of the task is made more meaningful. Once students know what, why, and how they are to learn, they will be encouraged to try harder. By specifying what is to be learned, written goals and objectives are motivating to teachers and result in direction and structure.

Written goals and objectives provide accountability by specifying what is to be learned within a specific time period. Teachers, administrators, parents, and the student are provided with a means of evaluating advancement along a continuum of progress. Performance in terms of goals can be examined to determine if progress is satisfactory.

Written goals and objectives facilitate team communication because each team member has a common point of reference. By specifying goals and objectives, each team member is aware of the critical areas in need of attention. When team members formally and periodically share information their thoughts will be directed toward a common set of goals.

In systematically establishing priorities the following six principles must be followed: Focus on the reason for referral.

Examine the student's present level of performance and note general areas in which progress is inadequate.

Examine the student's present level of performance and note areas of strength.

Determine what critical areas each team member considers to be educational priorities.

Examine each critical area with regard to the student's age, grade, rate of learning, amount of learning, likes, dislikes, strengths, weaknesses, abilities, etc.

Determine the prerequisite skills necessary to obtain more advanced skills in each critical area.

The determination of priorities is a decision-making process. It moves from general areas to specific goals. First, the team focuses on the academic and/or behavioral difficulties that led to the referral. Suspected and related areas of disabilities should be examined with this focus in mind. For example, in examining the assessment data and summary report of a student referred because of a reading problem, the team should center its attention on the referral problem (i.e., reading).

1. INTRODUCTION

Once the referral problem is established, the student's present level of functioning is examined and general areas in which progress is satisfactory or inadequate are noted. In this connection it is often helpful to have a list of academic and behavioral subskills on hand to enable the team to consider a wide number of skill areas and insure that the team zeroes in on general goals, while not overlooking important subcategories. The following is a partial list of content areas that might be examined:

a) *Reading Skills* - readiness, word attack, word recognition, vocabulary, and comprehension.

b) *Language Arts* - listening, speech, grammar, handwriting, writing, and spelling.

c) *Arithmetic* - numeration, addition, subtraction, multiplication, division, fractions, measurement, and time.

d) *Social Skills* - self concept, self help skills, interpersonal relationships, and self control.

e) *Thinking Skills* - comprehension, concepts, and problem solving.

f) *Behavioral Skills* - task completion, attention to task, hyperactivity, independent work, group participation, following directions, type/frequency of reinforcement, feedback, supervision necessary, preparation for work, time orientation, planning skills, aggressive/passive, handling of criticism, leadership, and rate of production.

After the general areas to be examined are determined, the team decides if progress in those areas is satisfactory or inadequate. Since "satisfactory" and "inadequate" are both relative terms, the student's present level of functioning in each general area is compared to a standard. Generally, there are three types of standards: norms, skill lists, and intra-individual scores. In utilizing norms as a standard, the student's present level of functioning is compared to scores from a population of students. With a skill list comparison between the student's present level of functioning and a fixed level of skill development is made; whereas intra-individual comparison contrasts the student's scores one against the other. One or a combination of these standards might be applied.

Once the general areas of strengths and weaknesses are determined, the next step is to target which general areas to incorporate into the annual goals. Since the parent, the regular classroom teacher, the specialist, etc. all view the student from a different perspective, it is expected that the team members will not select the same priorities. However, each area identified as a possible priority is examined and discussed.

For each critical area there are a number of conditions and constraints that will need to be investigated such as the student's grade placement, rate of learning, amount of learning, and previous teaching methods. For example, the goals for a fourth-grade student who has demonstrated a rapid rate of learning while receiving remedial instruction will be different from the goals for a similar student who has not responded adequately to remedial instruction. Similarly, the goals for a 17-year-old learning disabled student who cannot read will be different from the goals of a third-grade learning disabilities student unable to read. If it is known that the 17-year-old has received intensive remedial reading instruction during previous school years and made little progress, the team should consider alternatives to remedial reading.
the student's intellectual, social, and physical capabilities, level of motivation, and interests. The goals for a student with sensory deficits will be different from the goals for a student with depressed intellectual functioning. A highly motivated student working on skills that interest him will have different needs than a student who lacks interest and motivation.

Finally, the degree of severity of the disability and the type of services the student will receive must be considered. A correspondence should exist between the number of goals set and the amount of time available for instruction. Likewise, consideration should be given to where the goals will be met (i.e., regular class, resource room, etc).

With the above considerations in mind, the team will select those target areas most in need of educational instruction. For each selected area, scope and sequence charts and/or criterion skills checklists (i.e., Fountain Valley, Read On, Wisconsin Design, etc.) can be utilized to determine which skills the student has or has not mastered at his present level of functioning. Skills which the student has mastered, not mastered, or does not have at this level should be noted. Also, the prerequisite skills necessary to obtain a higher level of skill development should be determined. For each priority area, the prerequisite skills to be taught can then be arranged in the order in which they appear on the scope and sequence chart, thus insuring that prerequisite subskills will be developed before higher skills are taught.

Up to this point, the team has established general areas in need of remediation and maintenance. Furthermore, prerequisite skills in each of the priority areas have been delineated. The next step is to transform this information into annual goals and short-term objectives.

Annual Goals. When writing annual goals the team determines the competency to be demonstrated by the student on a skill cluster by the end of the school year. Clearly such judgments are difficult and, at best, annual goals are group estimates which may over- or underestimate a student's progress. To insure realistic goals, a relationship must exist between the annual goals and the student's present level of performance. An example of an annual goal derived from present-level statements is presented below:
Present level: The student can properly hold a pencil and make vertical, horizontal, diagonal, and circular marks on a paper.
Annual goal: The student will be able to write on a paper format from memory the capital and small letters of the alphabet.

In order to develop appropriate annual goals and short-term objectives the team will: a) determine the subcomponents of the skill to be taught, b) identify and name the behavior that the student will demonstrate once the objective is accomplished, c) define the conditions under which the behavior will occur, and d) state the acceptable level of performance. These criteria not only specify what the student will learn but also serve as a vehicle for monitoring pupil and program progress.

In writing annual goals and short-term objectives care must be taken to select appropriate behavioral terms to describe the required performance. Terms such as *understand* and *appreciate* are too general and vague to be useful; whereas *list, name, remove, identify, compare,* etc. exemplify appropriate behavioral terms specifying an observable and measureable activity.

Examples of inappropriate and appropriate annual goals and short-term objectives are presented below:
Inappropriate annual goal: The student will have a good understanding of the alphabet.
Appropriate annual goal: The student will be able to pronounce the names of the letters of the alphabet, A through Z.
Inappropriate short-term objective: The student will comprehend the letters A through F.
Appropriate short-term objective: The student will be able to pronounce the names of the letters of the alphabet, A through F with 90 percent accuracy.

In writing annual goals, the team leader should move the team through each of the priority areas identified. Starting from the lower-order skills and moving upward, the team should estimate what the student will be able to do in a priority area by the end of the year. With this estimate as a guide, annual goals can be written for each skill cluster within a priority area. Suppose, for example, that arithmetic addition is identified as a priority area for a third-grade learning disabled student. After examining and comparing the student's assessment data and summary report to an arithmetic scope and sequence chart, it is determined that the student has mastered whole numbers to 100 and addition involving two addends under 10 with sums under 10(e.g., 3 + 5 = 8). The student also demonstrates spotty mastery of addition involving two addends under 10 with sums under 20 (e.g., 9 + 4 = 13). By utilizing the scope and sequence chart, the team determines that in order to obtain a higher level of skill development, the student would need to master: (a) addition involving two addends under 10, e.g., 9 + 4 = 13, (b) ad-

1. INTRODUCTION

dition involving two-digit addends with no carrying, e.g., 14 + 22 = 36, (c) addition involving two-digit addends with renaming in the one's place, e.g., 14 + 29 = 43, and (d) addition involving three-place or more addends with renaming in one or more places, e.g., 295 + 78 = 373. Because of the student's present rate of progress, motivation, level of skill development, etc., the team decides that by the end of the year the student will be able to master (a), (b), and (c). For each one of these skill clusters an annual goal is written. An example of annual goal for each cluster is presented below:

(a) On a paper-pencil format the student will be able to add any two numbers from 0 to 9.

(b) On a paper-pencil format the student will be able to add any two-digit addends with no carrying.

(c) On a paper-pencil format the student will be able to add any two-digit addends with renaming.

Short-Term Objectives. Once the annual goals are written, the next step is to identify several short-term objectives for each annual goal. In developing these the team should examine each annual goal and determine the sequence of steps necessary to complete that goal. For each annual goal there should be at least four or five short-term objectives which may be viewed as milestones between the student's present level of functioning and the point the team hopes the student will reach by the end of the year (annual goals).

The following is an example of several short-term objectives developed for an annual goal:

Annual goal: When presented auditorially with a consonant sound the student will be able to write its corresponding letter.

Short-term goal # 1: When presented auditorially with the consonant sounds b, d, f, h, j, or k the student will be able to write their corresponding letters.

Short-term goal #2: When presented auditorially with the consonant sounds l, m, n, o, p, or q the student will be able to write their corresponding letters.

Short-term goal #3: When presented auditorially with the consonant sounds r, s, t, v, w, x, y, or z the student will be able to write their corresponding letters.

Short-term goal #4: When presented auditorially with the consonant sounds c and g the student will be able to write one of the letters corresponding to that sound.

While the annual goals should always be developed by the team, short-term objectives can be obtained from a variety of sources: curriculum guides, textbooks, teacher's guides, material manuals, grade-level objectives, etc. If these sources are used, care must be taken to insure that the short-term objectives reflect a logical progression of intermediate steps from where the student presently is to where it is planned he will be at the end of the school year.

DELIVERY OF SERVICES

With a clear understanding of the student's present level of functioning and the point he or she is anticipated to have reached at the end of the year, the team is ready to decide what services are necessary to implement the I.E.P., i.e., the team's task becomes one of arranging the appropriate educational and related services needed to support the process of moving from the present level of functioning toward successful attainment of the annual goals. The specific educational services needed by the student must be outlined in a statement which is to include:

(a) A statement of the regular, special education, and related services needed successfully to attain the annual goals. This list is determined without regard to availability of the services.

(b) A list of the special education and related services to be provided.

(c) The date when specific services begin and the length of time these will be provided.

(d) A list of the persons responsible for implementing services.

(e) A list of any special instructional media and materials needed.

(f) A description of the extent to which the

student will participate in regular education programs.

(g) A justification for the type of educational placement which the student will have.

In order to provide services that correspond to the specific educational needs of the student, a range of placement options should be available, thus, allowing for flexibility in matching services to the student's individual needs. Before any placement decision is made, the team must insure that to the maximum extent appropriate, the handicapped student is educated with children who are not handicapped. Special classes, separate schooling, or other removal of the student from the regular educational environment should occur only when the nature or severity of the handicap is such that education in regular classes with the aid of support services cannot be achieved satisfactorily. This concept is commonly known as the *least restrictive alternative*.

Regular, special education, and related services. Without regard to the availability of the services, the first step in the placement process is a listing of the specific educational services needed by the student. This includes a description of the regular, special education, and related services required to meet the student's unique needs.

A direct relationship should exist between the student's annual goals and their clusters of short-term objectives and the services listed. The team specifies the type of educational placement required to achieve those goals. With the student's present level of functioning, degree of severity, annual goals, and the least restrictive alternative as a focus, the team selects the educational option that most nearly corresponds to the student's needs. For example, for a third-grade learning disabled student with mild language difficulties, regular classroom instruction with support and resource room instruction would be appropriate, whereas for a sixth-grade learning disabled student with few academic skills, special class or resource room instruction would be appropriate.

Next, the team must decide which related or other special education services are required to meet the student's needs. Speech pathology, audiology, psychological services, physical and occupational therapy, recreation, school health services, social work, parent counseling, and diagnostic medical services comprise related services, while other special education services include special physical education and vocational education.

Once the team has determined the regular, special education, and related services needed, a statement of educational services is written. Based on the student's annual goals and short-term objectives such a statement might read:

The majority of the student's instruction should be within the regular classroom. The student should spend a minimum of five one-hour sessions weekly in a resource room receiving remedial instruction in reading and language skills. Twice a week the student should receive direct instruction on articulation from the speech therapist. The regular classroom teacher will require indirect support services to assist him/her in meeting the student's unique needs within the regular classroom.

Up to this point, services have been determined without regard to the availability of these services, but now the team's next task is to list the actual special education and related services to be provided. Under ideal conditions, no discrepancy should exist between needed and delivered services. An example of a list of special education and related services to be delivered is:

- Support by the L.D. teacher to the regular classroom teacher
- Resource Room, Learning Disabilities
- Speech Therapy

Date and length of services. When the special education and related services to be delivered have been listed, the team determines when the services will begin, end, and the amount of time per week for delivery of the services. The team decides when the student needs services and how soon these will be available. The duration of services can only be an estimate of the degree of time necessary satisfactorily to accomplish the annual

1. INTRODUCTION

goals. In Figure 2 the previous example of special education and related services to be delivered has been expanded to include implementation date, hours per week, and completion date.

	FIGURE 2		
	SERVICES AND THEIR DURATION		
Services to Be Delivered	Implementation Date	Hours/ Week	Completion Date
1. Support by the LD teacher to the regular classroom teacher.	October 3, 1977	2	May 28, 1978
2. Resource Room, Learning Disabilities	October 3, 1977	5	May 28, 1978
3. Speech Therapy	October 5, 1977	2	February 1, 1978

Individuals responsible for implementation. For each service, a list of persons responsible for the delivery of that service is developed, thus, providing the team with a quick and efficient means for determining who is responsible for what.

Media and materials. Included in the statement of educational services should be a list of any special instructional media and materials needed; however, only those highly "specialized" materials and/or media necessary should be listed since, otherwise, the team would be required to list all the instructional media and materials that will be used with the student. It is the responsibility of the implementing teachers and/or specialists to determine the media and materials that are not commonly a part of the special service option. Examples of special instructional media and/or materials are : Language Master, orthopedic aids, System 80, Gillingham materials, B.S.C.S. Science Curriculum, Slingerland materials, etc.

Extent of the student's participation in regular education programs. The concept of *least restrictive environment* requires that removal from the regular educational or related services be documented. Documentation of services includes a description of the extent to which the student will participate in the regular education program and a justification for the type of educational placement chosen for the student.

Specifying the extent to which the student will participate in the regular program can be done in straightforward manner. The team has already determined the amount of time allocated for special education and related services; thus, unless otherwise specified, the remainder of the time is spent in the regular classroom. An example of a description of the extent to which the student will participate in the regular education program might read:

The student is to spend approximately 50 percent (4 hours a day) of his/her instructional time in a regular 5th-grade classroom. Within the regular educational environment, the student will attend classes in art, physical education, science, spelling, and language arts.

Justification for placement. The justification for the type of educational placement corresponds to the specific educational needs of the student. If a discrepancy exists between services needed and delivered an explanation should be provided. In justifying the educational services provided, the team reviews the decisions and considerations that led to the delineation of specific services. These decisions and considerations are then listed in summary form. For example, a justification for an educational placement might read:

It was deemed necessary to provide the student with services in a part-time special class with regular classroom instruction because: 1) the student's chronological age is 12 years and 5 months; 2) the student's overall level of functioning is at the second-grade level; 3) the student evidenced an academic retardation of five years in math and reading; 4) the student needs individual-ization, success, and small group instruction; and 5) the student can suc-cessfully participate in art, physical education, and history classes.

EVALUATION

Ideally, instructional planning results in effective and appropriate learning; however, unless the student's progress towards annual goals and short-term objectives is evaluated, instructional benefits will be minimal. Similarly, without a strong evaluation component the I.E.P. can become a paper exercise of little practical value.

Systematic collection of data on the student's progress serves a double function by allowing the team to: (a) determine if annual goals and short-term objectives are being achieved, and (b) establish a basis for making adjustments in the instructional plan. Evaluation criteria for monitoring provisions of services, annual goals, short-term objectives, and consumer satisfaction must be specified.

Although standardized tests are often used, these are generally not appropriate for measuring student performance on specific short-term objectives since they seldom relate directly to the student's instructional plan. What is needed to determine if progress is adequate is a means of collecting infor-mation on specific objectives over time.

The student's daily work products plus the teacher's observation over time are two means by which student progress on specific objectives can be measured. By noting the time required by a student to complete instructional tasks, the teacher can estimate rate. Accuracy on daily work products indicates the degree of success the student is exhibiting on activities designed to facilitate the acquisition of the objective. When combined, rate and accuracy on daily work products allow for a good measure by which to adjust the student's daily instructional plan.

Observation of the number of trials per lesson is another means of evaluating a student's progress toward a specific objective. Graphs can be kept indicating the number of trials presented each lesson. This information will often reveal whether the task is appropriately sequenced and/or presented. A large number of trials per lesson would indicate that instructional revision is necessary.

Criterion reference testing is a commonly used method to examine a student's performance on a very specific behavior. The intermediate steps necessary to complete a certain objective are determined and each step is specified in performance terms whereupon a level of proficiency is established. For example, a criterion reference test item might read: When presented with a flashcard with the letters "sl", the student will be able orally to produce the "sl" blend with 85 percent proficiency.

The objective and its intermediate steps can both be written as criterion reference test items. At established intervals, progress toward the proficiency level can be tested and thus provide the teacher with a means by which to measure student progress.

A final means for assessing progress towards a specific objective is the use of a data-based system consisting of five es-sential elements: (a) specification of the objectives in performance terms, (b) col-lection of baseline data, (c) initiation of instruction, (d) collection of progress data, and (e) appropriate modifications of the instructional plan. This system provides a means by which the teacher can continually assess the appropriateness of objectives and instruction.

For each objective, the team decides the evaluation criteria to be used to determine progress toward the short-term objective. Rate, daily work products, trials per lesson, criterion reference tests, and/or a data-based system may be employed. In specifying the evaluation criteria, it is important that the evaluation activities relate directly to the student's instructional plan. In this respect attention must be given to the relationship be-tween the evaluation task and the instruc-tional activity, the time required for the

1. INTRODUCTION

teacher to conduct evaluation, the time required by the student to demonstrate task performance, and the value of the information derived from evaluation.

Besides evaluating progress toward short-term objectives, it is necessary to determine if long-range goals are being achieved. By viewing a long-range goal as the

---

FIGURE 3
REPORTING FORM FOR MONITORING SHORT-TERM SERVICES

Student's Name: _____ Date: _____ Grade: _____

Age: _____ District/Cooperative: _____ School Building: _____

Describe Special Educational and Related Services to Be Provided

Service	Implementation Date Hours/Week	Completion Date	Personnel Responsible

Describe Special Educational and Related Services Delivered:

Service	Implementation	Date	Hours/Week	Completion Date	Personnel Responsible

Reasons for Failure to Deliver Prescribed Services:

---

culmination of a series of short-term objectives, progress can be determined by examining the data collected on the intermediate short-term objectives. In conjunction with standardized pre- and posttest batteries this informal information will indicate the student's rate and amount of educational change.

In addition to evaluating goals and objectives, provisions must be established for monitoring provisions of services, parental participation (understanding and satisfaction) and student receptivity. A team member, the Instructional Coordinator, should be assigned the responsibility of monitoring service provisions and consumer feedback, including evaluation data from participating teachers and/or specialists, reports from specific educational services, and consumer satisfaction.

Monitoring of services. Information on two types of services should be collected: a) short-term, such as temporary direct instruction provided by a specialist, and (b) long-term, e.g., assignment to a resource room on an ongoing basis. For short-term services, teachers and/or specialists should submit a brief report every six to nine weeks to the Instructional Coordinator. This report (See Figure 3) should indicate what, where, and when services were to be provided and how, where, and when the agreed upon services were delivered. If the agreed upon services were not delivered, reasons why should be specified. For services of an ongoing nature, the Instructional Coordinator should consult with the participating personnel at the end of each six- or nine-week period. Based on this feedback, the Instructional Coordinator can determine if services are being adequately delivered and if they are not, make the necessary revisions.

Parental involvement. While the I.E.P. is not a binding contract, it represents an agreement for services between the school district and the student's parents. The involvement of parents as "equal partners" in making decisions related to special services for their handicapped child is implicit in PL 94-142. This involvement is viewed as a positive

movement in recognizing the rights of parents and should encourage professionals to be more sensitive to parental concerns and attitudes.

To insure that the concerns and needs of parents are recognized and considered in developing instructional plans for their child, a system should be implemented allowing parents the opportunity to respond to questions related to the quality of interaction. To assist in obtaining this information from parents, the *Staffing Conference Feedback (Parent Form)* was designed. Following each staffing, parents are provided an opportunity to respond to questions related to the quality of communication/interaction. School districts may modify or alter particular questions to reflect more nearly their needs. It is critical, however, that questions clearly reflect the philosophical intent of parent involvement (See Figure 4).

FIGURE 4
STAFFING CONFERENCE FEEDBACK
(PARENT FORM)

Student _____ Date _____

School _____ Grade _____

Parent(s) _____ Tele. _____

Home Address _____

Staffing Date _____ Time _____

Parents Attending Staffing Conference _____

TO THE PARENT: The purpose of this questionnaire is to obtain information that will assist the Special Service Staff in improving communication between parents and professionals.

Recently you participated in a staffing conference concerning your child's special needs. Based on your feelings about the conference please respond to the following questions. For each question, check either "yes," "partially," or "no." If you wish to provide additional information please print your statement. The last three questions are open ended; therefore, you may respond to them with a written statement.

I. ADMINISTRATIVE

A. Were you notified that your child had been referred for special education services prior to your invitation to attend the staffing conference?   ( )yes, ( )partially, ( )no

B. Was an effort made to have both parents participate in the staffing conference?   ( )yes, ( )partially, ( )no

C. Were you notified of the staffing conference early enough to insure your participation?   ( )yes, ( )partially, ( )no

D. Was the staffing conference scheduled at a mutually agreed upon time and place?   ( )yes, ( )partially, ( )no

E. Were you told who would be attending the staffing conference?   ( )yes, ( )partially, ( )no

F. Were you informed of the purpose of the staffing conference?   ( )yes, ( )partially, ( )no

G. Were you told that you could invite outside professionals retained by you?   ( )yes, ( )partially, ( )no

H. Were you informed of due process procedures and your rights to appeal decisions?   ( )yes, ( )partially, ( )no

I. Were you provided a copy of the I.E.P.?   ( )yes, ( )partially, ( )no

1. INTRODUCTION

II. PROFESSIONAL

A. Were team members knowledgeable of your child's emotional/social behavior? ( )yes, ( )partially, ( )no

B. Were team members knowledgeable of your child's academic status? ( )yes, ( )partially, ( )no

C. Was a variety of service options discussed relative to your child's needs? ( )yes, ( )partially, ( )no

D. Was the assessment information collected from a variety of sources? ( )yes, ( )partially, ( )no

E. Was the assessment evaluation conducted by a multidisciplinary team? ( )yes, ( )partially, ( )no

F. Do you feel that the test instruments used were culturally or racially discriminatory? ( )yes, ( )partially, ( )no

G. Did the team justify any removal of your child from the regular classroom? ( )yes, ( )partially, ( )no

III. PARENTAL

A. Did you feel comfortable attending the staffing conference? ( )yes, ( )partially, ( )no

B. Were you asked about your opinions? ( )yes, ( )partially, ( )no

C. Did you feel free to contribute suggestions regarding your child's needs? ( )yes, ( )partially, ( )no

D. Did the professional staff appear interested in what you had to say? ( )yes, ( )partially, ( )no

E. Do you feel that the professional staff felt your participation was important? ( )yes, ( )partially, ( )no

F. Were you provided ample time to express information that you felt to be relevant? ( )yes, ( )partially, ( )no

G. Did you understand the I.E.P. developed for your child? ( )yes, ( )partially, ( )no

H. Did you feel that your child should have participated in the staffing conference? ( )yes, ( )partially, ( )no

IV. GENERAL

A. Do you feel that the recommendations made were in the best interest of your child? ( )yes, ( )partially, ( )no

B. Are you satisfied with the decision made at the staffing conference? ( )yes, ( )partially, ( )no

C. Do you feel that support services other than those recommended are needed for your child's progress? ( )yes, ( )partially, ( )no

D. Did you feel free to ask questions regarding the contributions, evaluation, and suggestions of the:
  1. classroom teacher ( )yes, ( )partially, ( )no
  2. learning specialist/special teacher ( )yes, ( )partially, ( )no
  3. special education representative/administrator ( )yes, ( )partially, ( )no
  4. assessment team member ( )yes, ( )partially, ( )no
  5. school psychologist ( )yes, ( )partially, ( )no
  6. _____ ( )yes, ( )partially, ( )no

E. At the conclusion of the staffing conference, how did you perceive your child's problems in view of your previous understanding? _____

_____

_____

_____

_____

F. Remarks _____

_____

_____

_____

_____

Student receptivity. The Instructional Coordinator needs to collect information on the student's receptivity to the educational program. If the student is disinclined towards the program, success is unlikely. The Instructional Coordinator should consult with the student's teachers and, where appropriate, the student himself to determine if the student is: (a) responsive and motivated by his/her educational plan and (b) if the student feels that the plan is appropriate to his or her needs.

IMPLEMENTATION

With the completion of the written I.E.P., the services required to achieve the instructional program are activated and annual goals, short-term objectives, services, and evaluation criteria are operationalized. As mentioned earlier, the Instructional Coordinator is assigned the responsibility of coordinating classroom and/or special services in order to implement the instructional plan. This role is basically intended to: (a) foster cooperation and communication among teachers and specialists, (b) provide a liaison between the team and the teachers implementing the plan, and (c) assure that implementation of the plan actually occurs.

The Instructional Coordinator's first task is to meet with each teacher and/or specialist who will provide direct and indirect services to the student and familiarize them with the assessment summary document, annual goals, short-term objectives, services, and evaluation criteria specified in the written I.E.P. This information provides them with an understanding of the direction and purpose of the instructional plan. Furthermore, the Instructional Coordinator is responsible for initiating cooperation and communication among teachers and specialists who must be able to share information and work together in order to maximize instructional effectiveness. Each of these professionals are made aware of the roles and responsibilities of the others and a means of communication is agreed upon.

In addition to fostering cooperation and communication, the Instructional Coordinator acts as a liaison between the team and the individuals who implement the plan. Also, the Coordinator is responsible for reporting the student's progress to the team and insuring that the plan is adequately implemented. As the educational plan is operationalized and executed, flaws in the written I.E.P. will become apparent: the annual goals and short-term objectives may not be realistic; the length of time necessary to master objectives may be excessive; and all the objectives may be accomplished in half of the expected time. These and other problems will have to be resolved. For minor difficulties the implementers and the Instructional Coordinator should be able to work out an appropriate solution while it will be necessary to reconvene in order to resolve major problems. If, for example, a teacher is having difficulty accomplishing a specific short-term objective, the Instructional Coordinator, the teacher, and other concerned parties should determine a solution. However, if a student masters all of the prescribed objectives before the end of the year, the team will be reconvened to develop additional objectives.

As mentioned earlier, the Instructional Coordinator is also responsible for collecting evaluation data from each of the participating teachers and specialists. In order to determine if the plan is being implemented appropriately, evaluation data should be collected from the teachers at least every six or nine weeks. Progress on the prescribed goals is then reported to the team, parents, other teachers working with the student, administrators, and the students themselves. If progress is not adequate, the instructional plan is modified.

While the Instructional Coordinator initiates and monitors the written I.E.P., the essence of the I.E.P., classroom intervention, is administered by regular classroom teachers and/or specialists. Similarly, it is the responsibility of the participating teachers to select the methods and materials necessary successfully to attain the goals and objectives specified in the written instructional plan. For example, if the learning disabilities specialist is assigned the responsibility of teaching the student consonant symbol-sound associations, the specialist will have to refine this goal or objective and determine appropriate materials, reinforcers, and daily activities.

1. INTRODUCTION

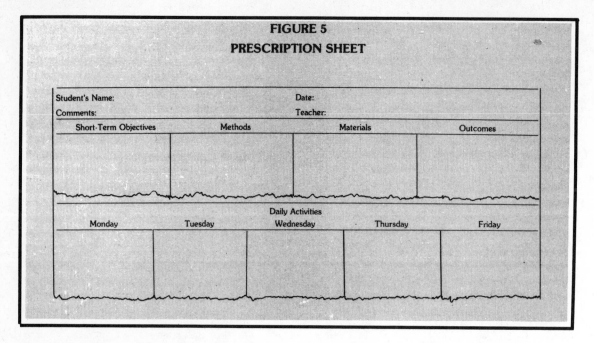

**FIGURE 5
PRESCRIPTION SHEET**

Student's Name: Date:
Comments: Teacher:

Short-Term Objectives	Methods	Materials	Outcomes

Daily Activities

Monday	Tuesday	Wednesday	Thursday	Friday

A valuable aid for refining the I.E.P.'s short-term objectives is a prescription sheet (See Figure 5). On this sheet the teachers write the assigned short-term objectives and specify the methods, materials, outcomes, and daily activities necessary to achieve the objectives. Initially, teachers refine only the objectives they are to work with immediately. As progress is achieved and short-term objectives are accomplished, additional objectives are refined. The prescription sheet provides the teacher with a written guide and the team with a summary of the teacher's activities.

While the scope of this article does not allow us to present an indepth discussion of appropriate teaching principles, it is necessary, however, to present a list of remediation principles that should be considered by the teacher when refining short-term objectives and delivering services. The proposed methods, materials, reinforcers, and daily activities should be realistic in respect to the instructional time available.

Suggested activities must be based on the recognition that the teacher's energy and time for preparation are not unlimited.

Remediation is a process of continuous evaluation. Evaluation data are used to determine if progress is adequate or if alterations in the instructional plan are required.

Successful remediation is based upon a flexible use of a wide variety of materials, techniques, and methods.

Remediation techniques and materials must be carefully selected and tailored to the student's unique needs.

Selected activities should be enjoyable and motivating to the student.

The teacher should dramatize student success through the use of charts, verbal praise, etc.

Activities must be provided which accomodate generalization of skills to other contexts.

CONCLUSION

Providing a handicapped student with an appropriate education is a complex task in view of the complicated nature of a handicapping condition and the variety of pressures brought to bear upon the student. Consequently, the education and remediation of the exceptional student require the resources and energy of a variety of education and/or noneducational personnel to resolve considerations concerning assessment, goals, objectives, services, evaluation, methods, materials, reinforcement, and organization. In this connection, the I.E.P. provides a framework through which personnel resources and educational considerations can be directed and, if properly used, assures a linkage between the student's needs and the education delivered.

PL 94-142 sets forth detailed requirements on what should be included in an I.E.P. and the conditions under which the plan should be developed. However, it does not specify the planning process to be followed. Due to the complexity of the requirements, it is clear that a systematic approach to the development and implementation of the I.E.P. is necessary. The approach presented in this article is intended to provide the team and participating teachers with a systematic guide from which to construct an appropriate educational program for handicapped children. Sample I.E.P. forms are presented on the following pages.

REFERENCES

Federal Register. Tuesday, August 23, 1977. Part II. Education Handicapped Children. Washington: Department of Health, Education, and Welfare, Office of Education.

I. SAMPLE
INDIVIDUAL EDUCATION PROGRAM
(Assessment Form)

School Year _____   District/Cooperative _____

Present Placement _____   School Building _____

Student's Name _____ Date of Birth _____ Age _____ Grade _____

Primary Area of Exceptionality _____ Dates of Meetings _____

Summary of Present Level of Performance:

_____

Assessment Team Members: Signatures   Date

II. SAMPLE
INDIVIDUAL EDUCATION PROGRAM
(Annual Goals and Short-Term Objectives Form)

Date _____   Student's Name _____

Annual Goals and Short-Term Objectives	Services to Achieve Objectives	Personnel Responsible
Annual Goal A _____		
Objective 1-A _____		
Objective 2-A _____		
Objective 3-A _____		
Objective 4-A _____		
Objective 5-A _____		
Annual Goal B _____		
Objective 1-B _____		
Objective 2-B _____		
Objective 3-B _____		
Objective 4-B _____		
Objective 5-B _____		

EDITORIAL: THE IEP

Editorial: The IEP

Public Law 94-142 is beginning to elicit reactions ranging from ecstasy to apoplexy around the country for a number of reasons, and some of it is understandable if not entirely justified. The law's prototypes in Massachusetts, Pennsylvania, Michigan, and Texas, to name several of the most prominent, have wrought profound changes in the assignment of priorities in the educational system, forced administrators and school boards to consider carefully their attitudes toward exceptional children, and released hordes of revolutionaries who have terrorized the countryside with threats of litigation and withholding of support money if exceptional children are not treated fairly. Through it all, most of the provisions of the precursors of 94-142 have affected only administrative line and staff personnel to any great extent. To be sure, beleaguered special education supervisors, school psychologists, principals, and other quasi-divine personages have had to arrange time for many due-process hearings and appeals, and have learned in exquisite detail about the physical and metaphysical inner features of the halls of justice. But these activities have scarcely touched the serene inner world of the classroom teacher. Outside a battle rages, but behind the classroom door it's pretty much business as usual—until recently.

The classroom is a temporary shelter, but it is now being swiftly penetrated by the thrust of the mighty events taking place in the real world, and teachers are beginning to notice. A year ago probably only one school administrator in ten knew what the initials IEP stood for, and the proportion of knowledgable teachers was much smaller. Now, thanks in part to a well conceived and conducted information campaign by the Bureau of Education for the Handicapped, with the help of CEC, most special education teachers and nearly all administrators are more or less intimately acquainted with PL 94-142. Terms like "least restrictive environment," "due process," and "multidimensional assessment" are more or less commonplace and will usually elicit at least comprehending nods when mentioned among any group of educators. However, the one term that appears to be nearly universally recognized and which has the most noticeable effect is the *IEP*. The reason is obvious: The IEP is a concept that will profoundly alter the domain of each teacher who has contact with an exceptional child. The IEP is the framework for the provision of educational experiences custom-designed for the individual handicapped child; it is the basis for the teachers' plans over the coming year; it is .a standard for evaluation of the interaction of the child and the education system.

The IEP is also the source of considerable anxiety among both teachers and administrators. There is concern that because of participation of the parents and the child in its development, the IEP might be held to be a contract in which the school agrees to produce certain behavioral change in the child for which it will be held accountable, and liable in the event the long-range goals are not met. There is also concern that the IEP may become the basis for evaluation of a teacher's competency, and a standard for determining merit pay. From the standpoint of both administrators and teachers there is concern that the process is too time-consuming and expensive, and may not be practical. There is even beginning a narrow but growing current of passive resistance on the part of front-line educators, in the hope that the IEP and other of the more controversial provisions of the law will atrophy and fade away due to neglect.

Well, at the risk of being accused of over simplification because of my own biases (which, you may notice, *do* exist), let me simply say that there is a very real possibility that the IEP may indeed be part of the basis for evaluation of some aspects of teacher performance, but this should worry only the ignorant, incompetent, inflexible individual. If the IEP includes an adequate monitoring system and provisions for modification as needed, the conscientious and capable teacher should perform more effectively and be able to show evidence of it. If teacher merit and salary increases are to be based on pupil progress, better to measure progress by an objective and reliable standard that everyone can read and understand than some obscure or subjective one that defies expression in behavioral terms.

The concern over the likelihood that the IEP will be considered a contract, with failure to reach stated goals possible justification for litigation or punitive action, is a serious one which may require further clarification by state legal officers or the courts. However, there is the real possibility that nonutilization of IEPs for exceptional children will not forestall such action. There were cer-

Editorial: "The IEP," Don L. Walker, *Education of the Visually Handicapped*, Vol. IX, No. 3, Fall 1977. © 1977 Association for Education of the Visually Handicapped Incorporated.

tainly no IEPs involved in recent cases where suits have been brought against public schools for their failures to teach high school graduates to read after 13 years in school. The "contracts" in those cases were implied, rather than explicit. Besides, most civil litigation is brought because of *ambiguity* in a relationship. Use of the IEP should reduce ambiguity, and therefore result in decreased, rather than increased, vulnerability to litigation.

As yet there is little research to show whether the IEP process can be carried out satisfactorily or whether the process will produce the desired improvement in educational effectiveness. However, a small but growing body of information from some of the state prototype programs suggests that the concerns may be exaggerated, and that the process is feasible. Evaluation of effectiveness will come in time.

One suspects that many teachers are resisting because they feel threatened by being force-fed a concept so foreign to their cherished, traditional style, and are insecure about their ability to learn the new skills required. However, there is a growing array of programmed materials for teaching the skills required for implementation of PL 94-142, in a variety of formats to fit nearly any in-service training model, including the individual auto-instructional approach.

The IEP is the law, it's necessary, it won't go away, the means are readily available to learn the skills, *and it's simply formalizing the individualization we've been claiming special education does anyway.* If you believe in the latter, *do it!* And while you learn, think about how to solve the *real* problem down the road:

What do we do when parents begin demanding equal services for non-handicapped children?

Have a good year.

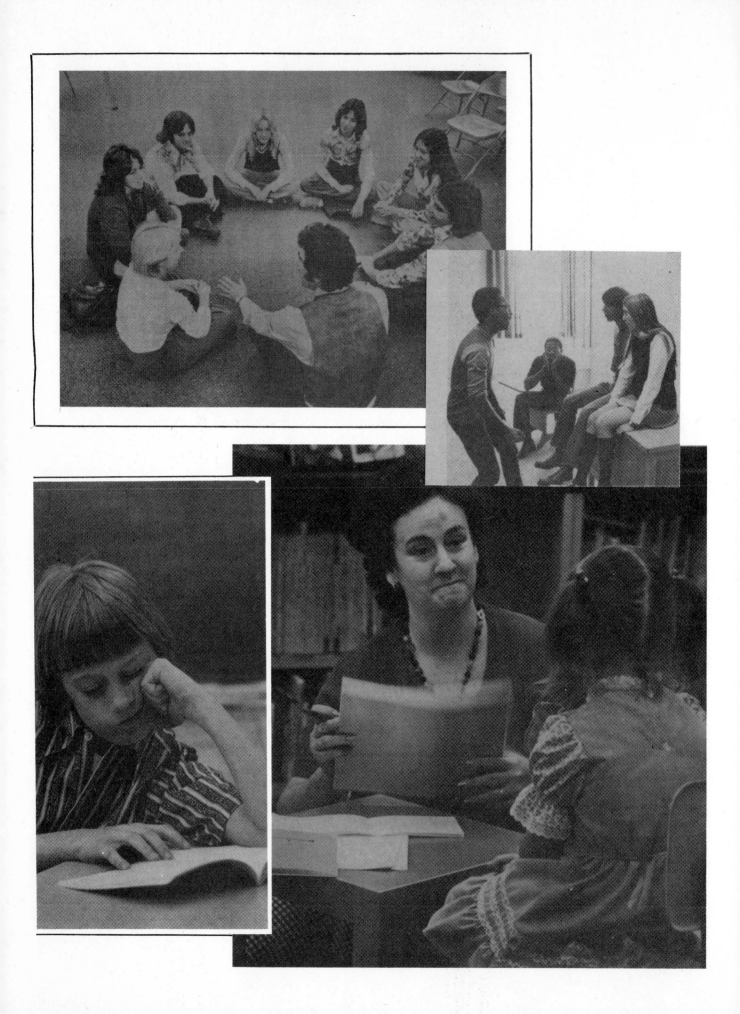

Goals and Objectives

Over the past five to ten years there has been an increasing emphasis on the use of specific behavioral objectives to organize and evaluate instructional units. Now this feature is required by federal regulation. As an accountability model the IEP process described in this book creates rather great expectations on special education teachers. The teacher is the person who is primarily responsible for the remediation of deficits that are revealed through criterion assessment procedures. For this reason, some anxiety have arisen among the many special education professionals.

The component of the IEP that these teachers appear to fear the most is the annual goals and specific instructional objectives element. This fear is primarily two-fold. One of the anticipated concerns is the amount of time teachers must spend delineating these goals and objectives and meeting with parents. Another difficulty teachers perceive is the potential of legal suits they may face if they don't meet the specified target objectives.

The first fear is real. Administrative arrangements have to be developed in order that teachers have the time to fulfill their time consuming responsibilities under the IEP provision of PL 94-142. A shortened instructional day once or twice a month, and the occasional use of inservice workshops are two alternatives administrators in some

local educational agencies have used. In regards to the second fear, teachers should be aware that the IEP is not a binding contract. Educators cannot be held personally responsible if a child does not achieve the contemplated growth mentioned in the IEP.

Despite some inherent problems the writing of annual goals and specific instructional objectives could provide the following benefits:

1. Structure the curricula, lessons, and services exceptional children receive.
2. Improve the parent-professional partnership.
3. Facilitate the evaluation process.
4. Increase communication among all professionals involved in providing services to handicapped children.
5. Insure continuity of programming as a student moves from one teacher to another.

Hopefully the following articles will provide special education teachers with assistance in the selection and writing of annual goals and short-term objectives for the children they must instruct. Emphasis has been given to the development of instructional sequences, involving students in the goal setting process.

Ten Guidelines for Writing Instructional Sequences

Ernest Siegel, Ed. D. and Rita Siegel, M.S.

Despite the fact that more courses are given and more literature is devoted to the overall topic of task analysis, teachers, though more than willing to implement, still seek more definitive guidelines for writing instructional sequences. This paper presents ten specific guidelines based on the pooled experiences and ideas of the authors and education majors in various colleges.

More and more, voices are crying out for greater precision in teaching. Both educators and practitioners readily agree that effective instruction begins when one matches the requirements of the task with the learning profile of the pupil. Despite the fact that there is no controversy regarding the desirability of instruction task analysis, in principle, current classroom practices simply do not reflect this awareness.

It is likely that teachers would be more willing to embrace and to *utilize* the concept of instructional sequencing if specific guidelines could be drawn up.

The following is a term paper that the senior author has assigned to students (in special education as well as in regular education, both graduate and undergraduate students) over the past ten years at various colleges:

TERM PROJECT ON LEARNING DISABILITIES

Children who present learning disabilities (i.e., problems in learning stemming from neurological impairment or emotional disturbance) often have difficulty in incidental learning and in "bridging gaps"; therefore, one of the principles for their education is to employ a sequential approach — i.e., a developmental hierachical set of activities and experiences leading to a specific, well-defined goal.

It is your task to list (and explain) the sequential steps necessary in teaching a child classified as "learning disabled" to master two of the following:

(a) multiply by 6
(b) perform subtraction with exchange
(c) read and understand a map's grid system (longitude and latitude lines)
(d) differentiate auditorially (and in spelling and reading) the S and S-blends: Sm, Sp, Sl, etc. (e.g., the difference between "sell" and "smell" and "sit" and "slit")
(e) ride a two-wheeled bicycle
(f) use a saw
(g) solve a simple algebraic equation (e.g., $5 \times ? + 1 = 36$)
(h) understand the alphabetizing system

"Ten Guidelines for Writing Instructional Sequences," Ernest Siegel and Rita Seigel, *Journal of Learning Disabilities,* Vol. 8, No. 4, April 1975. © 1975 The Professional Press Incorporated.

(use the dictionary — look up words quickly and systematically)

Choose any two (2). List all the sequential steps in order (explain when necessary). (Or, you may choose any of the above and one of your own). Note: Do not necessarily write a lesson plan (this need not be a single lesson, but a developmental sequence for one specific task; it may entail many lessons). Length: no more than 2 pages.

GUIDELINES

On the basis of various cross-currents which ensued while designing these sequences, evaluating them, criticizing and refining them, certain guidelines have emerged:

(1) *Avoid extraneous material.* For example, in a sequence design to help the pupil differentiate the S from an S-blend (e.g., Sm, Sp, Sl, St), a teacher proposed bringing in sugar, eggs, and an electric blender! The class agreed that while this might have some benefit in motivating a particular child, the connection between this and the task itself is an ethereal one at best. It is highly likely that the teacher got sidetracked with the word "blend." After all, the behavioral objective was not for the child to develop an appreciation for the phenomenon of blends generally, but to be able to distinguish auditorially Sm from S.

Likewise, some teachers, when asked to teach children to ride a two-wheeled bicycle, proposed having them begin by walking a straight line, walking on a balance board, or sitting on a wooden horse! Obviously, they are hung up on the word "balance." If this be the case, why not go all the way and ask the child to balance a basketball on his finger or a pointer on his nose? Clearly, the semantics of "balance" globally should not interfere with the teacher's concept as it specifically applies to bicycle riding.

(2) *Don't spend too much time in reteaching the prerequisite.* If the aim of the sequence is to teach the child to multiply by six, then one must assume that the child already knows that multiplication is a short-cut to addition, the meaning of the multiplication sign, the commutative quality of multiplication, and some of the prior "tables." If the child does not know all this and is in fact learning multiplication for the first time, then, why on earth would the teacher want to begin with the sixes?

Similarly, if the aim is to teach the child the alphabetizing system so that he will be able to look up words in the dictionary quickly and systematically, then one must assume that he already recognizes and can name all the letters.

Of course, there is a relationship between the sequence's aim — i.e., the behavioral objective, and the teacher's knowledge of the child — his level, learning style, intact and impaired modalities, etc. Even a good sequence is useless if the child isn't ready for it. Nevertheless, in designing sequences, the teacher must decide what the prerequisites are, assure herself that somewhere there surely must be a child who has mastered these, and then get on with the job of writing the particular instructional sequence, starting at the point of the child's entering behavior.

(3) *Use what the child knows — and this includes the prerequisites — to help him learn the new.* For example, it is a good bet that any given child has learned the "fives" in multiplying before the teacher attempts to teach the "sixes" — not because five comes first, but because the products always end in zero or five. Moreover, the fives are used in money, in telling time, scoring, etc. Therefore, a strategy for teaching multiplying by six might be to break up the six into five and one. Hence, 7x6 is approached as 7x5 and 7x1. The child should already know both of these answers. He may, of course, need help in adding 35+7 mentally — but that, then can be learned in a separate sequence.

(4) *Assume motivation.* In the never-ending debate between humanism and behaviorism, some teachers seem impelled to devote a considerable portion of the sequence (often more than 50% of it) toward motivation.

One teacher proposed teaching a child to ride a two-wheeled bicycle by talking about transportation and visiting a bicycle store. Another began his sequence for teaching a child to saw a piece of wood by discussing carpentry and furniture, and then asking the child to choose one of five pieces of wood and one of five saws.

Now, there is nothing wrong in attempting to motivate a child and, in fact, an insightful teacher would indeed recognize and make provisions for an unmotivated pupil. The reasons for the lack of motivation must be discovered, and a sequence for stimulating motivation, itself, can be developed. Behavior modification techniques are often helpful. The point, is however, that too much devotion to the child and his *presumed* lack of motivation often siphons the teacher's attention away from the instructional task. The net result is an ineffective sequence. At first glance, this writ-

2. OBJECTIVES

ten sequence may indeed *appear* valid, but if one subtracts all of the beginning motivation steps, the remainder generally is scant. It becomes apparent that in such a sequence there is no genuine attempt to *teach*. To put it differently, the teacher may succeed with motivating (even when it is not needed!) but fail with instruction.

Therefore, it is highly recommended that in writing instructional sequences, the teacher *assume* that motivation is present. Certainly there must be at least one child who is already motivated to learn but desperately needs systematic instruction. In the current vogue of "letting the child do his own thing," we must never forget that the handicapped learner has *already* demonstrated that he cannot learn on his own and, therefore, for him, instructional intervention based upon task analysis is of paramount importance.

(5) *Identifying sequential components.* In performing a task analysis, it is a good idea to look for specific areas which lend themselves to sequencing. There are general areas, of course, which obtain for all sequences: concrete to abstract, simple to more complex, proximal to distal, small initial doses to larger doses, a great deal of supervision to no supervision, etc. Besides these, a given behavioral objective will often have its own sequential components. They should be identified and incorporated into the written sequence.

For example, in teaching a child to saw a piece of wood, the direction should be from using soft wood to using hard wood, from pre-grooving the wood for the child to having him make his own groove, from holding the end of the wood for the child to giving him complete independence, etc. In teaching a child to ride a two-wheeled bicycle, it is easier for him to learn on a girl's bike. (The absence of the horizontal bar facilitates mounting and dismounting.) Other areas for sequencing would be for him to ride on hard-packed dirt first, then on pavement; for the teacher to run alongside and push the bicycle at first, then later let go; for him to ride on a straight path, then try curves; to ride in safe courses, then in traffic, etc.

In learning a task such as copying material from the blackboard, some sequential components are: from copying material which is familiar to the child to copying unfamiliar material, from copying material at his desk to copying from the board, and using a tilt board (at 45°) first in order to mediate transcribing from the vertical to the horizontal plane.

The handicapped learner needs support and structure. A consideration of sequentialized components of instructional tasks is a key means of affording him the "cushion" (physically as well as psychologically) he requires.

(6) *Avoid the "recipe" approach.* It is possible to write instructional sequences which are technically correct, yet are nonsupportive as far as the handicapped learner is concerned. Consider the cook's printed recipe. Obviously the steps are ordered, and the experienced cook will have no difficulty in following the steps. But the novice may not understand the meaning of "baste," "simmer," and "diced," and may require specific instruction in how to knead dough and to fold in beaten egg whites.

A carpentry shop may have the steps for sawing a piece of wood listed on a work chart in perfect sequence. However, since these did not take into account the child with perceptual and/or coordination difficulties, the pupil who needs help in actually gripping the saw, sawing on a straight line, making the initial groove, and in sawing for long periods of time will not find this kind of sequence adequate.

And in academic areas, instructional sequences must show a sensitivity for handicapped learners. Just as it is necessary to *teach* the inexperienced cook the actual motions involved in kneading and to include some supportive steps in a carpentry task analysis, instructional sequences in arithmetic and in phonics must likewise reflect teaching the needs of a handicapped learner.* For example, in teaching a child to "read" and "write" arithmetic sentences containing the "more than" and "less than" signs — >, < — a cardboard cut-out ≪ can be used first, since it is easier to *place* the sign than to *write* it. Or, in teaching the sounds of the long and short vowels, it might be easier initially to omit the Y as a vowel, inasmuch as this may prove to be a difficult concept to grasp at the onset.

(7) *Avoid substituting a variety of activities in lieu of an instructional sequence.* At times, a teacher submits an instructional "sequence" which has the aura of appropriateness since every "step" is related to the aim. Stated simply, there are no unrelated points — and this, of course, is to be admired. A closer inspection, however, may reveal that these are really not "steps" since one point does not lead into another. The order is entirely arbitrary, and there has been no attempt to *teach* any of

---

*Sequences should, of course, be designed for gifted students as well. However, the steps may be fewer, certainly the scope more advanced, and the subject matter geared toward enrichment.

the points. For example, there are many ways of teaching (or to be more precise, *practicing*) subtraction. One could construct a place-value chart in conjunction with squared material, one could use coins, one could use an abacus, one could practice the written algorism, one could read and solve problems requiring subtraction with renaming. None of these activities by themselves, actually *teach* the handicapped learner, which is the stipulated aim. For example, no strategy for recognition of *when* or *how* renaming is necessary was offered.

A variety of activities should indeed be utilized, but only as substeps at a given point. In other words, a particular step in an instructional sequence may well require massive practice in a variety of ways, but variety, per se, can never be a substitute for instruction.

(8) *Become proficient in technical aspects of the instructional task.* Besides being able to write educational sequences generally, the teacher must also be acquainted with all phases of the given task's requirements. In this way, she will be able to give the child the "fine points." For example, in learning to ride a two-wheeled bicycle, it is easier to balance if one looks straight ahead rather than down and if one goes a little faster rather than more slowly. Sawing a piece of wood is facilitated by the pupil standing and working the saw at right angles to the wood. Similarly, the teacher will be better able to instruct penmanship if she, herself knows the exact formation of each letter.

(9) *Avoid scientific jargon.* Since much of the literature regarding task analysis comes to us from psychologists, the written instructional sequence often exudes a scientific aura which can overwhelm, confuse, and finally discourage teachers. Some teachers are led to believe that a sequence can't possibly be of any value if it is written simply. The scientific semblance, if it exists at all, is to be found in the written behavioral objectives. This is so because one is attempting to define *precisely* what the child will finally do as a result of instruction. It may even be interpreted as a subtle attempt to chide teachers for having been somewhat imprecise in the past. This portion of the sequence generally contains a stipulated frequency of correct response (e.g.: when shown a list of 20 three-letter short E words and 20 three-letter short A words in random order, the child will read 90% of them correct within 30 seconds.)

Now, it is true that in some instances such as decoding, reading comprehension, arithmetic computation, etc., — it may be a good idea to stipulate correct-incorrect ratios. However, at other times, it is patently unnecessary. For example, a child can either ride a two-wheeled bicycle or he can't, he can write the letter H or he can't, he can form the plural of nouns or he can't. In fact, in these instances, the "behavioral objective" does not really differ from the aim (traditionally couched in relatively general terms). It does not even have to be written out and, more likely than not, can be found in the final step(s) of the sequence.

At any rate, one teacher, when asked to devise a sequence for teaching a child to ride a two-wheeled bicycle, offered: *"Behavioral Objective* — to determine the degree of visual/ motor development and physical integration to enable the child to mount and pedal a bike while maintaining balance and directionality."

To which the instructor inscribed the incisive comment, "Wow!"

(10) *Don't just present, teach.* If it is true, as we believe, that the "heart" of teaching is imparting knowledge or a skill, then this tenth guideline must be considered the heart of instructional sequencing. Most adequate learners learn when material is presented to them. The excellent student may even be able to figure out on his own that in the numeral 25, the 2 represents 2 tens and the 5 is really 5 ones. Out-of-school experiences with equivalencies in money and making change (quarters, dimes, and nickels) might well have given him this understanding and he may even have made the generalization into other two-place numerals.

For most of the other children a simple demonstration or verbalization by the teacher will serve to link up their previous experiences and they, too, will understand what the digits 6 and 7 in the numeral 67 represent.

The handicapped learner (in any particular area) is the one who doesn't "get it" when the teacher has only said it or shown it. He needs more than that. The instructional sequence is the "more" that he needs.

How does the teacher who has written a sequence decide whether or not she is really teaching and not just presenting? There are two specific pitfalls. First, if the sequence does not require the child to *do* anything, the teacher can have no certainty that the child has learned anything or that she has taught anything. If, in a sequence to "teach the difference between S and Sm," the steps enumerate only what the teacher will do and say (e.g., (1) teacher puts S and Sm on the board, (2) she speaks the sound of each, (3) she gives a word or several words

2. OBJECTIVES

beginning with S or Sm as examples for each), then she is merely presenting the material, not teaching it. And on the basis of this "teaching," the sequence writer may now expect the child to demonstrate what he has "learned" by doing the typical workbook exercise. This usually requires him to look at a picture, perhaps of a smoking chimney, and choose correctly from two or more answers. He will then mark an X in the box labeled "Sm" rather than "S" or "Sp," etc. This, then, becomes the second pitfall to avoid. It is an example of expecting the child to do something *without* instruction. If he can do it, then he didn't need any teaching in this area. He may already have known how to differentiate S from Sm. Perhaps he was able to make the correct generalization merely from presentation. On the other hand, the child who responds to the worksheet by saying "I don't understand," or who tries to complete the task and gets almost all of the items wrong, or perhaps just goes through the page and merely marks an X on anything he sees, is the candidate for a good instructional sequence.

Now the sequence writer is beginning to see the light. A glimmer may be coming through. Having presented the aforementioned material, the teacher recognizes that one or more children need more instruction. They are ready to learn this material but they will not be able to do so without direct intervention by the teacher. A possible sequence for *teaching* a child to differentiate between the S and the Sm sounds may be written such as the following example.

BEHAVIORAL OBJECTIVES

(1) Given 20 words beginning with S or Sm, the child will be able to identify the initial consonant sound or consonant blend with 90% accuracy.

(2) Given 20 letter clusters (e.g., ile, ort, ell) and told how each sounds, the child will be able to vocalize the whole word formed when S or Sm is put before the cluster with 90% accuracy.

Prerequisite for learning from instructional sequences. The child has demonstrated that he auditorially recognizes and can produce (vocalize) the sounds of all the consonants. (If the student who failed to learn the S-Sm lesson did so because he did not know the individual consonant sounds, then no sequence written to teach the former is good for him because he is not yet ready for it.)

PROCEDURES

I. Review sound of S.
    A. Teacher makes the pure sound (S is not attached to any word) and the child names the letter.
    B. Teacher points to the letter (on board or paper) and the child makes the sound.

II. Introduce the Sm sound.
    A. Teacher makes the pure sound and the child names the letters given. Both S and Sm are written prominently on the board or on paper.
    B. The teacher points to the Sm and the child produces the pure sound.

III. The child is required to differentiate between the pure S and Sm sounds.
    A. The teacher makes one of the pure sounds and the child is required to name the letter or letters she has sounded. (The teacher will require that the child do this five out of five tries before proceeding.)
    B. The teacher points to either S or Sm and the child is required to produce the sound pointed to. Five out of five correct tries are required before the teacher goes on.
    (Modification: Sometimes a child demonstrates that he cannot correctly reproduce the blended sound. He may put in extraneous sounds (e.g., "suh em") or even produce an Sn sound. At this point the sequence has to stop and a new sequence developed to teach the child *how to blend.*)

IV. Add a nonsense syllable to the pure S and Sm sounds.
    A. The teacher explains that she will be adding the sound "ah" to the S and Sm. She demonstrates how each will sound — "sah," "smah."

        1. The teacher makes the sound and the child tells which one he has heard (by pointing to it or if it is labeled by saying its number, e.g.: 1) sah, 2) smah). The child must be able to correctly identify five out of five before the sequence proceeds.
        2. The teacher points to the sound and the child produces it. The rule of five out of five correct holds true here. (It may be at this point that the blending ability breaks down and a new sequence must be introduced.)

V. Introduce S and Sm in actual words.
    A. The teacher vocalizes a word and the child is asked to tell whether it begins

with S or Sm. If he can do this with 90% accuracy when given 20 different words, then the first behavioral objective has been achieved.

B. A letter cluster is written on the board (or paper) and its sound is told to the child if he does not know it (e.g., ell).

   1. The teacher asks the child to tell what word it created when the S is put in front of the written "ell."

   2. The teacher continues this with 20 prepared letter clusters (or families) and varies the S and Sm placed before them. The consonant or the blend plus the cluster must make a real word.

      a) If the child can achieve 90% accuracy in this task, then the second behavioral objective has been achieved.

It should be noted that the above sequence is quite limited in scope. The best way to develop competency in sequence writing is to start with the tangible skill subjects such as phonics, math, or penmanship. These areas lend themselves to a circumscribed and well-defined aim. If the teacher's aim is simple and definite enough, it is more likely that her thinking will be focused upon component sequential steps. Later, more abstract subject areas can be approached.

It must be obvious that recognizing and producing the S and Sm sounds is a "splinter" skill. As an isolated sequence, it would have little meaning for the child who does not generalize easily. It isn't likely that even a superb young learner could make *all* the generalizations necessary to render this specific skill a useful one. However, building upon this sequence to include *every* S blend and to teach the child sequentially to differentiate among them, builds toward the ultimate goal of decoding new words phonetically. Similarly, when the teacher prepares an instructional sequence whose aim is that the child produce the cursive letter l, she knows, of course, that finally the child will be taught to write words, sentences, and paragraphs ideationally in cursive script. In organizing her thinking to write the sequence for the letter l, she develops her own skills in following through with further sequences geared towards the final goal. Hopefully, the teacher recognizes that the individual letters thus taught will be linked to form words,

then sentences, and finally paragraphs. First, the material is copied (from a paper on the desk and then from the chalkboard and ultimately from oral dictation). When competency has been achieved the child's creative writing will be done in cursive script.

If it seems to you that the above is really only simple common sense and not different from the way any good penmanship workbook is arranged, you are quite correct. But recall now guideline #6 — Avoid the "recipe approach — and remember that the handicapped learner will probably require insightful modifications: extra practice, initial short doses of written work, more experience in tracing, actual physical guidance by the teacher grasping his writing hand, directional and/or color-cuing, specially printed paper, cuing for correct word space (finger distance), etc.

All of these guidelines can be encapsulated in two prepotent principles: (1) Stipulate that the given child is absolutely ready for your sequence, but that (2) he is utterly incapable of learning it without specific instruction. The first insures that the teacher will not spend time in needlessly reviewing prerequisites; in projecting extraneous material which, however creative and clever in appearance, is totally irrelevant; or in attempting to motivate the already motivated child. The second enhances the likelihood that the teacher will not substitute a variety of unconnected and unordered activities (albeit pertinent to the lesson's aim) for ordered step-by-step instruction, will not offer a technically correct yet unmodified, nonindividualized, and nonsupportive recipe, will identify sequential components of the instructional module, will become aware of the technical aspects of the task, and, above all, will show a healthy respect for the difference between teaching and merely presenting.

Today, as always, there are numerous instances of superb, systematic, sensitive, master teachers. It is a tribute to them that they succeed despite the overall dearth of precise guidelines emanating from preservice or inservice sources. Call it love of children, instinct, creativity, a propensity to empathize with the handicapped learner and thereby glimpse his needs, whatever. Perhaps when we identify the forces which account for this spontaneous generation of excellence of teachers, we will come close to answering the final question: How can the "art" of teaching best be taught? — *14-16 217th St., Bayside, N.Y. 11360.*

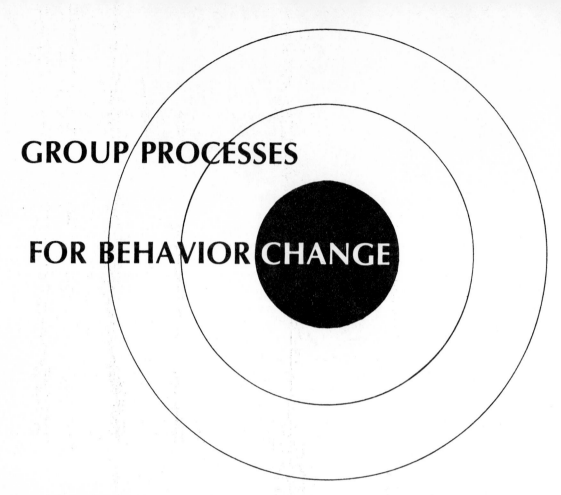

GROUP PROCESSES

FOR BEHAVIOR CHANGE

The pow-wow is an important part of classroom activity.

Robert Harth
Stanton M. Morris

*Robert Harth is Associate Professor,
Department of Special Education,
University of Missouri, Columbia.
Stanton M. Morris is Assistant Professor of
Special Education, University of Denver,
Colorado.*

*This article combines material independently written
by Dr. Harth and Dr. Morris. The section on the
pow-wow was contributed by Dr. Morris. Dr. Harth
authored the section on goal setting and the discussion of the relationship between cognitive control
techniques and behavior change.*

Goal Setting

■ Teachers of emotionally disturbed children have always set goals for the children with whom they work. These goals help the teacher focus on specific strategies to be used to move the child from a special setting to a regular setting. Without some sort of goal setting on the teacher's part, programs lack direction and tend to become vague.

The purpose here is not to talk about goal setting by teachers, however, but to develop procedures for helping children set goals for themselves. This is seen as the first step in their achieving cognitive control—the ability to identify their own problem behaviors as well as alternatives to these problem behaviors.

The notion of children setting goals for themselves carries with it two important implications: (a) It means that children need to become aware of their problem behaviors and be able to verbalize them. (b) In the process of goal setting the child makes a commitment to change as well as a commitment to be an ally of the teacher in the change process. It is possible to change a child's behavior without a commitment, but the changes are easier when a commitment exists.

THE PROCESS OF GOAL SETTING

Goal setting is the first activity of each week. It is carried out in a group on Monday morning. The setting is a circle of chairs with the teacher included as part of the circle. Rules of behavior are set up to insure the orderliness of the meeting. The rules have nothing to do with the quality of goals suggested or with whether or not a child sets

a goal. They refer only to the orderliness with which the meeting is carried out.

The purpose of the meeting is to help children set one goal for themselves relative to some aspect of their problem behavior. The child will work on the goal for a minimum of one week. To accomplish this the teacher goes around the circle asking each child to identify his goal. Occasionally, particularly when a child is new in the classroom, he may be unable to identify a goal. In this case, the teacher prods the child with some leading questions (e.g., What kinds of things do you have problems with in school? What things do you get in trouble for in school?). If this fails, the teacher could ask other group members what they think a good goal might be. If someone suggests a goal, the teacher should determine whether the original child will accept it. If the child does, then the goal is set. If there is still resistance on the child's part, the teacher should drop the issue and go on to another child. Later, when the group breaks up, the teacher should talk to

the child individually and attempt to set the goal then.

As each child presents his goal in the meeting, the teacher records it on chart paper. When completed, the chart is posted in the classroom to serve as a visual reminder to the children during the week.

Children may be allowed to carry a goal from one week to the next. However, this should occur only if the child demonstrated that the goal was not fully achieved. Some children want to carry a goal over even though they have achieved it. Under these conditions the teacher encourages the child to select a new goal, explaining that the old one has already been accomplished.

The goals selected should always represent a challenge for the child. If the goal is too easy the child will not be truly involved in the program. If the goal is too hard it will be impossible for the child to achieve and frustration will occur. Figure 1 presents examples of goals set by children in an intermediate class for the emotionally disturbed.

FIGURE 1
SAMPLE GOALS

Linda: I will not talk to my neighbor during study times.

Rusty: I will not "bug" anyone when they have told me to stop doing so.

Carol: I won't cuss at anyone—including the teacher.

David: I will work in my Open Highways book more.

Tom: I won't shout so much.

Sara: I won't lose my temper when dumb things come up.

The Pow-Wow: Rationale and Objectives

■ Classroom teachers often have problems in managing behaviors on an individual basis due to the number of children in the class. The size of the class may limit the amount of time a teacher can spend with individual pupils. It has been stated that a teacher with problem children spends more time with these children anyway, so time spent in individual management programs is time well spent. This is true of course, but if teachers could use groups to accomplish behavior change, it might be possible to spend a little less individual time. The pow-wow technique may aid teachers in this area. Most teachers who have tried it

report noticeable results in relatively short periods of time.

The pow-wow is not new nor is it inflexible. In fact, one of its advantages is that it can be modified fairly easily to fit a variety of situations. With only minor changes it can be used effectively with all school age children and with groups of varying size. Although it was designed for use with relatively small groups of 8 to 12 children, with some modification it could be incorporated into groups as large as 30.

Based on a theory developed by Glasser in his book *Schools Without Failure* (1969), the pow-wow is a classroom method that

aids students in the development of personal responsibility for individual behavior. The pow-wow achieves this objective through a group process which:

● Requires each student to determine his own behavior goal.
● Aids each student in examining which specific events bring about certain behaviors.
● Provides a stimulus to students to become more observant of the positive behaviors of others.
● Provides an experiential setting for improvement of a student's self image.

2. OBJECTIVES

SETTING UP THE POW-WOW

1. Seat the children in a circle.
2. Explain that this is a pow-wow and that they will each make a behavioral goal which they should attain by the next pow-wow.
3a. At the first pow-wow, begin with the child on your left and state something like the following to each child in turn: "If we had done this before you would now tell us whether or not you achieved your goal, and then we would ask the others if they thought you did. Since this is the first time we are doing this, you should make a goal for next time. Explain to the children what a goal is, giving examples if necessary. Goals must be stated in observable behavioral terms and must be observable in the classroom. At the first pow-wow, proceed to step 8 after the child has stated his goal.
3b. At the second and all following pow-wows, have the child on your left restate his goal. Read it for him if he does not remember it.
4. Ask the child if he achieved the goal. The child may only answer "yes" or "no" and may offer no excuses if the answer is "no."
5. Go around the circle asking the other children in turn if they feel the goal was achieved. If the answer is "no," elicit a specific instance. If none can be given then it is assumed that the child has achieved his goal.
6. After all the other children have been asked, return to the first child and ask him again whether or not he achieved his goal.
7. Ask the child to make a new goal.
8. Go around the circle asking the other children if they think the new goal is a good one. If someone says "no," elicit the reason.
9. Ask the child if he wants to keep the goal as stated or if he wants to change in light of the other children's comments. If the child wants to change, he may.
10. Write the goal on a large piece of paper next to the child's name.
11. Go around the circle asking for suggestions on helping the child achieve the goal.
12. Go around the circle and have each child make one positive comment about the child who just finished making a goal.
13. Go to the next child and proceed with steps 3 through 12.
14. After the last child has finished, post the goals on the bulletin board or some other place where they can be seen by the class.

SOME SUGGESTIONS

Keep the pow-wow comfortable and flexible, but keep the following suggestions in mind.

Keep all students involved with the pow-wow. If a student leaves, the pow-wow stops and everyone waits until he returns. If someone cannot think of a goal, everyone waits until a goal is decided on. After a period of time, the teacher may ask for suggestions from the other children.

Discourage extraneous talking. Only one person at a time is allowed to speak. No side comments or arguments are permitted. Not accepting excuses and requiring specific examples tends to minimize this.

Keep groups heterogeneous. All the problem children should not be placed in one group. Divide up the class so that the students with problems are together with those who have few or no problems. This will give the problem students positive models while providing the nonproblem students with a better understanding of the problems of others.

When a group is formed, it should stay together in the pow-wow for a period of time. It is not a good idea to change groups often since students in one group may not know the goals of those in another group.

Encourage students to set goals that consist of observable behaviors that occur in the class in which the pow-wow is held. As long as the behaviors can be observed by those in the group, behavioral goals can include almost anything. If the group has recess together, for example, then recess behavior can be used. In departmentalized classes, only behaviors that occur in that class are appropriate.

Do not expect instant results. Some children will have a harder time than others with the pow-wow. They will need more time to learn what is expected. Do not give up. It may take five or six sessions before you begin to see results.

Feel free to modify the procedures. Although the pow-wow is a ritual and should be conducted in the same way each time, it is sometimes necessary to modify the process. However, remember the previous suggestion and give modifications a chance before changing again. Reports from teachers who have instituted the pow-wow in their classes indicate that nearly all of them have achieved positive results.

The pow-wow must be done on a regular basis. A pow-wow done once and then not repeated for a few weeks will achieve few, if any, results. The frequency of occurrence is up to the teacher. Many teachers hold the pow-wow on a daily basis, but if this is not possible, it should be held at least once a week.

The teacher should be fully committed to the pow-wow. Unless there is a fire drill, pow-wows should be held as scheduled. If it is at all possible, neither assemblies nor testing should displace the pow-wow. If the students know that the pow-wow is important, then they will treat it as such. If it is treated as something done only as a time filler, the students will pick this up and progress will be slow, if it happens at all.

The teacher should participate in every pow-wow. Although there is much repetition and children can eventually proceed unaided, the teacher must be there in order for the children to have a model to copy. If only nonacceptable models are available, the children may not be able to formulate acceptable goals. The teacher participates fully except that he does not make a goal. It has been found that when teachers make goals, students tend to spend too much time watching the teacher and too little time watching themselves and each other.

If you think the pow-wow method might work for you, try it. It may take a little time to organize and to plan for those students who are not in the pow-wow group, but it can be a useful technique to aid you in changing behaviors in your classroom.

Relationship Between Goal Setting, Pow-Wow, and Behavior Change

■ Cognitive control techniques such as goal setting and pow-wow are facilitators of behavior change. They identify problems for children, offer solutions, and indicate commitment to change. But by themselves they will not bring about behavioral change.

It is not sufficient to set goals and suggest alternatives to existing behavior. To increase the probability that behavior will change, we need to teach the child how to perform the new behavior that has been

FIGURE 2
STUDENT POINT SHEET INCLUDING
THE WEEKLY GOAL

Behavior and point value

Task	Start promptly (3)	Be neat (3)	Follow directions (3)	Complete work (3)	Attend to task (3)	Sit at desk (3)	Raise hand (2)	Work quietly (5)	Goal:	Bonus points	Other points

Keep all students involved in the pow-wow.

identified in the pow-wow, and we need to provide the child with reinforcement for the new behavior when it occurs.

As an example, consider the case of a child who, in goal setting, decides that his goal for the week is to fight less. In pow-wow the child decides that he will count to 10 and walk away from situations that previously led to fighting. The teacher may point out models to the child of other children walking away from fights and make sure that the child's behavior is reinforced when he walks away from a fight.

These things are most important. Without the teaching procedures and the reinforcement as supports, cognitive control techniques will be relatively ineffective.

Cognitive control techniques are enhanced by a classroom which operates on a point or token system. The child's goal can be listed as one of the behaviors for which points or tokens may be earned. For each time period in which a child is given points or tokens, extra points or tokens are earned if he met his goal. An alternative is to give bonus points or tokens for achievement of the goal. Figure 2 presents an example of a point sheet with space provided for the goal.

In order for these meetings to achieve their purpose they must be orderly. As a result, ground rules must be set up to include such things as not interrupting, raising hands, and so forth. Rule setting is facili-

tated with a point or token system. A list of rules can be identified, with point or token values assigned for each behavior on the list. An example of such a list appears in Table 1.

It should be noted that points are not taken away or given for interactions around the content of the meetings. Points relate only to surface behavior that facilitates the orderliness of the meeting.

Hobbs (1966) indicated that disturbed children can and should be taught cognitive control. According to Hobbs:

The emotionally disturbed child has fewer degrees of freedom in behavior than the normal child, yet he is not without the ability to shape his own behavior by self-administered verbal instruction. He can signal to himself if he can learn what the useful signals are. The teacher-counselor works constantly to help a child learn the right signals.

Hobbs is saying that children can be taught to instruct themselves about appropriate behavior, and that children should be able to administer self instructions whenever they get into situations where problem behaviors occur. The management techniques of goal setting and the pow-wow can aid the teacher in developing successful group processes for behavior change.

REFERENCES
Glasser, W. *Schools Without Failure.* New York: Harper & Row, 1969.
Hobbs, N. Helping disturbed children: Psychological and ecological strategies. *American Psychologist,* 1966, *21,* 1105-1115.

TABLE 1
BEHAVIORS REINFORCED DURING POW-WOW
AND GOAL SETTING

Behavior	Point Value
Raising hand to speak	20
Not interrupting others	20
Not laughing at others	20
Not whispering while others are talking	20
Keeping to the subject	20

GOAL ANALYSIS FOR BEHAVIOR PROBLEM LEARNERS

Esther L. Hill

Esther L. Hill, EdD, is an associate professor of special education at Loyola
College, 4501 North Charles Street, Baltimore, Maryland 21210.

Prescribing attainable goals for behavior problem students has been a perpetual problem for many educators. The direct overt resistance these learners demonstrate handicaps their performance even in areas where they could succeed. Particularly challenging are children with long-term aggressive acting-out behavior who refuse even the initial involvement of opening a book. With such symptoms, any plan for change must give serious consideration to what R. F. Mager (1972) has called "the indefinable and intangible aspects of the learning process" (i.e., those related to motivational patterns and to attitudes). These nebulous facets of learning fall within the affective domain, where feelings, interpersonal relationships, and expectations of self and others are all major determinants in shaping responses to teachers and school.

Each resistant learner presents his own complex of variables. The majority have not only failed to meet the expectations of the school, but have been unable to cope successfully with social learning in the broader environment of the community. These students are a particular source of discomfort in any classroom because their constant disruptions, fighting, and devaluing of academic activity threaten the teacher's self-esteem as a classroom manager and interfere with learning for those who find this rebellion either contagious or annoying.

The present study was one aspect of a more comprehensive program established by a guidance clinic in a public school system to treat multiproblem boys and their families (Hill and Morrison 1969). Antisocial boys in elementary and junior high schools, grades three to nine, were identified by teachers and guidance counselors as those who had serious behavior problems of a long-standing nature in home, school, and community. Their school records presented lengthy histories of underachievement in relation to grade placement even though they had intelligence

"Goal Analysis – For Behavior Problem Learners," Esther L. Hill, *Academic Therapy*, Vol. 13, No. 3, January 1978. © 1978
Academic Therapy Publishers Incorporated.

within the normal range and no physical difficulties which would interfere with learning. Most outstanding were endless notations of poor relationships with classmates and teachers, aggressiveness, negativism, general depression, anxiety, and often hyperactivity. These boys had been overtly resistant to school learning since early grades, and little success had been gained from any intermittent intervention. Even individual remedial tutoring seldom achieved positive results, since any direct attack on learning deficits elicited active or passive resistance, and the yearly achievement scores of these boys showed constant plateaus or losses. It was obvious that a more comprehensive diagnosis of their learning styles was needed to obtain baseline data from which more realistic goals might be delineated.

A Case Study

The complexity of factors involved in the learning responses of these boys is more vivid when one such case is examined in detail (Hill and Morrison 1969). Gary, aged ten, had had difficulty in school adjustment and social relations from kindergarten days, but was capable of good work "when he felt like it." In first grade, he was considered a "bully" and "needed a very firm hand." His work was erratic, he couldn't concentrate, he was continually in difficulty with other children, and he frequently upset the class. Gary constantly tested limits, interrupted the teacher, and dominated class proceedings.

In third grade, his provocative behavior became worse. In spite of being punished at home, Gary's attitude about school, his stubbornness, unchanneled energy, and his limited attention span resulted in poor school achievement. By fourth grade, he was two years retarded in reading and spelling and more than a year behind in math, although his intelligence quotient (IQ) was

115 (WISC Verbal 106, Performance 122). An interview with Gary's teacher disclosed that she was unable to control him and frequently had to suspend him from school because of behavior problems. He couldn't be trusted, would run around the room, throw pencils into the air, threaten and bribe other children, and fight boys of any size or age. He was irresponsible, tried to boss others, lied, cheated, stole, and was always spoiling the fun of the group. He defied authority, would do anything to be recognized, and had poor work habits in all subjects. Gary's learning style was one of continual provocation and resistance, short attention span, and hyperactivity, all suggesting tremendous anxiety.

The social worker pointed out that, at three, Gary had had an operation on both eyes for strabismus, and he continued to have visual problems. He had been hospitalized for a glandular difficulty and had meningitis when he was five, had a tonsillectomy in which he had hemorrhaged and had to go back to the hospital when he was seven, and continued to have various allergies.

Gary's parents were very defensive about him. They felt he had no problems and that the school difficulties were caused by the external environment. He was an only child. His mother did not really see him as a separate object from herself; she mothered, indulged, and protected him. She was constantly defending herself against overwhelming anxiety and panic and kept repeating the theme, "What is going to happen?" She related to others in a suspicious, fearful, distrustful, and aggressively hostile manner, had little to do with her neighbors, and perceived only two kinds of people: those who were for her—mainly medical doctors—and those who were against her, such as school personnel. Gary's father had better reality perception than the mother but seemed detached and withdrawn. He spent time with Gary, let him help with tasks around the house, seemed rather patient with him, but used beatings and strappings as discipline.

Analysis of Learning Responses

Additional data from education evaluations and from pilot attempt to involve boys like Gary in tutoring indicated that a more precise analysis of the tasks required for school learning was crucial. It was clearly evident that these students had not yet satisfied even these following preconditions for school learning:

1. They had not learned to sit still or focus attention, for they were activity-oriented.
2. They had not mastered basic impulse control, and much of their energy was devoted to immediate gratification of basic needs and desires.
3. They could not deal with symbolic materials or ideas, for they responded positively only to concrete rewards in the form of food, money, or immediate attention.
4. They had not learned to trust adults to give consistently, either in concrete ways or in learning methods, and they refused to accept anything from them.

Early and continual clashes with authority figures both at home and in school made these boys particularly averse to accepting the teacher's values or recognizing the teacher as a desirable model for identification. In addition, most of these boys had few friends, poor relationships with peers, and basically felt themselves to be the "bad ones" both at home and in school. They had to strike out and run away from any frustrating situation, of which reading was one.

These fundamental relationship conflicts, poor self-concepts, and fear of failure resulted in rising anxiety in any interpersonal learning situation. Self-instruction programs, even on mechanical devices, were accepted only briefly by these students until the novelty of the machinery failed to intrigue them, as they lacked any internal motivation to progressively increase their skills. Even contingency reinforcement was of little value since many of them would not accept the freely available supplies of candy and food, and praise or affection was discredited. Their most prevalent way of handling anxiety was by constant activity which prevented sustained attention or concentration on any learning task.

Preconditions of Learning Goals

Since no program could be maintained when the students steadfastly refused to take part in it, early cognitive goals were set aside in favor of more practical ones of attendance. Knowledge of each boy's learning strengths and his interests was critical as the focus for early discussion and action. These frequently centered around cars, motors, mechanics, or sports. Of primary importance was an estimation of the boy's ability to relate to a teaching adult on a one-to-one basis. If his conflicts about himself and his inadequacies in school and relationships were too threatening to permit much interaction, goals had to reflect this and permit distancing, even in the limited learning space between tutor and student. Keeping discussions more impersonal for a time and using activity sessions rather than passive sittings all helped gain some acceptance of the program.

An individual psychoeducational approach was used in which a combination of learning and behavior needs was reflected in the primary objective: involve the boy in any learning experience that provided some pleasure and satisfaction for him. The highest priority was given to dealing with negative feelings about learning, impulsive outbursts, and interpersonal conflicts. Academic topics took second place for some time, until a practical need led to a newspaper or catalogue. Hence, early goals pertaining to the preconditions of learning first defined behaviors that focused on *personal interaction and acceptance of the tutor.* They included such hoped-for responses by the student as:

1. Coming to sessions and staying at least half of the time, in this case 30 minutes.
2. Taking off his coat and trying a game or craft materials, such as clay, car models, paints, or puppets.
3. Accepting candy or food or interaction with the adult, suggesting a positive response to the giving, supporting relationship between tutor and student.
4. Becoming involved in action-oriented sessions, such as taking walks or trips to local places of interest, science-nature hikes, or working with structural materials (construction of cage for gerbils, etc.).
5. Displaying less hyperactivity and fewer repeated motoric patterns, such as running about the room, banging on tables, stomping feet.
6. Accepting the required limits regarding striking out at people or equipment.
7. Using verbal release of feelings of anger and hostility, rather than destruction of his own or other students' belongings.
8. Talking about his conflicts in the school situation and expressing his feelings about learning or the whole school system.
9. Indicating better acceptance of himself as worthwhile, as capable of succeeding in some activities, and with fewer expressions of "I'm stupid!"

Since these boys were as reluctant to relate to symbolic material as they were to people, the second category of goals in the preconditions of learning stage gradually emerged as *appropriate responses or behaviors in learning.* These two separate goal categories were obviously not independent of each other in their development, but, at this second level, the observable changes in student responses included:

1. Listening while tutor read short selections to him.
2. Accepting short periods of looking at books and magazines (such as *Popular Science, Popular Mechanics, Life, Hot Rod, Sports Illustrated* and others in his particular areas of interest) and talking about the pictures.

3. Reading directions to play a game or make a model.
4. Evaluating ideas from magazines or newspapers in terms of his own experiences.
5. Relating a story or activity in sequence to be typed or taped for later use.
6. Losing a game without overreacting or leaving; strong verbal expressions of feelings were acceptable.
7. Expressing more curiosity and willingness to continue in learning experiences.
8. Accepting his mistakes without complete loss of confidence or feelings of worthlessness and rejection.
9. Willing to try new materials, new games, or crafts.

Data regarding these two categories of goals were kept in process notes of tutoring sessions and later summarized in a predetermined outline for the academic year or a selected span of sessions.

Achievement Goals

Although academic-type learning was tried intermittently, actual achievement in developmental skills in reading and math became secondary to gains made in the aforementioned preconditions of learning. Acceptance of books for informal reading, practice lessons for study-type skills, or practice in needed math areas was often undertaken in a compromise plan of alternate times for work and free-choice activity. With each boy, the reward schedule was different, depending on his ability to attend and perform. Work periods were increased as the relationship became more secure and successes in learning became more numerous and attainable. Although some boys began with actual flight from many of their sessions, or missed alternate ones for a time, they eventually were able to accept a closer relationship with the tutor through games, crafts, or sports activities. Other boys resisted involvement by constant talking, peripheral interaction in games, or indifference to all activities. As time passed, however, most boys actively accepted this therapeutically oriented educational model and their sustained attention to academic tasks gradually increased. At times, there were regressions to physically active sessions as boys responded to reality pressures or inner conflicts. Tutors had to be flexible and secure enough to accept ambivalence and angry rejection in interpersonal relationships as well as in school achievement. Yet, this third category of goals could begin to include *more academic-achievement tasks* after the earlier preconditions of learning had been mastered. These tasks included:

1. Reading from books and magazines related to special interests.
2. Working math problems related to experiences and money and, later, from worksheets and books.
3. Concentrating on school-related tasks for extended periods of time.
4. Accepting direct teaching of skills when needs were evident in reading or study.
5. Having confidence enough to admit errors and try again.

6. Reading a whole book and writing a book report.
7. Attempting more complex learning tasks, such as two- and three-step problem solving in math.
8. Moving from concrete materials to verbal and more abstract approaches in math and science problems.
9. Indicating increased willingness to search out information for himself and carry on some projects with little tutor assistance.

For most boys, these gains resulted in some increase in reading and math scores on achievement tests. However, standardized tests were not readily accepted, even when given individually as opportunities for identifying areas for additional help. In spite of modifications in subtest order, in timing, and in test length—to accommodate some anxiety about testing—the boy's behavior in testing, his feelings of adequacy, and his relationship with the examiner all influenced his scores.

Of 23 boys who had participated in this specialized tutoring, six refused testing at various times, so comparisons were feasible for only 17 boys. Because of the wide variation in the number of tutoring sessions (from 30 to 150) and time span (one to three years), it was more meaningful to look at individual scores and to use each boy as his own base line for any changes that might have occurred. For this reason, expectancy scores were calculated for each boy based on the differences between his grade scores on the *Metropolitan Achievement Test* (MAT) and his actual grade placement in school. Since all the boys were within the average or above-average range of intelligence, they were expected to achieve within their grade-level continuum. The discrepancy in the expectancy score upon initial testing, and in the expectancy score at final testing, was used as evidence of gain (if smaller at end-of-project testing) or loss (if larger at final testing than upon initial testing).

Evaluation

Although most boys made measurable gains on achievement tests following their tutoring sessions, it was important to question what these changes reflected since much of the tutoring time focused on maintaining a positive feeling about self, others, and

TABLE 1
Achievement Test Gains

Gross Change in Achievement Test Scores from Initial to Final Testing

	Composite Reading (N = 17)	Composite Math (N = 17)
Gain 1 year to 4.5 years	13	14
Gain 0 to .9 years	3	2
Loss 0 to .3 years	1	1

As a group, 64 percent were at or above expectancy upon initial testing, while 42 percent were included in this range at final testing in reading.

learning. These changes are shown in Table 1. When considered as a group, the expectancy scores indicated that the boys had not closed the large gaps that had existed between present performance and grade placement, even though some made gains of as much as 4.5 years. These test results suggested increased knowledge or skill in dealing with academic subjects, but was there any way to show an improvement in the desire to learn, in the ability to concentrate, or in self-esteem that led to an increased effort to achieve and make better use of skills?

E. Zigler's (1969) studies emphasized that a child's history of deprivation and failure, his desire for attention and affection from adults, his views of himself, and his expectancy of success are all as important as determinants of how he functions in intellectual activities as his cognitive skills. In the tutored samples, case study data of more positive interactions both at home and school suggested improved relationships and self-concepts. An attempt to evaluate more completely what goals might be realistic for multiproblem boys led to a more thorough study of changes in the "preconditions of learning." From each file of process notes on tutoring sessions, a yearly summary had been compiled by the tutor on 15 points related to behavior, affect responses to tutoring, and reactions to the total project. These essay-type reports were rated by three independent judges who had no contact with the boys or the project.

The ratings were made on a five-point scale developed to evaluate responsiveness and involvement in tutoring:

1. Marked positive response
2. Usually positive response
3. Generally passive and uninvolved
4. Usually negative response
5. Marked negative response

In a manual prepared for the judges, each point was described in behavioral terms in regard to relationship and interaction, attendance, and verbal responsiveness of the boy. The average of the judges' rating became the involvement score for each boy. Reliability of the judges was .89, .77, and .71, even though the summaries were written by many different tutors in varied styles and mixed writing quality.

Of the 23 boys involved in the educational program, 60 percent (14) were rated as positively involved in tutoring, 22 percent (5) were judged as rather passive in their learning, and 15 percent (4) were judged as responding negatively to tutoring. From the records, it was evident that the boys who were most involved attended more sessions and could be expected to make gains in relationships, behavior, and achievement. These positively involved boys became more verbal and outgoing with their tutors in earlier months and eventually could discuss fairly reasonably their feelings about school work and school personnel. At times, they could even admit their own responsibility for achieving success or for getting into trouble. Active verbal interchange on a generally reasonable level seemed related to those cases where boys were able to continue in positive trusting relationships with tutors in spite of crises and regressions.

Summary

Although these measures of affective and relationship responses were global and unrefined, they demonstrated that changes were occurring in areas most essential to school adjustment. The preconditions of learning, categorized in this study as interpersonal relationships and overt response to learning activities, become crucial elements of any goals that define changes in learning responses of antisocial children. Evaluation related primarily to school achievement as measured on standardized tests denies the deeply entrenched negative learning style that often requires extensive modification before measurable gains in achievement scores can be expected. Goal priorities for acting-out, resistant learners are well stated by E. Simpson (1971):

> The inhibition of destructive antisocial tendencies begins with a socialization process far more fundamental than the acquisition of cognitive skills or a body of knowledge. It begins with interactions to build health, lessen vulnerability to stress and provide ability to cope with normal life stresses.

The varied levels of goal performance required for resistant learners reinforce the imperative demand for early treatment of significant antisocial behavior, when not only negative interactions are more amenable to change, but there are fewer years of failure to counteract. The serious educational problems of these children are comprehensive in scope, involving networks of factors in physical, social, emotional, and intellectual domains. Because of this, goals should not be primarily in areas of school achievement but, first of all, in terms of more satisfying relationships and increased attention and acceptance of active learning in student interest areas.

References

Hill, E., and Morrison, M. 1969. Juvenile delinquency field demonstration and training project: Newton-Baker. Project of the Judge Baker Guidance Center, Volume 1. *Evaluation Report.* Boston (supported by Grant number 2-R-11-MH11-2 from the National Institute of Mental Health): pp. 99-158.

Mager, R. F. 1972. *Goal analysis.* Belmont, California: Fearon Publishers.

Simpson, E. 1971. Other ways of knowing—educational goals. *Teachers College Record* 72:559-565.

Zigler, E. 1969. Developmental versus difference theories of mental retardation and the problem of motivation. *American Journal of Mental Deficiency* 73:536-555.

Session II

Consequences For Instruction: The State of the Art of Individualizing

Richard E. Snow

Richard E. Snow is Professor of Education and Psychology, Stanford University. Ph. D. (Psychology), Purdue University, 1963. Author of (with L. J. Cronbach) *Aptitudes and Instructional Methods: A Handbook for Research and Interactions;* New York: Irvington, in press.

Adaptation of instruction to the individual learner has long been a slogan for educators. One can trace the idea back at least as far as Quintillian (c. 35-95 A.D.) in Ancient Rome; he observed that learners clearly differ in their characteristics so teachers should take account of these differences in their teaching methods. Binet's test was originally an attempt to identify students who needed different types of instructional treatment. Unfortunately, as the test was developed thereafter, classification on this basis never has been very adaptive. Schools have sought to individualize instruction on the basis of general ability measures only by streaming. (I use the English term instead of "tracking" because the metaphor is better and is consistent with the term "mainstreaming.") Some students are allowed to try the rapids to open water, some are diverted into calmer and duller canals, and some are left to splash around in the shallow backwaters. Within each of these streams and pools, some teachers try, however intuitively, to adapt their methods to individual differences; some students learn to swim under these conditions, and some do not. Such adaptations (or maladaptations) are harmful at worst, misguided at least, and unsystematic at best because no one yet knows the psychological principles that govern the matching of learner and instructional environment.

Any systematic adaptation of instruction to individual differences rests on an hypothesis that one or more student attributes predict response to instruction differently under different instructional conditions. Attributes that offer such prediction are called "aptitudes," and differential prediction under different instructional treatments exemplifies aptitude-treatment-interaction, ATI for short. An ATI hypothesis is implicit in the practice of streaming on the basis of prior achievement or IQ: On some general criterion, high scorers are expected to do better in the rapids and low scorers, in the pools. Similar hypotheses underlie the various inventions of special education, the development of programed instruction, and the more recent approaches to individualization. In short, whenever a teacher aims two students at the same general goal and tries to help them in different ways en route, (s)he is acting out an ATI hypothesis. Yet, despite its central role in evaluating attempts at individualization and analyzing the nature of individual differences in learning, concentrated research on ATI is only about 10 years old. ATI also has not been applied to the evaluation of special vs. regular educational treatment for exceptional children, which is really a special and massive form of individualization.

In this review of the state of the art of individualizing from the ATI perspective, the particular frame of reference is the Conference theme: the problems and possibilities associated with the mainstreaming of children previously classed in special education. A sketch of some recent history of individualized instruction shows what ATI looks like in this context and how ATI may be used in the development and evaluation of improved individualizations. This groundwork should help to identify the ATI concepts and research methods that bear on the central concerns of this Conference. A mixture of real and hypothetical examples are needed to elaborate these points. A list of other findings from previous work may suggest further considerations in the design of instruction for tomorrow's mainstream schools. Some implications for the teacher and teacher educator, and for the view of education that ATI suggests are also noted. Most of my remarks and cited references come from a recent review of the whole field of ATI by Cronbach and Snow (in press).

Keep in mind that ATI research is rather new and underdeveloped. It is an area in which methodology is still often inadequate, hypotheses are still exploratory, and there are as yet no solid generalizations or real theories. Even if there were, however, I am here extrapolating to a population of students and a school situation not yet studied by an ATI approach. Clearly, much of what we can say today must be quite tentative. At best, hypotheses worth examination can be shaped as our work proceeds. Perhaps the most important immediate application of the ATI approach here is not to propose solutions to the problem of individualizing instruction but to provide a methodology for evaluating individualized instruction in this new context.

ATI and Individualization— Past and Present

In traditional and conventional teaching situations, typically, the relation between the measured mental ability or prior achievement of learners before instruction and achievement outcome after instruction is positive and strong. There is no stronger generalization in all of educational psychology. The student who is low initially achieves less than the student who is higher initially. This finding is best displayed as a regression line, as in Figure 1, for some hypothetical children in one school year. The line shows the positive relation between aptitude scores plotted on the abscissa and later achievement scores plotted on the ordinate. It is labeled "RI" for the regular or recitation instructional treatment that has been the routine fare in most conventional classrooms. As learning accumulates over school years, the low student falls further and further behind the high one. The traditional response of schools to this situation has been some form of homogeneous ability grouping or streaming. Added to Figure 1 is one such plan; three streams have been arbitrarily defined by cutting the ability continuum at convenient points. The lowest or most unusual children probably have been removed already from this picture into special education classes. Instruction then proceeds in more or less the same form in each stream in the earlier years of schooling, although each stream moves at a different pace. In later school years, each stream leads to different occupational and higher educational preparation, again at its own pace. So the lower streams go slower and, therefore, not so far.

This adaptation is minimal, if it can be called adaptation at all. In these streams, teachers may try to adapt further by choosing text material which is less abstract, with larger print size or more pictures, but the effect is usually to bring instruction down to the student rather than to find new routes to higher achievement for her/him. Remedial and tutorial work also usually appear to be just more of the same at a slower pace. What data there are seem to indicate that streaming of this sort accentuates the regression line: The fast go faster and the slow go slower than they other-

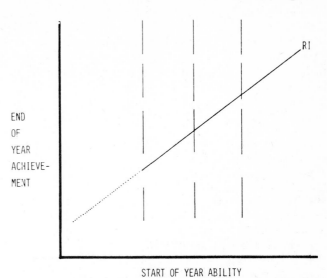

Figure 1. Regression of achievement on ability under regular instruction (RI) showing conventional ability grouping plan (vertical divisions).

wise would in homogeneous groups. Even if this conclusion were solidly supported by many studies (which it is not), it would be impossible to improve individualization by using it because it tells us that it is best for fast learners to keep them together in homogeneous groups, whereas for slow learners it is best to mix them with faster learners. Someone would always have to be sacrificed. However, neither this possibility nor the hypothesis that streaming helps everyone in some way has been put to sufficient test. This neglect is strange, given the long and wide use of streaming and its ultimate social consequences. Through it, the educational system supports a more general social stratification: "Them as has, gets." I can assure you that this situation is not unique to the United States; it is more or less the same in many other countries. The situation is aggravated here, however, because streaming begins rather early, at least in subjects like reading, and disproportionate numbers of ethnic minority children are often found in the lowest streams.

Now consider the implications of mainstreaming—of special education children re-entering the picture. If everything else remains more or less in place, they enter the lowest stream. I would expect this placement to be only slightly beneficial to them and, perhaps, slightly detrimental to those children already in the streams. The general consequences remain unchanged for everyone. Without belaboring this point let me just say that I believe strongly that traditional streaming plans should be abolished; they offer no real adaptation to individual differences at all. This statement, of course, should not be taken to rule out elective streaming in pursuit of specialized personal talents in later years, once everyone has developed the societal, common talents to her/his fullest. But we are concerned here with how schools can form talent development programs that will meet each child where (s)he is and bring her/him to

2. OBJECTIVES

prescribed levels on the common goals. I note that many schools are now postponing formal streaming for the first three elementary years and some even have ungraded plans in this age range; but if you visit such schools you still see implicit ability grouping without much adaptation of instruction.

Next, consider programed instruction, or PI, which offered a greater hope for improvement through individualization than the streaming of regular instruction. When it came on the scene around 1960, it was expected to be superior to regular instruction for all students and to do away with individual differences in learning as well. That is, it was hoped that PI would give both a higher average on outcome measures and a lower regression slope on ability measures, as shown in Figure 2. But this expectation was not realized. Although many inconsistencies appeared in the research on this question over the last 15 years, the most likely expectation seems to be that when PI has an effect on achievement different from that of RI, it is beneficial to students low on prior ability or achievement and, if anything, detrimental to high-ability students. The effect appears mainly when PI is of the linear, small-step form with overt, constructed responses. This form may be too restrictive for high-ability students, since they seem to do less well in this stream than in regular instruction. A number of studies have shown results like that depicted in Figure 2 (Cowan, 1967; McNeil, 1962; Porter, Note 3; Stukat, 1965; Wittrock, 1963).

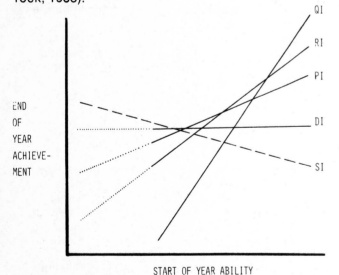

Figure 2. Regressions of achievement on ability under five methods of instruction.

Key: QI = Inquiry Instruction.
    RI = Regular Instruction.
    PI = Programed Instruction.
    DI = Drill Instruction.
    SI = Special Instruction.

The relation of achievement to ability is different under the two instructional treatments. As it stands, this difference is not large enough in the populations studied to be of practical importance.

If it were large, one could expect to improve overall achievement by dividing learners on ability at the crossover point, giving PI to low-ability students and RI to high-ability students. This finding would imply a rather large main effect favoring PI, however, if we could extrapolate these regression lines into the range of special education children. More extensive research is needed to test this hypothesis as mainstreaming proceeds. The main point here is that research and evaluation studies on this and similar questions will need to examine regression slopes, not just averages, since minor changes in slope can shift the crossover point significantly up or down the ability continuum.

I know of no study that has examined this hypothesis in detail using EMR or other learning disabled children. One miniature study of adolescent retardates (Cartwright, 1971) is relevant, however, since it introduces some further complications. It contrasted a program giving an orderly progressive sequence on the arithmetic of fractions with a more haphazard programed sequence, which was probably more akin to the kind one might observe in regular classrooms. There were faint indications that prior verbal achievement and IQ scores might relate more strongly to immediate learning and to retention in the haphazard program. Thus, orderly linear PI would be best for low-ability students in this group. But a transfer measure gave the opposite indication; transfer was better on average after the haphazard program, and regression slopes were steeper in the orderly program. Specific arithmetic pretests also gave such results on immediate as well as transfer criteria. This study can hardly sustain any conclusion. But it introduces the idea that general vs. special aptitude variables and learning vs. transfer outcomes may give contradictory messages. Clearly, then, both kinds of variables should be included in evaluation studies.

Further, this and many other studies of PI and, more recently, of CAI (Computer Assisted Instruction) seem based on an assumption that the way to individualize instruction for low-achieving or low-ability students is to concentrate on smooth, orderly, small-step drill in content skills. This idea is reasonable enough. But if a smooth progression of fractions, for example, gains its achievement advantage by promoting rote learning, the gain comes at the expense of transfer, as Cartwright (1971) found. This result is reminiscent of several older studies contrasting rote and meaningful instruction in primary arithmetic, of which the Brownell and Moser study (1949) is the most important. They demonstrated that children taught by rote in Grades 1 and 2 proved unable to benefit from explanations in Grade 3. Despite apparently adequate learning under rote conditions, they were unable to transfer to meaningful conditions to continue their advance; in effect, they had developed an inaptitude for meaningful instruction. Some other studies have also shown that high-IQ children benefit from meaningful instruction while low-IQ children do better on direct tests with rote drill (Orton, McKay, & Rainey, 1964; Thiele, 1938). This finding is, in turn, consistent with some of Jensen's theorizing. Again, of course, the findings are not altogether consistent, but we can add a regression line, DI, for drill instruction, to Figure 2 to represent the most likely conclusion.

Here, then, is a basic problem in need of careful attention in the mainstreaming movement. Earlier, we saw that simply reducing the pace of instruction, while it might relieve some feelings of frustration and failure, does not improve immediate learning for students low in prior ability or achievement. Now we see that removing the need for thinking from the instruction may improve immediate learning for these low students but may not develop the aptitudes that will eventually be needed to apply this learning in more complex situations or to absorb new learning in these situations. If some students do not have the basic skills to handle meaningful instruction, it is reasonable that a school will try to advance these skills without relying on comprehension. But limiting individualization to these steps still dooms such students to menial lives.

To complete Figure 2 and to introduce some other ideas, two other regression lines have been added, one empirical and one hypothetical. The line labeled QI stands for inquiry methods and other novel or innovative curricula, such as new math or science. Most of the more substantial studies contrasting these kinds of treatments with RI show them to yield the steepest regression slopes of all. That is, IQ is essential for QI, and the less able student is served very poorly here. (This is not to say that some innovative curricula might not be especially designed to benefit lower ability students; some have been.) The line labeled SI stands for specialized instruction; it represents the hypotheses of most interest for us.

One can imagine treatments that identify special weaknesses in cognitive skills among low-achieving students and then either build these skills directly with specially designed training conditions or circumvent them with conditions designed to make them unnecessary, for some learning situation. These instructional treatments are the kind I envision for the future of special education, that is, individualized education, in mainstream schools. But it is difficult to discuss these ideas in abstract form. The content of such treatments may be clearer when we look at some examples of ATI findings in the following section. Let it suffice to note here that these treatments can be expected to show zero or even negative regression slopes for achievement on general ability. They are special treatments fitted to the particular weaknesses of low-ability students, so they should be useless, even dysfunctional, for more able students. It is odd to think of negative relations among cognitive variables, but they are occurring in ATI research and may well be more frequent in mainstreaming schools.

Figure 2 now shows the full array possible of ATI results, ranging from treatments that are particularly good for the lowest students to those that are valuable only for the highest students. Certainly we could add other kinds of instructional treatments to the picture, but they would give regression slopes similar to those already shown. Some of these other treatments are themselves valiant attempts at individualization. IPI, IGE, and PLAN, for example, are each descendants of PI and are successful programs to some extent in their own right. Although they have not yet been extensively evaluated using ATI methods, the data so far reported suggest that their regression slopes would not differ substantially from those shown for PI. They need to be evaluated by ATI to determine how best to develop later instruction (e.g., RI and QI).

Also not shown are treatments based on behavior modification approaches. They too assume ATI, as, for example, when different reinforcers are chosen for different children. But they also have not yet been evaluated from an individual differences point of view, except in a few limited studies.

In most discussions of ATI, it is common at this juncture to emphasize that the points where regression lines intersect define empirically the places at which the general ability continuum can be sliced. Students within each slice can then be assigned to the instructional treatment with the highest elevation in that region, and overall achievement is thereby maximized. In effect, the collection of ATIs define an empirical grouping plan with treatments that are genuine alternatives to the traditional, arbitrarily defined streams with their hollow variations in pace. Since the ATI findings likely would vary from subject to subject, so would the group membership. And, with the classification scheme based on multiple aptitudes, including personality and style variables instead of general ability alone, this form of classification would not carry the negative stigma of streaming. Thus, no one would be locked into a "slow" or special group and labeled as such. Please note that for simplicity I have used only a general ability or prior achievement construct as the aptitude variable in this discussion. Although it is regarded as the most important aptitude, it is not the only one. Similar pictures could be drawn using special ability, personality, and cognitive-style aptitudes as well, except that there is less research on these variables. I also differentiate students as "high" or "low" for simplicity although I recognize that these terms are rather unfortunate. Keep in mind that we are concerned here with students who "score low" on mental measures, for whatever reasons, not with absolute values.

This kind of individualization based on ATI is sufficient in some instructional settings—at the college level or in military training, for example—when the data supporting it are strong enough. But this use of ATI is far into the future. The col-

2. OBJECTIVES

lection of relations depicted in Figure 2 is itself only a crude generalization. Many individual studies are not at all this consistent; results vary markedly with local conditions, kinds of students, subject matter, and other such factors. Besides, although this form of classification system is a vast improvement over most previous attempts at individualization, it is insufficient for mainstream public schools because it does not explicitly provide for aptitude development or for the particular problems of the re-entering exceptional child. Here is where, I hope, the hypothetical treatments labeled SI come in.

ATI and Individualization—The Future

A collection of instructional treatments that gives the regression pattern shown in Figure 2 can be viewed as a set of alternative treatments, as I have shown with rather global treatments as examples. But it can also represent a gradient or sequence of treatments. This point is better seen in examples using more specific, special treatments. Four such examples follow:

1. In a study of phonics skill training as part of reading instruction, Sullivan, Okada, and Niedermeyer (1971) trained some children on single letter (SL) grapheme-phoneme correspondences and others with letter combinations (LC). Using a pronunciation test as pretest and a parallel form as posttest, a striking ATI was found: steep regression slope for LC, shallow slope for SL. The implication of this finding is to give SL to low-pretest students and LC to high-pretest students. But skill in SL must lead to skill in LC, since ultimately the child must handle letter combinations. Thus, low-pretest students should start with SL, but their aptitude development should be monitored until the crossover point is reached where a switch to LC will lead to higher continued skill development.

2. An isolated finding by Tanaka (Note 8) suggests a parallel between the training gradient of Sullivan et al. (1971) in phonics skills and some of the classification skills needed in simple concept learning. Tanaka found that verbal concept instruction gave a steep regression slope with ability, but a more concrete manipulative treatment showed a shallower slope. Because all children need to be brought to the verbal level, the implication is, again, that the less able child should start with manipulative instruction and aptitude development should be monitored to find the best switching point to the more verbal abstract treatment.

3. In another context, Salomon (1974) used film demonstrations of perceptual-cognitive skills in improving the performance of students low in the skill to begin with. A zoom technique served as a model for discriminating stimuli in complex visual arrays and a filmed spatial transformation demonstrated solutions to spatial visualization tasks. In each case, the film model helped promote adequate performance in less skilled students but hindered the performance of those who were more highly skilled initially. These treatments may or may not represent actual skill training; they may simply prompt learners to apply skills they already possess but do not recognize as relevant, removing a "production deficiency" in Flavell's term (Flavell, Beach, & Chinsky, 1966, p. 284). Other studies also have shown the superiority of attention-directing demonstrations to verbal descriptions for younger vs. older learners (Corsini, 1969). Again, a gradient of training treatments with periodic aptitude monitoring is suggested.

4. Finally, Keislar and Stern (1970) showed that in concept attainment tasks, a single-hypothesis strategy was best for low-IQ children and a multiple-hypothesis strategy was best for higher IQ children. Here again a gradient idea may be involved; the less able learner may be brought eventually to use multiple-hypothesis strategies effectively if single-hypothesis training and aptitude monitoring are appropriately arranged.

In each case, then, two alternative treatments form a progression. The learner who can manage it starts with the second treatment; the learner who cannot is given the first treatment, and this one is designed in part to promote readiness for the second. But aptitude is measured periodically along the way. The ATI pattern provides a decision rule for when to shift each learner to the later treatment. One chief goal of the school becomes the locating of each child in the kind of instructional treatment (s)he needs at first and deciding when (s)he can best accommodate the next most demanding treatment. A major task for educational research, then, is to design these sequences of aptitude development. Some of the individualized systems now being developed try to design such sequences.

But this kind of development, too, is insufficient. Even assuming that successful aptitude development sequences can be designed, they require considerable time and effort of the learner. Is the school to withhold all other instruction while certain requisite skills are developed? Shall the teaching of social studies be delayed until Sullivan's sequence and more advanced reading instruction have done their work, or of science until Keislar and Stern's and Salomon's treatments have been fully developed, or of mathematics until Tanaka's lead has been fully played out? Clearly not. The school must circumvent the learner's weaknesses while removing them. This circumvention, or compensation as I call it, requires that the school find and use some strengths in each learner, while it is diagnosing weaknesses, to use in getting around the weaknesses. Some examples of this kind of compensation follow:

5. Both Cromer (1970) and Budoff and Quinlan (1964) have reported data to suggest that poor readers can equal good readers in comprehension when they receive information via ear rather than the printed page. This example of compensation is simple and obvious but good. Audiotape serves

to circumvent the poor reader's weakness, just as it does for the blind. The poor reader cannot forever be taught by audiotape but (s)he need not be held back in other learning while reading ability is being developed.

6. Some studies also contrast verbal instruction with one or another kind of substitute. We find among the mixed results some evidence that using simplified symbolic systems in place of verbiage helps low-ability students. Visual-figural material, on the other hand, can be detrimental to these students even as it is being particularly helpful to more able students (e.g., Fredrick, Blount, & Johnson, 1968; Gagné & Gropper, 1965). A distinction probably can be made here, though, between ideographic materials that provide diagrams or schema for abstract ideas, and pictographic materials that communicate concrete information. There is some evidence that concrete pictures are more effective than words in simple learning, particularly for low-ability students (Rohwer, Note 4). Some related work has found high-imagery children to be faster at learning names, but slower at seeing them as names for abstract concepts, than low-imagery children (Kuhlman, Note 2; Stewart, Note 7). Here, then, is an instance in which an individual difference variable is both a learning ability and a learning disability, depending on the nature of the task.

7. There is evidence that experience with a medium of communication helps the learner to profit from later instruction via that medium. Some studies have demonstrated this finding for filmed instruction, for example Vandermeer (Note 9). There is also evidence that television builds some cognitive skills (Salomon, Note 5). Thus, an examination of the special learning history and daily habits and preferences of each child may give clues to the strengths to build upon.

8. Finally, the work of Dunham and Bunderson (1969) and their colleagues has shown the role of rules taught to the learner to help organize information, and of memory supports to help retain previous instances, in concept attainment tasks. With neither device, memory ability seems required for learning. With either device included in the treatment, memory ability is no longer relevant, but reasoning ability then controls the degree of achievement. The implication is that instruction can be arranged to avoid whichever ability is weakest.

Thus, we see that effective individualization must accomplish two objectives: build particular aptitudes and, at the same time, avoid particular inaptitudes. Both require the identification of some other particular strengths in each individual to build upon, so there are actually three instructional design functions at work: (a) *remediation* of weaknesses, (b) *compensation* of weaknesses, and (c) *capitalization* of strengths. A fairly pure example of remediation is the study by Sullivan et al. (1971) of SL and LC training. The clearest example of compensation is probably the Cromer (1971) use

of audiotape with poor readers. Capitalization is implicit in all the studies cited; a certain degree of auditory skill must be assumed for the Sullivan and Cromer treatments to work, for example. But it is easier to see the way capitalization operates by looking at the effects of instructional treatments on high-ability learners. Note, in Figure 2, the ladder-like progression for able learners. Each step up involves removing some structure or control from the treatment and allowing the learner to provide that structure for her/himself. The learner is progressively allowed to use abilities that (s)he possesses, and inquiry methods probably maximize this freedom, at least within the range of present classroom-teaching methods. Independent library research might be an out-of-class example. I would speculate that a capitalization process is or should be at work along with compensation as one moves up the steps on the left side of Figure 2 with low-ability learners. Here, each step up compensates by adding some structure or control to the treatment in order to avoid some inaptitude. Increasingly, the treatments do things for the learners that they cannot do for themselves. The treatments remove information-processing burdens as they capitalize on something each learner can do well. But substantial long-term improvement is probably only realized, as I suggested earlier, when remediation is also included in this development.

The last point of this section is made briefly. Many collections of instructional treatments seem to yield the regression pattern exemplified in Figure 2. One rarely finds a treatment that is highly effective for everyone, no matter what treatments or aptitude variables are studied. So there is always a kind of saddle point in the middle around which regression slopes seem to pivot. I have fallen into the habit of summarizing this observation in what I facetiously call the first law of conservation of instructional effectiveness: "No matter how you try to make instruction better for someone, you will make it worse for someone else." Consequently, we should expect to provide many varieties of specialized treatments. Individualization in the mainstream school will not be a set of simple grouping rules or hierarchically arranged content units. There will have to be alternative routes at many points in the hierarchy. The need for alternative routes, of course, will make things much more difficult for the teacher.

Other Kinds of ATI

Some other ATI findings may be of use in extending the previous points or giving other specific ideas for instructional design. Again, I warn that the data are not always consistently supportive of the statements that follow:

9. Some more examples from the reading area may be helpful since it is a central concern. A great deal of research has contrasted different methods of instruction in reading. It is a pity that

2. OBJECTIVES

much of this work has ignored individual differences in aptitude, especially since almost all reading studies collect readiness test data before starting instruction. Nonetheless, some findings exist and it is sometimes possible to probe for ATI even when the original research report ignored this aspect.

(a) The large Cooperative Research Program (Bond & Dykstra, 1967), for example, shows some reasonably consistent ATI. Students low on prior ability appear to be somewhat better served by a whole-word treatment (WWM—the baseline condition), and the various innovations and combinations that were tried by different projects seemed to benefit the higher ability students. This was the case regardless of the innovative instruction tried —ita (Initial Teaching Alphabet), phonics-linguistics, enriched language experience, and so forth. A similar finding came from a more recent study by Stalling and myself (Stallings, Note 6).

Figure 3 shows the regression lines for WWM and PLM, the latter a phonics-linguistics approach. The aptitude here is a special ability called "sequence memory," drawn in part from the ITPA subscales, but there is reason to believe that this result should be thought of in somewhat more general ability terms. Again, the slopes are extrapolated into the lower range to suggest the unorthodox hypothesis that whole-word methods may be better for very low students than phonic-linguistic methods. This is not to say that some form of phonics skills training would not be better than WWM for low students, but only that these particular classroom PLM programs were not. Recalling the finding of Sullivan et al. (1971) and assuming that PLM is more similar to their LC, I have added a hypothetical slope to show where their SL treatment might fall. It is possible that by adding that treatment WWM would cease to be a viable first treatment for low students. But it is also possible that whole-word instruction provides a better model or advance organizer for the overall reading task. Ausubel's work (Ausubel & Fitzgerald, 1962) with older students shows advance organizers to be primarily of help to low-ability learners.

(b) Some other studies of reading suggest that certain kinds of ability grading or grouping may help lows (Brady, 1970; Marita, 1966), and that lows can benefit from readiness training applied within a grouping plan.

(c) In the reading section, there is also some interesting evidence on teacher variations. One of the Coop Projects (Heilman, 1965) provided inservice training for some teachers and then compared their results with control teachers. The training included discussions of research results and much sharing of ideas and methods. Subsequently, the trained teachers apparently tried a lot of individualization and enrichment in their classes. The basic method for both groups was WWM. Training seemed to reduce the slope, especially

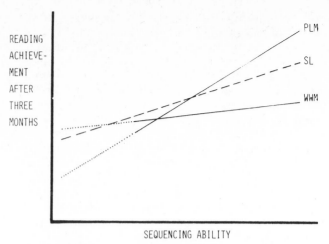

Figure 3. Regression of reading achievement on sequencing ability under two methods of instruction (data from Stallings) showing hypothetical position of Sullivan's single letter training condition.

Key: **PLM** = Phonics Method.
     WWM = Whole-Word Method.
     SL = Single Letter Training

for boys. In other words, trained teachers obtained more achievement, particularly from boys who had been low achievers, than did control teachers. Incidentally, there is also evidence that boys are better off with teaching-machines, another form of individualization, than with conventional human teachers, in primary reading (McNeil, 1964).

(d) There is also evidence that a common adaptation for low students, adding pictures (Samuels, 1967) or sentence-context embellishments (Hartley, Note 1) to reading materials, can actually be detrimental to low-IQ children. These embellishments apparently are distracting to the children, a finding that is consistent with the House-Zeaman (1967) theory that the critical difference between normal and retardate learning is attentional; lower IQ children take longer to identify the significant stimuli. Kulm, Lewis, Omara, and Cook (1974) also found that pictures can distract low-IQ students. Pictures tended to cause these learners to use incorrect methods in mathematical problem solving.

(e) An old study by Grimes and Allinsmith (1961) shows that personality variables also interact with teaching methods in reading. The more structured phonics approach seemed to serve compulsive and anxious children better than the whole-word approach, which seemed particularly problematic for them. A follow-up analysis of these data and some later work by Grimes seem to call this finding into question and to suggest, instead, an ability interaction that is inconsistent with the cited findings of Bond and Dykstra and of Stallings and her associates. Again, note the complexity of the problem we face in reaching practical decision rules. But the threads of evidence on both ability and personality deserve further attention. A three-way interaction of ability X personality X treatment may not be unlikely since it is suggested by evidence from studies in other content areas.

10. A study of ability grouping by Atkinson and O'Connor (1963) implied that grouping was disadvantageous for able, constructively motivated boys. In a second study, low ability but constructively motivated students benefited from grouping, and there was no benefit or loss for other students. This result suggests an ability X motivation X grouping interaction.

11. Another study of personality dealt with primary schooling in general, not just reading. This is the famous Heil, Powell, and Feifer (1960) work which has never been adequately pursued. Fifty teachers were classified on the basis of questionnaire data as turbulent-spontaneous, orderly, or fearful; they were further subdivided as superior (warmer-democratic) or inferior on the basis of observations. Their fourth to sixth graders were identified by questionnaire as conformers, strivers, opposers, and waverers. Looking, then, at achievement adjusted for IQ, the results were complex but appear to boil down to the following: Anxious students had a great advantage with superior orderly teachers; the opposers did well with inferior orderly teachers but very badly with superior spontaneous teachers; the latter teachers did well with the other types of children, particularly with conformers; and constructive strivers were least affected by teacher type. This study is provocative because it deals with observed types of teachers and children, suggesting that the matching or mismatching of certain types is important.

12. Other studies also suggest teacher-student matching. Several studies show permissive teachers to give steeper regression slopes of achievement on student ability. Dominant teachers seem better for low students. Cleare (1966) and Yamamoto (1963) both showed that achievement outcomes were higher when teachers and students were similar in ability profiles. And Hutchinson's (1963) data suggest an ability X teacher X treatment interaction. Teachers trained to elicit independent thinking in students differed from control teachers and also among themselves; some showed shallower regression slopes for student ability.

All this work reminds us that teachers differ in as many ways as students. Teachers are not interchangeable. Thus, teacher training and teaching assignments will likely have to be based on these kinds of matching ideas. Furthermore, alternative treatments will be needed in teacher training; and there are some studies that support this idea. Needless to say, much further research is needed in this important area.

Conclusion

It is impossible to summarize my discussion in a few neat sentences. I hope the ideas do not seem too disorderly but, frankly, that is the present state of the art of individualization and it will be some time before continuing research can sort out the useful ideas. The mainstreaming movement promises to be a unique and important test for the ATI approach. For the immediate future in that movement, ATI can make two concrete contributions: (a) an evaluation methodology, which is indispensible for examining individualization attempts; and (b) an emphasis on more intensive analysis of individual differences in learning processes than has been typical in the instructional research of the past. The latter is largely a laboratory research job, although it is helped greatly by the descriptive data and diagnostic insights of real school experience. Beyond this, whether teachers, instructional designers, and researchers come to find ATI suggestions of the sort reviewed here useful in real schools remains to be seen over a more extended period.

One general point is clear from the ATI work to date: Equal educational opportunity, for the wide range of children that must be served, will never be attained by superficial individualizations that merely assure each child a fair race from the start. However, more adaptive alternative treatments, which are much better for some children, are much worse for others. Equal education means carefully diversified teacher training and assignment. Judging from the papers in this report, we can expect a lot of argument in the near future about *who* should choose what treatment for which child —the teacher, judge, parent, community, or others. Note that most of these decisions will be made without benefit of the sort of evaluative ATI analyses proposed here. It will be unfortunate if variable pacing becomes the only form of individualization acceptable to all. Variable pacing is the safest but the least valuable adaptation from an ATI point of view. Truly effective individualization must concern itself with the details of individual differences and instructional processes all along the route, paced or not. I hope that mainstreaming will bring the special educator's talents for devising specialized treatments to bear on this general problem of individualization.

EFFECTIVE USE OF OBJECTIVES AND MONITORING

CORINNE E. CRUTCHER
ALAN M. HOFMEISTER

Corinne E. Crutcher is Assistant Professor of Special Education at the University of Wisconsin, Oshkosh.

Alan M. Hofmeister is Project Director, Exceptional Child Center, Utah State University, Logan.

■ Mastery of sequentially arranged objectives may serve as a continuous progress approach for student advancement through the curriculum. For the slower students it may be a kind of insurance policy against eventual failure in the upper grades. Early diagnosis and placement in a continuous monitoring system should prevent the child's problems from being neglected until they reach proportions too serious to allow for full remediation later in the school program.

The need for such diagnosis and monitoring has been evidenced by the estimated 5 to 20% of students in grade school classrooms who are failing (Rockford & Brennen, 1972). Sanders and Hansen (1971) have observed that students who are slow in the early grades are often hopelessly behind their peers in the fifth and sixth grades. The use of behavioral objectives in a monitoring system to insure continuous progress for slower students may be seen as a valuable failure prevention device.

DISCREPANCIES IN USE OF BEHAVIORAL OBJECTIVES
Over the past 10 years there has been a growing emphasis on the use of behavioral objectives as a means of curriculum organization. This emphasis is only a starting point. According to Conroy (1973), "The incredible irony seems to be that even though there is broad agreement about the benefits of using behavioral objectives in education, relatively little systematic use is being made of behavioral objectives" (p. 29).

Research suggests the contradictory effects of using behavioral objectives on student performance. Several studies (Parker et al., 1972; Semb, Hopkins, & Hursh, 1973; Miles, Kibler, & Pettigrew, 1967) suggest that use of behavioral objectives does increase student performance on tests of knowledge in specific subject areas. Other studies (Jenkins & Deno, 1971; Baker, 1969) have produced generally nonsignificant differences between students using behavioral objectives and those not using the objectives.

A major reason for the discrepancies in findings may be related to whether the emphasis is placed on the statement of objectives or on the use of the objectives to improve treatment processes. For adequate use of the objectives, emphasis must be placed on evaluation devices for determining task or objective mastery in the prescriptive program that follows the initial diagnosis.

SPECIAL EDUCATORS AS MONITORS
In many school systems the role of the special educator is changing from that of teacher to that of resource person to the regular class teacher. In this new role the use of a monitoring system will allow the special educator to stay close enough to the child to allow for effective decision making regarding the child's program.

In order to investigate the effects of the application of monitoring with slower math students in the early elementary grades, a continuous monitoring system was devised and field tested. The material necessary for implementation of this system included all elements of a set of behaviorally stated objectives for the math curriculum for first and second grades.

Materials used in the system included:
1. The two math text series for first and second grades. (These were the ones in use in the classrooms' studies.)
2. A master list of the objectives taught in each textbook series including page references for locating practice examples of each concept. Objectives were arranged in related clusters. Each cluster was designated by a letter, and each objective within the cluster was designated by a numeral.
3. A placement test, which included one or two examples from each cluster.
4. A set of criterion tests including five items for each objective in a cluster. These tests assessed mastery after instruction.
5. A class record form kept by the teacher. This form indicated which students had mastered the objectives and allowed the teacher to monitor each child's progress through the curriculum.

ORGANIZING THE MATERIAL FOR CLASSROOM USE
All consumable materials within the system (placement test, criterion mastery tests, and class record form) were printed so that they could be duplicated on "quickie dittos." Copies were then filed for easy retrieval.

The teacher began by giving the placement test to all students. The placement test results provided the teacher with a fairly accurate estimate of where to start teaching. For each item passed, the teacher filled in the appropriate spaces under the letter designated cluster on the record form. This indicated that the student had demonstrated competency in that group of objectives.

INTERPRETATION AND APPLICATION OF THE CONTINUOUS RECORD
After the placement test results had been entered on the record form, the teacher could see which students needed remedial help in specific objective clusters. Some students had common

"Effective Use of Objectives and Monitoring," Corinne E. Crutcher and Alan M. Hofmeister, *Teaching Exceptional Children* Vol. 7, No. 3, Spring 1975. © 1975 Council for Exceptional Children.

needs and were organized into small groups for instruction, practice, and criterion testing. Other students showed deficits unique to the individual and required separate instruction and assignments to fill the need.

The teacher used the page references on the master list to locate appropriate practice examples of the objective for the student. Specific teaching procedures were left to the teacher's own resources. When the teacher estimated, on the basis of informal assessment and daily work, that the students had mastered an objective, the number designated space for the objective in that cluster was filled in for that student.

When all objectives in the cluster had been completed, the teacher gave the test for the letter designated cluster. When a student failed to meet the 100% criterion for any objective within the cluster, immediate remediation was indicated before he was advanced to the next cluster. After the student mastered the missed objective, the teacher filled in the T (test) space for that cluster.

This system has been described by teachers as a time saving aid in the organization of materials and students for behaviorally based individualized instruction. More specifically, teachers have used the record to plan learning activities one objective at a time and to determine when to advance or remediate students. Other effective and appropriate uses have been to reinforce students by showing them how far they have progressed, to report student progress to parents and to next year's teacher, to give the teacher some ready suggestions for parents who ask what they can do to help their child, and to aid the teacher in requesting classroom materials to enhance the teaching of difficult objectives.

VALIDATION EFFORTS

After formative evaluation and revision of the classroom materials, a controlled study was undertaken. The experimental period was 10 weeks. The sample for the study was drawn from the lower 20% of 19 classes. The experimental group of 32 students from nine first and second grades took pretests, participated in the treatment, and took posttests. The control group of 37 students from 10 first and second grades received the pre- and posttests. A stratified random assignment procedure was used to place students in the control and experimental groups.

An analysis of covariance for both the Wide Range Achievement Test and a criterion test indicated significant differences in favor of the experimental group for the second grade ($p <$ .0005, achievement test; $p <$ .001, criterion test) and the total

group ($p <$ .001, achievement test; $p <$ .0005, criterion test). The second grade experimental group gained almost half a grade level over the control group in the 3 month treatment period. The gains made by the first grade pupils, while not as substantial as those made by second grade pupils, favored the experimental group.

The results of this study suggest that the monitoring system not only provides the teacher with a method for keeping track of student progress using the behavioral approach, but it further provides valuable information on the relationship between a curriculum sequence and the entering behaviors of the students. The validation data collected to date clearly indicate that substantive gains in achievement are associated with use of the monitoring system.

REFERENCE

Baker, E. L. Effects on student achievement of behavioral and non-behavioral objectives. *The Journal of Experimental Education*, 1969, *37* (4), 5-8.

Conroy, C. C. The synthesized behavioral objective. *Educational Technology*, 1973, *13* (10), 29-32.

Jenkins, J. R., & Deno, S. L. Influence of knowledge and type of objectives on subject matter learning. *Journal of Educational Psychology*, 1971, *62* (1), 67-70.

Miles, D. T., Kibler, R. J., & Pettigrew, L. E. The effects of study questions on college students' performance. *Psychology in the Schools*, 1967, *4* (1), 24-26.

Parker, R. K., Sperr, S. J., & Rieff, M. L. Multiple classification: A training approach. *Developmental Psychology*, 1972, *7*, 188-194.

Rochford, T., & Brennen, R. A preference criteria approach to teacher preparation. *Exceptional Children*, 1972, *38*, 635-639.

Sanders, R. M., & Hansen, P. J. A note on redistributing a teacher's student contact. *Journal of Applied Behavioral Analysis*, 1971, *4*, 157-161.

Semb, G., Hopkins, B. L., & Hursh, D. E. The effects of study questions and grades on student task performance in a college course. *Journal of Applied Behavioral Analysis*, 1973, *6* (4), 631-642.

Assessment
and
Evaluation

According to P.L. 94-142, The Education for All Handicapped Children Act, future services for the handicapped must stress educational programs that are designed to meet the individual needs of each handicapped child. An individualized educational plan (IEP) must be developed for each child. Paramount to the development of the IEP is the assessment and evaluation process. The identification of learning problems and the prevention of potential problems requires formal and informal assessment techniques prior to the remediation and intervention procedures. Although assessment should precede remediation and intervention it should have implications for programming and instruction. Assessment, no matter how exacting and precise, has relatively little value if it offers no information for remediation.

Assessment is often viewed as a means of determining deficits and strengths of a child at a given point in time. In this context, it may be looked upon as a prerequisite to

programming. However, it is unlikely that this initial assessment would yield adequate information for ideal programming. The assessment process does not and should not end when the child is placed in an instructional setting. There is a critical need for ongoing evaluation of the program and the child within the instructional setting to ascertain whether desired outcomes are being achieved. When necessary, programs must be modified, revised, or completely altered when ongoing evaluation proves programming to be ineffective and/or inefficient.

The articles chosen for this section are offered the hope that the reader will recognize assessment and evaluation as integral components of individualized programming. By itself, the IEP is meaningless and will serve no useful purpose unless the assessment information, upon which it is built, is closely interwoven with intervention and ongoing evaluation procedures.

Educational Diagnosis with Instructional Use

JAMES B. DUFFEY
MARK L. FEDNER

JAMES B. DUFFEY *is Director, National Learning Resource Center of Pennsylvania, King of Prussia; and* MARK L. FEDNER *is a Psychologist, Montgomery County Intermediate Unit, Norristown, Pennsylvania.*

Abstract: American education, though haphazard at times, has proved successful for many children. However, a large population of students, especially those regarded as exceptional, has not been able to benefit from such instruction. Part of the problem has been the almost exclusive use of norm referenced testing as a diagnostic tool for instructional purposes. A different approach is needed, one that de-emphasizes standardized norm referenced testing in favor of a measurement that is truly instructionally diagnostic. The approach suggested is criterion referenced assessment. Implementation of this technology will be no overnight task. But successful implementation is within the educator's grasp. Accurate educational diagnosis and instruction based on such assessment is beneficial for diagnostician, teacher, student, and parent.

ADVANCES in educational technology have historically been slow and difficult. With a host of educational panaceas available, educators have found making the best choice of methods and procedures to be understandably perplexing. In the last few years, new technology has been widely publicized in the professional literature, and yet field demand has been minimal. In addition, publishers have been rather slow to refine evaluative instruments and curricula related to this technology. The new technology of note, criterion referenced measurement (Carver, 1974; McClelland, 1973; Proger & Mann, 1973), is designed to determine what a student has and has not mastered, leaving the comparison of individuals to the statisticians.

Educational Diagnosis Experts

School psychologists, reading specialists, and learning disability specialists, among others, have been considered the experts in educational diagnosis. When faced with a referral of a nonachieving student, teachers have relied on these specialists for general consultation and for special instructional materials. It has often been obvious that these experts were not fully equipped to assist teachers in the remediation of academic deficiencies when they were restricted to their wits and to norm referenced tests.

Queries to school psychologists, for example, frequently were answered by written reports that indicated IQ and achievement grade levels. School psychologists were especially proficient at the identification of a problem that was substantially the same as the one described by the teacher. Reading specialists have found themselves lost in curriculum materials. Ready and willing, they

"Educational Diagnosis with Instructional Use," James B. Duffey and Mark L. Fedner, *Exceptional Children*, Vol. 44, No. 4, January 1978. ©1978 Council for Exceptional Children.

supply classrooms with innovative reading series for children who are having comprehension difficulties. To the teacher's dismay, however, curricula prescriptions are often made without appropriate evaluation, that is, without indicating what the child has learned and must still learn. Learning disability specialists on the other hand, are sinking in the mire of proprioceptive, perceptual motor training. Research has repeatedly demonstrated that such training leads to little or no transfer to academic areas, and yet educators have continued to use the "magic" methods of Kephart, Frostig, and others (Hammill & Wiederholt, 1973).

Use of Norm Referenced Testing

Educational diagnosticians have spent much of their energies in attempting global diagnoses (e.g., minimal cerebral dysfunction) and global remediations (e.g., self contained classrooms) and have received little in return (Forness, 1976). Experience has shown that the days of "love the child," "segregate him," or "expose him to a new reading series" have come and gone, and yet they are still with educators. Myriad factors have contributed to the unfortunate situation of the educational diagnostician. One salient factor has been the exclusive use made of norm referenced testing. Even though these tests are designed primarily to separate and order individuals, they have been used as diagnostic tools for instructional purposes by the educational specialist. In using these instruments for testing on a group or individual basis, the educator's efforts have produced as little as a grade equivalent score.

For example, like the teacher, the specialist now knew that Johnny Jones was achieving lower than the majority of his classmates, but what could be done instructionally to remediate the problem? Where should Johnny and his teacher initiate their efforts? What does he know? What does he need to learn? Few answers were available.

If a norm referenced standardized achievement test is better than most, it provides information concerning a child's independence, instructional, and frustration levels. With such a test, the teacher will know approximately at which grade level he should start seeking clues that indicate learning deficits. But few norm referenced instruments

provide such information. In most cases, the teacher is informed that a student is reading at a certain grade equivalent level. If this is a student's frustration level rather than his instructional level (which is often the case), and a teacher begins instruction at this point, no progress is made. In fact, the teacher may contribute to Johnny's academic frustrations. What is required, in addition to an accurate instructional level, is to determine if Johnny has competence in areas such as letter and word recognition, word attack skills, and reading comprehension (Woodcock, 1973). These areas can be assessed and appropriate curricula indicated by criterion referenced methodology.

Types of Experts

Partly because norm referenced tests have yielded so little instructional information about skill areas like the ones cited, specialists have developed modes of operation that allow them to avoid dealing with the frustration and disappointment of their educational colleagues. One such strategy is employed by the "hit and run" expert. These specialists rush into the classroom and administer some quickie standardized tests. They then shower teachers with IQ and grade equivalent scores. Some months later, after the teachers have attempted to unravel the meaning of the scores by examining them with puzzling reference books by their side, they realize that they have been told little of value. The specialists have long since gone.

The "judge" is another type of evaluation "expert." These specialists shed their feelings of inadequacy by adopting an accusatory, Genghis Khan posture. Upon learning that a child is functioning below level, they search for the educator or the parent responsible for mishandling the child's educational program. The referring teacher or parent is a handy culprit.

The "savior" might characterize one more humanistic, educational, evaluation specialist. Consistent with their intensive training, they administer, scrutinize, and interpret with care the child's standardized tests. Their big scene, usually completed within 20 minutes, is to describe the child and make far-reaching recommendations. Saviors have no hesitation in doing this, even though they have not really identified the child's instruc-

3. ASSESSMENT AND EVALUATION

tional difficulties. Teachers are initially so impressed with the specialists' jargon and their bent toward child advocacy that they are permitted to escape, sometimes even with praise. It is not until the teachers have tried to implement the recommendations a few times that they realize the diagnostician, rather than being a child advocate, was self serving.

At this point, some saviors might vehemently retort, "O.K., so our medical model labels, self contained special education classes, and perceptual motor training have not provided us with the answers we had anticipated, but what about the specification of ability strengths and weaknesses based upon tests and subtests analyses? We've been doing this for years—informing the teacher how best to present instructional materials considering the processes of input, output, and integration." Meager evidence is available to validate this strategy (Ysseldyke, 1973; Ysseldyke & Salvia, 1974). A major problem is that of reliability. Ysseldyke (1973), in his review of the diagnostic-prescriptive model, revealed that the standard error of measurement associated with most standardized tests and subtests makes process specification quite a shaky venture, a phenomenon also noted by Hammill (1971). In essence, exhibited deficits in auditory processing or visual motor integration may well be the result of chance factors. Why would a teacher want to plan skill instruction to circumvent a deficit based on chance factors? In considering this and other data, Ysseldyke (1973) proposed, as one option, that educators abandon the use of standardized tests for more informal assessment procedures. If this is not enough to discourage the saviors (let alone the conscientious diagnosticians) from using standardized tests, political opposition will certainly have a dramatic effect in dampening their enthusiasm. Specifically, the use of standardized IQ tests is in jeopardy for labeling special students, especially those considered to be members of minorities.

Although not all researchers are convinced that labeling a child (e.g., educable mentally retarded) is aversive (MacMillan, Jones, & Alora, 1974), a considerable political force in the United States is extremely reluctant and, in some cases, appalled by the labeling process as it is presently being used (Guskin, 1974). The implications are obvious in California, where IQ tests have been at least temporarily banned (*Larry v. Riles*, 1974), and a master plan for special education has been advanced that eliminates diagnostic categories (Forness, 1976). It appears that norm referenced tests offer limited instructional information and that IQ tests can be a source of intense negative affect. Educators must explore supplementary procedures.

Skill Assessment and Development

It is time to rescue the diagnostic specialist. As suggested earlier by McClelland (1973) and Carver (1974), school diagnosticians have not had sufficient tools for their trade. They have been in a difficult situation from the beginning. The present technology, norm referenced measurement, seems to cause innumerable problems when it is used in isolation. Supplemental procedures and models that emphasize skill assessment and development (Mann, 1971) and social, vocational, or academic competence (McClelland, 1973) should be considered.

Educational diagnosis should reveal what a child knows and does not know. It should specify the next appropriate step for instruction and should assist the teacher in avoiding unnecessary review for certain students. Diagnosis must be content specific. It must refer to the information that is, or should be, taught in an educational setting. One way to meet these objectives is to de-emphasize the use of standardized norm referenced testing and to emphasize the use of testing that is truly diagnostic in an instructional sense. In recent years, diagnostic technology has been developed that allows for the exact identification of specific skill deficits and strengths of criterion referenced measurement. At last educators have a bona fide diagnostic technology with real instructional use.

Criterion referenced devices are designed to evaluate mastery of specific educational objectives that have been determined before instruction. Thus, these devices can determine whether instructors and their curricula have been successful in accomplishing specific objectives. They do not attempt to compare students to their peers through a normative approach. Educators have been accustomed to thinking in norm referenced terms and have failed to realize that the statistical qualities they require in norm referenced testing make this type of evaluation less sensitive to real educational gains (Carver, 1974). In a typical situation, where educators might be using a criterion referenced instrument to measure mastery of skills before and after an instructional unit, they would expect most students to score uniformly low on the pretest and uniformly high on the posttest. These characteristics would be judged statistically inappropriate for a norm referenced test, for 50% of the population would always be below the median no matter what is being assessed at any particular age level.

Measurement of mastery as provided in criterion referenced methodology suggests a model for the teaching and evaluation of student progress (Proger & Mann, 1973). Before offering an instructional unit to a class of children, the need for that instruction should be justified. By presenting a criterion referenced instrument and by designating an arbitrary mastery level of perhaps 80%, the teachers might find that the majority of their students do not have mastery of the unit material. Some students may perform exceptionally well on the pretest and thus are provided with enrichment material or moved on at an accelerated rate. The majority of the students receive the instructional unit. When a task is completed, the teacher readministers the mastery test as a posttest. The results indicate which students have achieved mastery and can move on to the next instructional unit. Students who have not achieved mastery, as indicated by the posttest, are recycled through the instructional material, perhaps with an alternative instructional approach. Maintenance of the instructional approach can be monitored through repeated posttesting and review if necessary.

There are a number of strategies that the classroom teacher or the educational specialist can implement and materials are currently available to accomplish criterion referenced methodology. They are described elsewhere (Proger & Mann, 1973) and thus will not be presented here. However, in selecting from existing procedures, it is important to remember that they must be appropriate to the educational level currently being presented. Furthermore, if criterion referenced tests are used without inherent curricula, they should have a high correlation to the objectives being used in the educational setting. Ideally, test items should be identical to instructional objectives. The suggestion that available procedures be used is not intended to rule out the possibility of teachers' designing and using their own criterion referenced instruments or systems (Millman, 1970).

Criterion Referenced Methodology and Application of Special Services

If parent group pressure and subsequent litigation proceed on their present course and dissatisfaction among educators regarding special education and IQ testing continues, the educational system will require reorganization. Efforts in this direction have already been proposed or implemented. Noncategorical special education programs based upon a behavioristic approach are among the first to report some success (Forness, 1976). However, noncategorical education is just as easily conceptualized by a Piagetian/cognitive, affective/social or eclectic orientation. Instead of the widespread use of medical model categories and self contained special education classes, criterion referenced methodology can be employed to group so-called special and regular children. This grouping would be based upon those skills students can demonstrate and those they need to demonstrate, rather than on ability quotients. Mastery levels in social, self help, readiness, and academic skills would be used to allocate educational services. Under such a system, all children would be guaranteed an appropriate and educationally relevant program to meet their specific needs. It is important to note that criterion referenced methodology, as it is conceptualized here and elsewhere (Proger & Mann, 1973), is a continuous evaluative process. Children singled out as needing to enhance skills thought to have been mastered by their chronological age could literally work their way out of special attention by mastering identified criteria. Futhermore, the child would gain skills considered to be essential in educational, social, and vocational situations.

Assessment would emphasize skill competence that could be readily explained to parents without much of the IQ jargon to which they are presently subjected. The IQ test might be degraded to a minor role in placement and be used simply to provide an *estimate* of a child's ability to learn. IQ's might be referred to as academic quotients

3. ASSESSMENT AND EVALUATION

(Kagan & Haveman, 1976) because they estimate academic success and do not describe innate, unchanging, hypothetical constructs.

The positions set forth in this article have up to this point ignored the clerical time and effort necessary to implement a criterion referenced system. Again the technology is available to solve the problem. The simpler approach involves embedding criterion referenced principles in curriculum materials and procedures, an effort that is under way. A second but more complex solution lies in the marriage of computer technology and present educational needs.

The implementation of the procedures proposed here is no overnight task. Tests need to be developed and issues resolved. One particularly significant issue brought up by Drew (1973) relates to assessing minorities with criterion referenced tests. He suggested that, even with criterion referenced instruments, bias is incurred when criteria and mastery levels for different skill areas are determined. Drew was asking who would select the standards of success and on what basis. The answer can be found in criterion referenced methodology, but this solution requires that educators determine what is important to include in their curricula. Perhaps this selecting can be empirically based upon criterion sampling (McClelland, 1973). What values will the educator employ to shape the future? Will cooperation with peers be one of the behavioral objectives? These decisions and value judgments will have to be formalized, for criterion referenced methodology and haphazard education are mutually exclusive.

It is anticipated that teachers and schools will be accountable for assessing needs and developing objectives and curriculum plans for each child that would be acceptable to parents, as per the requirements of the Education for All Handicapped Children Act of 1975 (Public Law 94-142). Thus, a need for a system of checks and balances in which society and education work together to determine what education should attend to is imminent. This objective is within the grasp of educators, for they have the necessary technology.

Concluding Comments

The thrust of this article is to encourage educational specialists and teachers to make use of and to refine the technology available to them. They are capable of measuring each student's individual progress within the limits of clerical time and of adjusting instruction appropriately. Miraculously, haphazard education has been successful for many children. We educators do, however, have a large population of students, especially those regarded as special, who have not been able to benefit from haphazard instruction. It is primarily these students who should receive the benefit of accurate educational diagnosis and instruction based on that assessment.

References

Carver, R. P. Two dimensions of tests: Psychometric and edumetric. *American Psychologist,* 1974, *29,* 512-518.

Drew, C. J. Criterion-referenced and norm-referenced assessment of minority group children. *Journal of School Psychology,* 1973, *11,* 323-329.

Forness, S. R. Behavioristic orientation to categorical labels. *Journal of School Psychology,* 1976, *14,* 90-95.

Guskin, S. L. Research in labeling retarded persons: Where do we go from here? *American Journal of Mental Deficiency,* 1974, *79,* 262-264.

Hammill, D. D. Evaluating children for instructional purposes. In D. D. Hammill & N. R. Bartel (Eds.), *Educational perspectives in learning disabilities.* New York: John Wiley & Sons, 1971.

Hammill, D., & Wiederholt, J. Review of the Frostig Visual Perception Test and the related training program. In L. Mann & D. Sabatino (Eds.), *The review of special education* (Vol. 1). King of Prussia PA: Buttonwood, 1973.

Kagan, J., & Haveman, E. *Psychology: An introduction.* New York: Harcourt, Brace, Jovanovich, 1976.

Larry, D., et al. v. Riles, W. United States District Court, Northern District of California. No. C-712270 RFP, 1974.

MacMillan, D. L., Jones, R. L., & Alora, G. F. The mentally retarded label: A theoretical analysis and review of research. *American Journal of Mental Deficiency,* 1974, *79,* 241-261.

Mann, L. Psychometric phrenology and the new faculty psychology: The case against ability assessment and training. *Journal of Special Education,* 1971, *5,* 3-14.

McClelland, V. C. Testing for competence rather than intelligence. *American Psychologist,* 1973, *28,* 1-14.

Millman, J. Reporting student progress: A case for a criterion-referenced marking system. *Phi Delta Kappan,* 1970, *52,* 226-230.

Proger, B. B., & Mann, L. Criterion-referenced measurement: The world of gray versus black and white. *Journal of Learning Disabilities,* 1973, *6,* 18-30.

PUBLIC LAW 94:142—A FOCUS ON ASSESSMENT

Nancy E. Dworkin*

The author wishes to acknowledge with profound gratitude the background for this article provided by Joesph Ballard, Assistant Director for Policy Implementation, the Council for Exceptional Children, Reston, VA.

Why is this education law, Public Law 94-142 different from all other education laws? In what way has the introduction of new legislation revolutionized the structure within which our society is committed to delivering educational services to young citizens considered handicapped or disabled? How have the specifics introduced through the new legislation redirected the commitments and obligations of professional educators? What protections have been delivered to the tax paying consumers who are both the supporters and users of public education?

Since the turn of the decade the private and class action suits have challenged the right of state and local education agencies to exclude children on the basis of handicapping conditions. Although the post war years witnessed an increase in the delivery of special services to handicapped children, the U. S. House Subcommittee on Select Education and the U. S. Senate Subcommittee on the Handicapped, in reviewing the Education of the Handicapped Amendments of 1974 (Public Law 93-380), brought to light the following facts:

- Over 1.75 million children with handicaps in the U. S. were not receiving a public education.

- Over half of the estimated 8 million handicapped children were not receiving appropriate educational services.

- Many children went with their handicaps undetected and, therefore, lost out on the possibility of taking advantage of (even) those educational facilities which did exist.

The magnitude of the problem as well as two decades of commitment to civil rights, has led to the development of a legislative structure which brings education into consonance with general civil rights and constitutional ethics. Much of the litigation challenging the right of state and local schools to deny specific children access to educational services turned to the Fourteenth Amendment of the Constitution of the United States as precedent through the structure of equal rights. Parents and child advocates argued that under Constitutional law,

where a state has undertaken to provide a benefit to the people, such as public education, these benefits must be provided to all of the people unless the state can demonstrate a compelling reason for doing otherwise (Ballard, J. and Zettel, J. "Public Law 94-142 and Section 504: What They Say About Rights & Protection," p. 47).

The net result, characterized as the "Bill of Rights for Handicapped Children" was signed into law by the Senate on June 18, 1975, the House of Representatives on July 29, and by President Gerald Ford on November 29, under the title Public Law 94-142: The Education for All Handicapped Children Act. Many of the major provisions, such as the assurance of non-discriminatory assessment and education in the least restrictive environment, were required in an earlier law—P. L. 93-380, the Education Amendments Act of 1974. P. L. 94-142 was enacted approximately one year and three months later, refining the rights mandates initially stated in P. L. 93-380.

The thrust of P. L. 94-142 has recently been underlined by the decision of HEW Secretary Joseph Califano (April, 1977) to begin aggressive reinforcement of the baseline civil rights mandate for all handicapped Americans, namely Section 504 of P. L. 93-112, the Vocational Rehabilitation Act Amendments of 1973. In effect, while P. L. 94-142 guarantees the right of appropriate education to all handicapped children, Section 504 safeguards qualified handicapped individuals against exclusion from federally funded programs solely because of that handicap.

I. PURPOSES & DEFINITIONS

Public Law 94-142 addresses itself to the following major areas:
1) Special education programming to handicapped children and youth ages 3-21.
2) a. Assessment and decision-making **process for the provision of special education programs where appropriate.**
   b. Parental and lay participation in the decision-making process.
3) Management and auditing require-

3. ASSESSMENT AND EVALUATION

ments.

4) Financial assistance to states and local government through the use of federal funds.

Within the general framework of those five areas the legislation also undertakes the task of defining specific operational procedures and the identifying characteristics necessary to them.

Handicapped children are defined by the Act as children who are:

mentally retarded, hard of hearing, deaf, orthopedically impaired, other health impaired, speech impaired, visually handicapped, seriously emotionally disturbed, or children with specific learning disabilities *who by reason thereof require special education and related services.*

Special education is defined in P. L. 94-142 as:

specially designed instruction, at no cost to parents or guardians, *to meet the unique needs of a handicapped child,* including classroom instruction, instruction in physical education, home instruction and instruction in hospitals and institutions.

Related services are defined in P. L. 94-142 as:

transportation and such developmental, corrective and other supportive services (including speech pathology and audiology, psychological services, physical and occupational therapy, recreation, and medical and counseling services, except that such medical services shall be for diagnostic and evaluation purposes only) *as may be required to assist a handicapped child to benefit from special education* and includes the early indentification and assessment of handicapping conditions in children.

II. ASSESSMENT

The purpose of "Evaluation," as defined in the P. L. 94-142 Rules & Regulations is:

to determine whether a child is handicapped and the nature and extent of the special education and related services that the child needs. The term means procedures used selectively with an individual child and does not include basic tests administered to or procedures used with all children in a school, grade or class.

States and local educational agencies are mandated to insure that, at a minimum (12 1 a. 532 of the P. L. 94-142 Rules & Regulations):

A. Tests and other evaluation materials:
1) Are provided and administered in the child's native language or *other mode of communication,* unless it is clearly not feasible to do so;

2) Have been validated for the specific purpose for which they are used; and
3) Are administered by trained personnel in conformance with the instructions provided by their producer.

The provision, in effect, orders that assessment procedures be multi-factored, multi-sourced and carried out by qualified personnel. The regulations governing this provision should therefore be carefully reviewed (refer to Section 612 (5) (C) of the Act). Children should be evaluated as soon as possible following referral according to evaluation-placement procedures established and implemented by public agencies.

Interpretation:

In terms of the evaluator, this means the following:

1) Where children whose primary language is not English, or in the case of children who have difficulty with different modes of communication, evaluation instruments must be selected not only on the basis of their diagnostic content, but on the basis of guarantees that the child can understand and respond to test items. In short, the burden of proof is on the evaluator vis-a-vis the applicability of test instrumentation.
2) Single test instruments may not be used for multi-purpose diagnosis, nor is it legitimate to use findings about a specific condition in order to generalize about other conditions. This issue may become particularly critical where the specialist is asked to predict or project future behavior, achievement, etc. In effect, every diagnostic and predictive statement made by specialists must be supported by the findings of demonstrably appropriate instrumentation. Further, tests may not be used to cross lines, nor may the evaluators assume that a given instrument can be used with a child unless there is either a) a directly stated diagnostic objective and a quotable validating statement in the original test development substantiating that usage, or b) every diagnostic statement made by the tester is related to test instrumentation clearly identified and validated for that objective.
3) In effect, there are two constraints placed upon the evaluator. First, they may no longer modify or change individual test items or sections since such actions would constitute a violation of the original format and intent of the instrumentation and second, not only must evaluators relate their diagnostic findings to specifically appropriate instrumentation, but they must also

provide evidence that they have been trained, either through certification or other form of evidence, to use such instrumentation.

B. Tests and other evaluation materials include those tailored to assess specific areas of educational need and not merely those which are designed to provide a single general intelligence quotient.

Interpretation:

In brief, a projection of intelligence regardless of how soundly derived, is no longer sufficient in the development of diagnostic or programmatic statements. Additional test materials must be included addressing themselves to the examination of specific academic or behavioral areas in education. These additional instruments must conform to all of the conditions identified above.

C. Tests are selected and administered so as best to ensure that when a test is administered to a child with impaired sensory, manual or speaking skills, the test results accurately reflect the child's aptitude or achievement level or whatever other factors the test purports to measure, rather than reflecting the child's impaired sensory, manual or speaking skills (except where those skills are the factors which the test purports to measure).

Interpretation:

This section of the legislation focuses on two issues. First, an evaluator must be careful to avoid instrumentation where the derived scores depend on specific physical or other skills with which the child is having difficulty—unless the specific purpose of the testing is to identify and characterize those difficulties. Second, any complex instrumentation may be used only for the purposes of identifying scores and diagnostic characteristics explicitly stated in that instrumentation. The evaluator is cautioned to avoid projected assumptions beyond the framework of the test. Although the language is written to safeguard the child against unprovable assumptions, it also lays the burden of proof for the applicability of instrumentation on the evaluator. Perhaps the most critical issue is the prohibition against using intelligence and other projective techniques without the support of specifically oriented test evidence and without proof that the child is technically capable (i.e., physiologically) of handling the test.

D. No single procedure is used as the sole criterion for determining an appropriate educational program for a child.

Interpretation:

This legislative item is related to the above, implying simply that a single source may provide an inaccurate view of a child's current or future capabilities.

E. The evaluation is made by a multi-disciplinary team or group of persons including at least one teacher or other specialist with knowledge in the area of suspected disability.

Interpretation:

The thrust in this legislative item is again dual. On the one hand requiring diagnostic input from a variety of professional sources and on the other guaranteeing that the individual most likely to be carrying out an individual program be a part of the diagnostic team. For many evaluators such a team would require a revision of their general procedures, especially as it relates to interaction with the classroom teacher. This may be particularly true in the case of private evaluators who have traditionally delivered diagnostic information to the school system.

F. The child is assessed in all areas related to the suspected disability including, where appropriate, health, vision, hearing, social and emotional status, general intelligence, academic performance, communicative status and motor abilities.

Interpretation:

The complexity of this item is related to the multi-disciplinary mandate. Quite evidently, where complex diagnosis is required, it is necessary that a multi-disciplinary team determine what kinds of examinations are necessary and then carry them through in terms of their professional expertise.

Note:
Children who have a speech impairment as their primary handicap may not need a complete battery of assessments (e.g., phychological, physical or adaptive behavior). However, a qualified speech-language pathologist would 1) evaluate each speech impaired child using procedures that are appropriate for the diagnosis and appraisal of speech and language disorders and 2) where necessary, make referrals for additional assessments needed to make an appropriate placement decision.

The general framework of the legislation concerns both safeguards for individual children and guarantees for the appropriateness of evaluative instruments and techniques. In terms of safeguarding individuals, the law clearly mandates the avoidance of approaches which, a priori, penalize specific individual children on the basis of their group affiliation.

According to the law, children may no longer be identified as dull or incapable on the basis of either cultural differences, use of non-standard English or other languages, phys-

3. ASSESSMENT AND EVALUATION

ical handicaps, ethnically different behavior, etc. While school systems may recognize such differences, they may not place a lower value on the child as a consequence of such differences. In popular terms, what the law warns against is the use of culture bound tests and the imposition of white, middle-class values as a single standard value of measurement.

A more subtle thrust deals with the nature of test instrumentation. Aside from the issues raised above which deal with the origin of instrumentation, the revolution in the new laws deals with the internal structure of the instrumentation. The law explicitly states that:

1) The relationship between diagnostic statements and characterization of the child must be supported by instrumentation designed for that purpose.
2) Test segments requiring specific types of input may not be imposed on children who have overt and obvious problems with that form of input. This issue is particularly poignant where a child's intelligence may be identified on the basis of a complex of interactive parts where some of those parts are clearly beyond the child's physical capabilities but do not necessarily relate to the intellectual ones.

Explicitly stated, an intelligence test which requires fine motor manipulation and is administered to a palsied or dystrophic child, may deliver a skewed and inaccurate intelligence score and does little to help the self esteem of the child, just as a standardized test normed against a White, middle-class student population may not be a legitimate way of examining the total school population.

PROCEDURAL SAFEGUARDS

Procedural safeguards have been established by Congress to protect the interest of parents, guardians, children and the schools and agencies involved. Those which pertain to evaluation are as follows:

1) Written notification before evaluation. In addition, the right to an interpreter /translator if the family's native language is not English (unless it is clearly not feasible to do so).
2) Opportunity to present complaints by parents and guardians regarding the identification, evaluation, placement or any other issue touching on the appropriateness of the procedures.
3) Notices written in layman's terms so that they may be understood by a general nonprofessional public, containing a description of each evaluation procedure, test, record or report the agency uses as a basis for a proposal or refusal.
4) Opportunity to obtain an independent educational evaluation of the child. Public agencies must, upon request, provide parents information concern-

ing where independent educational evaluations may be obtained. Parents of a handicapped child may inspect and review all educational records with respect to the identification, evaluation and educational placement of the child and have the right to obtain an independent educational evaluation of their child (i.e., from a qualified examiner who is not employed by the public agency which is responsible for the education of the child in question) at public expense should they disagree with the evaluation obtained by the public agency. The public agency, however, may request a hearing to contest this. Should that prove to be the case, the parents may indicate additional evaluation at private expense. Regardless of who pays for the assessment, however, the results must be considered in regard to decision-making for the child.
5) Access to all relevant records.
6) Right to the protection of confidentiality of personally identifiable information at collection, storage, disclosure and destruction stages as stated by this and other legislation dealing with right of privacy. (See Section 615)

PLACEMENT PROCEDURES (121a.533 of P. L. 94-142 Rules & Regulations)

In interpreting evaluation data and in making placement decisions, each public agency shall:

1) Draw upon information from a variety of sources, including aptitude and achievement tests, teacher recommendations, physical condition, social or cultural background and adaptive behavior.
2) Insure that information obtained from all of these sources is documented and carefully considered.
3) Insure that the placement decision is made by a group of persons, including persons knowledgeable about the child, the meaning of the evaluation data, and the placement options.
4) Insure that the placement decision is made in conformity with the least restrictive environment rules in 121a.550-121a.554.

If a determination is made that a child is handicapped and needs special education and related services, an individualized education program must be developed for the child in accordance with 121a.340 121a. 349 of Subpart C.

III. INDIVIDUALIZED EDUCATION PROGRAMS (IEP)

To insure that handicapped children have

access to appropriate educational services the Congress included, as part of P. L. 94-142, a requirement that individualized educational programs be designed for each child. The IEP is considered to be the central building block of the Education for All Handicapped Children Act and constitutes the most radical departure in educational legislation.

What are the Basic Concepts of the IEP?

The term "individual education program" itself conveys important concepts that need to be specified. First, "individualized" means that the IEP must be addressed to the educational needs of a single child rather than a class or group of children. Second, "education" means that the IEP is limited to those elements of the child's education that are more specifically special education and related services as defined by the Act. Third, "program" means that the IEP is a statement of what will actually be provided to the child, as distinct from a plan that provides guidelines from which a program must subsequently be developed.

What are the Basic Components of an IEP? (121a.346)

The individualized education program for each child must include:

- A statement of the child's present levels of educational performance.

- A statement of annual goals, including short term instructional objectives.

- A statement of the specific special education and related services.

- Appropriate objective criteria and evaluation procedures and schedules for determining, on at least an annual basis, whether the short term instructional objectives are being achieved.

Who Participates in IEP Meetings?

At the initial planning meeting it is necessary that a professional knowledgeable about the test instrumentation and the results specific to that child be in attendance. This may be any member of the evaluation team, a representative of the evaluating agency or the child's teacher. At all meetings it is necessary to include a representative of the public agency other than the teacher who is qualified to provide or supervise the provision of special education, the teacher(s) and one or both of the child's parents. Other individuals may also be invited at the discretion of the parent or agency.

Is the IEP an Individual Plan?

No, it is a management tool. Its function is to state appropriate educational goals and objectives, identify the services within the system for those objectives and develop a timeline for delivery of services.

Is the IEP a Contract?

This question lies at the heart of every professional's concern regarding the new legislation. There is no simple response, although the language of the legislation indicates that the IEP is an agreement, not a contract. An examination of the various facets of the legislation, including the sections dealing with programming would suggest a number of lines of reasoning. From the point of view of the school system, it can be assumed that ... "if a local system decides as part of the individual planning process, that a child should receive a certain service, there is the assumption that such services be provided..." (U. S. Commissioner of Education Ernest Boyer's address to Congress July 14, 1977.)

To this extent, planning and programming have a quasi-contractual character and it would be rational to deduce that both the system and individuals would be held responsible at least to the extent of future funding, although specific accountability does not seem to be called for. In essence, both the system and the professionals would be expected to be able to support programmatic suggestions with appropriate documentation and reference to "state of the art" standards.

As far as resolution of the educational and other problems of individual children are concerned, however, there is a marked difference in approach. At no point does the legislation indicate personal or system liability for outcome. Throughout the entire development of P. L. 94-142 the emphasis is on the professional legitimacy of diagnosis and planning. In short, the system and the individuals are expected to identify needs and service within the best and most ethical frameworks of current knowledge. They are also expected and mandated to take into account the input of those agents in the child's life whose insights and rights may seriously affect successful delivery of services. They are not, however, contractually or otherwise, expected to guarantee "... that such treatment will cure the ... problem." (Commissioner Boyer)

Indeed the language of the legislation clearly indicates that an IEP is not necessarily the final or definitive program for the child. Thus the planning must be reviewed on an annual basis. Unfortunately there is a potential softness in the review process since it is not necessary for one of the original diagnosticians to be present nor is there a requirement for re-diagnosis of the child.

What is the Least Restrictive Environment?

Underlying all of P. L. 94-142 is an environmental commitment which stands in sharp contrast to much of former special education practice. Namely the assumption that the standard classroom is a model for the least restrictive school environment and is, therefore, a point of departure for all program development. Thus, any IEP which calls for services

3. ASSESSMENT AND EVALUATION

outside this environment or additional to it must be supported by hard evidence. The law represents a swing of the pendulum. No longer do we posit that separation of supposedly standard learners and special education children is positive for either group. On the contrary, the law clearly implies that handicapped children and non-handicapped children will benefit from each other's presence. In addition, each state must establish procedures to insure that, to the maximum extent appropriate, handicapped children, including children in public and private institutions or other care facilities, are educated with children who are not handicapped and that special classes, separate schooling, or the removal of handicapped children from the regular education environment occurs only when the nature or severity of the handicap is such that education in regular classes with the use of supplementary aids and services cannot be achieved satisfactorily.

What then in summary are the rights and protections of P. L. 94-142 (which, for the most part, are also affirmed in Section 504) that must be guaranteed?

P. L. 94-142 makes a number of critical stipulations that must be adhered to by both the state and its local and intermediate educational agencies:

- Assurance of the availability of a free, appropriate public education for all handicapped children, such guarantee of availability no later than certain specified dates.

- Assurance of the maintenance of an individualized education program for all handicapped children.

- A guarantee of complete due procedural safeguards.

- The assurance of regular parent or guardian consultation.

- Assurance of special education being provided to all handicapped children in the "least restrictive" environment.

- Assurance of nondiscriminatory testing and evaluation.

- A guarantee of policies and procedures to protect the confidentiality of data and information.

- Assurance of an effective policy guaranteeing the right of all handicapped children to a free, appropriate public education at no cost to parents or guardian.

- Assurance of a surrogate to act for any child when parents or guardians are either unknown or unavailable or when such child is a legal ward of the state.

BIBLIOGRAPHY

For further information regarding individualized education programs, the reader is referred to the following resources:

- A Primer on Individualized Education Programs for Handicapped Children by Scottie Torres, 1977, 60 pp. Available from the Foundation for Exceptional Children, 1920 Association Dr., Reston, VA 22091.

- "Teacher Issues Regarding Individualized Education Programs" by Scottie Torres and Josephine Hays (forthcoming in the January 1978 issue of Exceptional Children).

For further information regarding related service the reader is referred to The Council for Exceptional Children:

- Public Policy and the Education of Exceptional Children edited by Frederick J. Weintraub, Alan R. Abeson, Joseph Ballard and Martin L. LaVor, 1976, 288 pp., Stock No. 123, $13.95.

- P. L. 94-142, The Education for All Handicapped Children Act of 1975 by Joseph Ballard, Jean N. Nazzaro, and Frederick J. Weintraub, (Multimedia package), 1976, Stock No. 136, $50.00.

- Special Education Administrative Policy Manual by Scottie Torres 1977, 175 pp., Stock No. 164, $27.50.

For further information regarding procedural safeguards, the reader is referred to the following resources available from The Council for Exceptional Children:

- A Primer on Due Process: Education Decision for Handicapped Children by Alan R. Abeson, Nancy Bolick and Jayne Hass, 1975, 77 pp., Stock No. 104, $4.95.

- Procedural Safeguards P. L. 94-142—A Guide for Schools and Parents, produced by The Council for Exceptional Children in conjunction with the Children's Television Workshop, (multimedia package), 1977, Stock No. 167, $90.00.

Informal Assessment during Clinical Teaching

David C. Loe

David C. Loe, PhD, is an assistant professor of special education and learning disabilities at Arkansas State University, State University, Arkansas 72467.

EDUCATIVE PROCESSES, I believe, should result in anticipated changes in the behaviors of those involved in the procedures. Circumscribed behaviors are best evaluated before, during, and after implementation of educational experiences; comparisons might well be made with behaviorally stated objectives in order that progress rates can be determined. It is the responsibility of a *clinical* teacher (one who teaches according to a child's unique needs and abilities) to determine goals, initiate the learning process, and evaluate results. A clinical teacher can determine individual ability hierarchies by longitudinal beharior assessment during learning situations, supplementing such information with standardized test results provided by ancillary personnel. Conventional psychoeducational evaluation yields some measure of an individual's functional competencies within the limits of an evaluative environment; but I feel that the results may have limited practical applicability for educational purposes. It appears that eventual classroom success can be predicted more reliably than failure.[1] For example, a young child who scores well on a reading readiness test has a rather high probability of becoming a competent reader; however, a young child who does not do well on a readiness test may become a successful reader, particularly if the problems are caused by simple immaturity. Multidisciplinary evaluations can, however, facilitate development of individual teaching and learning strategies intended to optimize school learning, if the evaluations cluminate in school-relevant behavioral suggestions.

A developmental concept of biological-environmental interaction indicates that the learner and the learning environment continuously influence one another, resulting in a process of ongoing mutual adaptation.[2] Academic success is a primary goal of educative processes; success is relative to the particular characteristics of an individual and the learning environment in which he functions. Success cannot be measured without assessment of individual learner characteristics, of tools and techniques, of the general instructional milieu, and of the stated learned objectives.

Informal assessment during learning situations has been recommended as a necessity for true educational diagnosis; advantages derive from the large behavioral sampling at the disposal of a teacher and the unobtrusive nature of such observations.[3] Educators must identify the needs of each child for whom responsible and adopt programs to fit those needs.[4]

Informal assessment is a necessary function of clinical teaching. When a child's characteristics differ significantly from community averages, the need for individualized programing increases; however, clinical teaching need not be reserved for the exceptional, for each learner is a unique case. Clinical teaching is a systematic attempt to facilitate individual learning processes, an effort to enhance achievement within the framework of personal abilities. Individual teachers should be as much concerned with the specifics of education as with the generalities. Whether teaching a group or a single person, a clinical teacher must determine their specific circumstances, such as learning integrities, motivation, and abilities hierarchies. Intuition and creativity will always be factors in a truly stimulating learning situation; the two factors coexist within a system of behavioral analysis and goal specification. Incidental learning is appreciated, but it should not be the mainstay of an educational program. A sophisticated teacher will incorporate individual preferences in order to provide each learner with viable avenues to desirable goals.

Assessment Strategies

Two general types of assessment may be employed: process analysis and product analysis.[5] Process analysis is an immediate study of how a student approaches a task. Variables to be considered include rate of work; what the learner does when approaching a difficult task; whether he implements problem-solving strategies, escape devices, or a combination of both; specification of what a learner can and cannot do in particular situations; and what a student will select when given a choice of relevant tasks. Observations are recorded objectively, accurately, and explicitly. Process analysis involves observable behaviors; learner thought processes can only be approached inferentially. One might correctly note that "Tommy completed only three math problems today." The teacher would not really know how many problems Tommy was able to complete, or whether he learned during that time. A teacher can, and usually should, make judicious clinical assumptions concerning individuals. Assumptions can only be tested on the basis of observable evidence, however.

Product analysis is the study of what a student has accomplished: review of samples of work done, test results, group participation, success. Products can be analyzed without process analysis. Product analysis identifies concepts the student appears to have mastered and yields specification of conditions correlating with success and/or failure. Product analysis can be used to measure the effectiveness of strategies incorporated according to interactions identified through process analysis. Both types of evaluation are valuable tools, necessary for reliable clinical teaching; process analysis, however, may be more critical for success, as a result of its focus on the learning characteristics of individuals.

Educational assessment applies to all areas of function, and should continue during instruction. Operationally defined behavioral observations may be used to verify the educational validity of formal test results, to acquire further information concerning specific behaviors under varying conditions, to study behavioral consistency, to direct intervention, and to obtain a baseline for measuring progress.[6]

Meaningful information can be reliable only if precision structuring is the basis for all observational assessment. A teacher should plan for the behavior to be observed. Time parameters must be consistent for results to be comparative; and recording procedures must be consistent, perhaps allowing for the possibility of another observer. Total circumstances should be controlled as much as possible. Inconsistency of task characteristics, for example, seating arrangement, teacher behaviors, materials activities prior to the assessment period, all introduce confounding variables which seriously reduce the effectiveness of assessment. The teacher should learn what a child does under specific conditions, how frequently, and at what times, and must reach conclusions regarding the continuation of the behavior. The teacher should understand the contingencies of each recurring behavior that is considered noteworthy, whether the behavior is desirable or not. Precision observations need not be time consuming, nor are they necessarily exhausting. The critical requirement is teacher attention. If the teacher consciously attempts to be open to the environment and actively seeks to be aware of classroom events, observations can be registered for several students over a period of time. As a teacher becomes familiar with significant patterns of behavior, appropriate observations will require even less time and effort.

It must be emphasized that a skillful teacher can achieve reasonable control over observational conditions without creating an atmosphere of restriction of regimentation. Subtle manipulations can occur without learner concern, resulting in an atmosphere of structure that is beneficial for most young learners, particularly those with disorders of attention or concentration. The prevailing structure must be individualized, based on child proclivities, recognizing unique needs preferences, and abilities.

The ability to assess and define salient behaviors should preclude dependency upon checklists devised prior to interaction with a child. What is required is the ability to assess behavior operationally in terms of distinct components, under relatively limitless sets of circumstances. General checklists may be devised as starting points for any of several broad performance areas; increasing familiarity with a particular child would lead to continuing revision of each checklist so that critical behavioral interactions are identified. Such an approach leads to observational flexibility and precision, avoiding a static orientation. Figure 1 presents an example of two checklists for a hypothetical child who has experienced difficulties while working independently.

Initial Assessment Examples

Individualized behavior lists can serve as bases for beginning analysis of a child's performance in selected school-related areas. Further individualization would result from identification of sequences or conditions meriting more refined annotation. Individ-

Figure 1

Initial Checklist	Revised Checklist
Name	Name
Date	Date
Task	Task
In-seat	Location in class
Out of seat	Looking at task
Looking at task	Looking at teacher
Time___to___	Looking at classmates
	Looking at bulletin board
	Amount of work correct
	Time___to___

ual behavioral specifications can enhance the instructional process by causing a teacher to focus attention on performance details that might be overlooked in more casual circumstances.

The significance of independent environmental variables cannot be overestimated; dependent variables (student responses) indicate learning progress, or its absence. Selected dependent variables will differ according to the teacher's determination of priorities. For example, a handwriting inventory might include evaluation of the following characteristics: posture, pencil grasp, rate of writing, and quality of response (legibility, formation of letters, spacing of letters and words). Each process may be studied as it interacts with external variables such as time, reinforcer, or physical location.

Emotional indices are more difficult to guage because subjective teacher interpretations may be either erroneous or inconsistent; however, one could record characteristics of speech and language, of group behavior, or of conversation content.

Reading behavior may be reduced to its various components. Physical posture, characteristics of errors, and preferred material are examples of the potential range of noteworthy qualities.

Other types of behavior may be rather easily assessed: attending, language, work completion, outbursts, and general behavioral response level.

Informal assessment records may be used to guide operant attempts to elicit or extinguish particular responses. Pupils can be taught to record certain of their own behaviors; self-monitoring of desirable events is likely to acquire reinforcement properties, increasing the probability of behavioral progress. Process analysis does not offer an answer to the question of intervention strategies. Procedures of informal assessment serve to pinpoint problem areas, enhancing the ability of an individual teacher to use his or her preferred techniques in a given situation.

Multiple benefits may derive from application of informal assessment procedures in a classroom. Empirical observation allows intra-individual comparisons of the quality and level of any behavior, making it possible for the clinical teacher to employ meaningful experimental methods in the classroom.

Informal Diagnostic Procedures: "What Can I Do Before the Psychometrist Arrives?"

Jennie J. DeGenaro, MS

WHY INFORMAL ASSESSMENT?

In this age of educational specialization, many teachers assume they are not qualified to diagnose children who are suspected of having a learning disability. They feel they must wait for the psychometrist, or another specialist, who may not be immediately available. Meanwhile, valuable time is lost.

Although classroom teachers are often unskilled in formal assessment procedures, the continued rise in the number of children who can be identified as learning disabled makes the generalist an essential member of the diagnostic team. In situ assessments may be helpful.

Smith (1969, p. 10) states that "most university and college teacher-training programs do not provide opportunities for learning informal classroom evaluation." Suggested in this paper are easily learned, informal testing procedures for assessing each child's strengths and weaknesses.

Diagnostic information is essential in planning an individualized program for each child. Also, procedures are needed by the classroom teacher for identifying children who should be referred for more extensive (formal) evaluations. Further, informal assessments place the teacher in the professional position of accepting accountability for the pupils in his or her charge.

Often there is a question about the level of performance a teacher can reasonably expect from a given pupil. Group intelligence test scores for the majority of the children assigned to a teacher are generally available. Thus, rough estimates of each child's potential may be ascertained. Mental maturity tests, such as the California Test of Mental Maturity, may be administered if the above information is lacking. Lerner (1971) suggests three different formulas which can be used to quantify a learning disability. The simplest was provided by Harris (1961). The formula is: RE (reading expectancy grade) = MA (mental age) – 5.

In working with learning disabled children, however, the teacher must be extremely cautious in accepting student potential as measured by standardized instruments or informal assessments. Further, any test is only as good as the professional who uses it. An accurate assessment depends upon seeing the child in a total context. And any instructional program based on these tests must be carefully supervised and monitored, lest the child be misclassified and perhaps unjustly condemned. According to Kirk and Kirk (1971, p. 5), "... some children who appear mentally retarded in the classroom and on intelligence tests may be children with learning disabilities rather than children who are mentally retarded."

Various publications suggest remedial exercises which help to alleviate deficit areas uncovered on such tests as the Stanford Binet Intelligence Scale and the Illinois Test of Psycholinguistic Abilities (see Ferinden et al. 1970). Deficits uncovered by informal assessments may also be remediated in a like manner. Children whose performances fall substantially above or below that expected will need personalized instruction. But these may well be the children who should be considered for referral for more in-depth evaluation, where intra-individual strengths and weaknesses can be more closely analyzed.

WHERE TO BEGIN

Information on each child can be obtained by the classroom teacher without the use of formal instruments. Thus, the teacher will have valuable diagnostic information on every child under her tutelage within a few days.

I shall now discuss informal methods for assessing the fourteen following areas:

 (1) Visual discrimination and memory
 (2) Auditory discrimination and memory
 (3) Letter identification
 (4) Writing the alphabet sequence
 (5) Phonetic knowledge
 (6) Tactual ability
 (7) Reversals and rotations
 (8) Verbal skills (oral)
 (9) Copying at near and far points
(10) Reading levels
(11) Self-concept

(12) Eye-hand coordination and written language
(13) Following directions
(14) Gross motor skills

Testing should begin with the visual and auditory channels, inasmuch as these are the two major avenues for learning. The teacher proceeds until the level is reached where the child's skills "break down." Generally, the instructional program, both developmental and remedial, should begin slightly below the instructional level, thus enhancing the learner's chances for success.

(1) VISUAL DISCRIMINATION AND MEMORY

The teacher can assess the visual modality for discrimination and memory ability. Children suspected of physiological deficits should be referred through the proper channels.

Visual Discrimination. Assess visual-motor ability by displaying geometric forms for the child to reproduce. Present individually a circle, cross, square, triangle, and diamond. Request the child to copy the design. Before he commences, explain that he will have five designs to copy on the page. According to the Gesell Developmental Schedules, children are expected to copy a square at four and a half years, a triangle at five, and a diamond at six.

Visual discrimination is further assessed in a more academic (task-oriented) manner. An exercise such as the following is appropriate for the child with some reading ability: The teacher writes a short sentence of four or five words, and places the sentence at the top of the page. In succeeding "sentences," the words from the original sentence are scattered among similar words. Children are to underline only the words found in the sample sentence. *Example:* "Where was that black cab?" is written at the top of the page. The next sentence may be written as follows: "Where When saw was what that black back cat cab car?" Include six or eight examples with different, but similar words interspersed in the sentences.

A small group of children may be tested in this manner. The time required to complete the exercise and the number of words correctly marked determine response adequacy.

Visual Memory for Letters, Digits and Pictures (objects). To assess memory for letters, print from two to eight letters (not in alphabetical sequence) on each card. Make several sets of cards containing the same number of letters per card. Display the card for one second per letter. *Example:* A card containing letters "b, l, c" is displayed for three seconds. Remove the card from view and ask the child to name the letters in the same order as on the card.

To reach the level expected of a nine-year-old on the Detroit Tests of Learning Aptitude, a student must recall all letters presented up to and including five letters in the exact sequence. The child is given four chances to succeed, if needed, at each level.

The visual memory of children who cannot read letters may be assessed by using pictures or objects.

Paste pictures of common objects on cards. Make two sets for each series. Two pictures will appear on the first card, three on the second, four on the third, and so forth, up to ten. *Example:* individual pictures of a dog, cat, mouse, car.

Start the test by displaying a card containing two pictures. Use both sets of cards for each series. Increase the number of pictures per card until the child errs. Allow him to look at the cards for one second per picture. *Example:* Four pictures on a card are studied for four seconds. Remove the card from view. Ask the child to name the objects (pictures) on the card. Consider the response correct regardless of the order given.

To achieve at a seven-year plus level on the Detroit, a child is required to recall all of the items presented, using two sets of each series, through six objects.

(2) AUDITORY DISCRIMINATION AND MEMORY

To assess auditory discrimination and memory, the teacher works with each pupil individually in a room free from noise and distraction.

Auditory Discrimination. Compile a list of word pairs which are alike except for one phoneme. The phoneme that is different occurs at the beginning of some words, in the middle of some, and at the end in others. *Example: men-fen, bend-band, lose-loose.* Words may be actual or nonsense. Occasionally include the same word twice. *Example: walk-walk.*

The teacher calls word pairs. The pupil indicates when the words are different by holding up a paper flag, or by giving some other agreed upon signal. The child faces away from the teacher.

As a normative guide, note that the Wepman Auditory Discrimination Test rates as unsatisfactory the performance of an eight-year-old who makes three errors out of a total of 30 items.

Auditory Memory (words). To test auditory memory, select one-syllable nouns. The same procedures are followed as for Visual Memory for Pictures (above).

Commence with two words. *Example:* The teacher says *dog-bird.* Two sets of words are prepared and presented for each series. The most difficult set includes eight words.

The Detroit has a similar subtest. The child is required, however, to remember more words presented auditorially than objects presented visually to achieve at the same proficiency level.

Auditory Memory (digits). Digits may be used to test a child's auditory memory. The teacher works with individual pupils and calls out a series of digits which the child is to repeat verbatim.

The teacher begins by calling two digits and increases the number called until the child can no longer recall them in the exact order given. *Example:* The teacher calls, "2 – 7," then "5 – 1 – 0," then "6 – 3 – 8 – 4."

According to the Stanford-Binet Intelligence Scale (1973) a seven-year-old is expected to recall five digits forward and three reversed.

(3) LETTER IDENTIFICATION
To determine which pupils do not know the letter names, the following procedure is used. Mimeograph a page of letters not written in alphabetical sequence. This task is accomplished individually. The child names the letters while the teacher records the exact error response above the letter attempted.

(4) WRITING THE ALPHABET SEQUENCE
To determine if the children can write the alphabet and the length of time required, instruct each to write the alphabet using small (lower case) letters. No copy is provided. When each child finishes, the teacher records the time required in minutes and seconds on his paper. Note the number of omissions, letters out of sequence, and reversals. Mixing of capital and lower-case letters constitutes an error.

There is no apparent agreement in the limited literature available concerning the length of time acceptable for writing the alphabet. From experience, a rough guide as to the approximate time for a child to perform this task, by the end of the third grade, is 38 seconds for girls and 42 seconds for boys.

(5) PHONETIC KNOWLEDGE
Phonetic ability is generally assessed by asking the children to write the beginning sounds or vowel sounds, etc. of letters and words. However, phonetic ability to transfer graphemes (print) to phonemes (speech) should also be assessed. Some children are successful on the first but not the second task.

To test the child's ability in phonics, direct him to write the sound specified in each word. *Example:* "Write the beginning sound in 'sun.'" Give no further clues and allow only enough time for an immediate written response. Select words to assess beginning, medial and final sounds and consonant blends. For the more advanced pupils, include special vowel sounds, final blends, and digraphs. The children may be tested in a group.

The same phonetic elements which were given auditorially should be presented visually.

Prepare a card containing the same elements as above. A marking sheet is necessary for each child. The child names aloud the sounds of the letters. The teacher records incorrect responses. Individual testing is required.

(6) TACTUAL ABILITY
To determine whether a child uses his sense of touch, other modalities are excluded. Blindfold the child, or present objects in a manner to prevent his viewing. Use geometric shapes and ask him to identify the objects by touch. The child reproduces, or names, these forms.

Accurate tactual ability is usually developed in children by five years of age, according to Benton and Schultz (1949).

(7) REVERSALS AND ROTATIONS
To determine whether a child reverses letters (*b* for *d*) or makes rotational errors (*u* for *n*) when identifying letters, the teacher should spend a few minutes with him.

The teacher prints the following letters on a card: *b, d, q, p, n, u, w, m.* An exact copy is used to score each child. The child names the letters as quickly as possible. All incorrect responses are recorded directly above the letter called.

Prepare a card with words which are frequently reversed. *Example: was-saw; dad-bad; men-new; on-no.* Use the same procedures as for letters.

To assess written reversals or rotations, have the child write from dictation the same letters and words, which had been presented visually. Children may be tested in groups to ascertain whether written reversals occur.

(8) VERBAL SKILLS
Identify the pupil who is weak in language skills by requiring individual responses in a structured situation.

Hand the child a common object and ask him to describe it. He is praised for his correct responses. If the child omits the name, color, composition, function or size, these are stated by the teacher on the practice item.

Select a different object, such as a toy car, eraser or other familiar object. Hand it to the child and ask him to describe it, giving no

3. ASSESSMENT AND EVALUATION

further cues. Record each child's response verbatim. The same objects should be used for testing each child. The child should not hear another's response prior to being tested.

Delayed language development is identified by the quality of responses. The teacher may wish to devise a point system for each relevant descriptor supplied by the child.

The Illinois Test of Psycholinguistic Abilities provides a detailed scoring procedure for a similar measure of verbal ability.

(9) COPYING AT NEAR AND FAR POINTS

Children may have difficulty copying from the board (far-point) but may achieve success when copying from a book (near-point). Teachers are able to assess these abilities in a small group by using the following techniques. Both performances are timed.

To test far-point copying, write 3-5 short sentences on a large chart. Place the chart in front of the group to be tested. Direct the children to copy the sentences on lined paper. Scoring involves accuracy of punctuation, capitalization, spelling, letter formation, organization on the page, and the time required to complete the task.

To test near-point copying, use short sentences as for far-point copying. Sentences are written at the top of the page and mimeographed to allow one page for each pupil.

Blank lines are provided below the sentences for the child to copy the material. Scoring is the same as for far-point copying. The teacher should compare the child's far- and near-point samples for an intra-individual measure.

Slingerland (1970) states that a seven-year-old who has received "one year of adequate instruction and practice" should be able to copy satisfactorily.

(10) READING LEVELS

A teacher should be aware of the reading material that is appropriate as to level and interest for her pupils.

The informal reading inventory is effective and available, and should be used. The directions for giving an IRI are found in most college textbooks on the teaching of reading. The material is mimeographed to allow a sheet for each child tested. Each teacher should use an inventory based on the basal series she plans to use.

Using Goodman's (1973) miscue analysis procedure, in conjunction with the IRI, enables the teacher to gain further insight into each child's reading ability.

The "cloze" technique may be used to sample silent-reading comprehension for a group of children. The "cloze" procedure is a technique whereby words are omitted at predetermined intervals; the child is expected to fill in the missing word by using the context.

To use the "cloze" procedure, the teacher selects a parallel paragraph, or page, to that used in the oral reading inventory. Omit every fifth word and draw lines of equal length to reflect each missing word. Direct the child to read this and to fill in the blanks. The exact word, when supplied, is preferable; however, synonyms may be accepted as correct.

(11) SELF-CONCEPT

To appraise the child's self-concept, a simple device may be used. Draw "faces," using a scale of five, from the "saddest" to the "happiest" face. These faces are mimeographed with a statement below each set of five faces.

Read the statements to the group or to an individual child. Direct the children each to circle the one of the five faces which demonstrates his true feelings. Statements, such as the following, are used below each row of five faces: "This is how I feel," "This is how my teacher — friends — mother — father feel(s)," and "This is how I feel about school."

This simple scale, when used judiciously, appears to be as valid as most subjective instruments for measuring the child's self-concept, his feelings concerning others, and how he believes others perceive him. The negatively responding child should be observed more closely, however, before a judgment is actually made.

(12) EYE-HAND COORDINATION AND WRITTEN LANGUAGE

The following activity measures the child's eye-hand coordination, creative writing ability, vocabulary development, handwriting skills, and a sampling of spelling ability. Interests and attitudes are suggested by both the child's picture and his story.

Ask the child to draw a picture and color it. When the picture is complete, direct him to write a story about his picture. No help is given with spelling. (The child who cannot write may dictate a story to the teacher.) Drawing and coloring efficiency, content and length of story, vocabulary used, handwriting and spelling ability serve to measure performance adequacy.

(13) FOLLOWING DIRECTIONS

To determine whether a child has the ability to comprehend and execute one or more oral directions in exact order, the following procedure is used. Test children individually.

Give directions only once. Increase the number of commands until the child can no longer carry them out in sequence. A format similar to the following may be used:

"Walk to the window." (One command)

"Go to the door. Say 'hello.'" (Two commands)

"Go to the bookcase. Get a book. Bring it to me." (Three commands)

Anderson et al. (1963) expects a five-year-old to follow a three-part command in the exact order given.

Directionality Concepts. A group of children may be tested. Use paper and pencil tasks to determine the children's ability to follow simple commands involving directionality.

Direct the children to write their names and ages and specified geometric figures. Indicate where the writing and drawing of each should be placed. *Example:* top, middle, above, below, and so forth. The children may be told: "Write your name on the left side of your paper." "Draw a triangle in the middle of the page." Only one-part commands are given and time is allowed for each child to perform after each direction.

(14) GROSS MOTOR SKILLS

O'Donnell (1969) states that "... too little is known about motor development beyond the age of infancy." He suggests that, "While some portions of an instructional program can be based upon empirical data, other portions must be based upon common sense."

Gesell (1949) expected a typical five-year-old to skip on alternate feet. Gutteridge (1939) found that 81% of the five-year-old children in his sample were proficient at jumping and 74% were proficient at throwing a ball.

These activities may be used as a rough measure of the child's gross motor development.

Ask the child to hop on each foot, skip across the room and throw and catch a ball. Five times for hopping and throwing and catching a ball should be sufficient to determine whether or not he can perform. Skipping should involve the equal use of both feet.

PROFILE OF ABILITIES

A matrix (Table I) is recommended for recording each child's performance. To quickly identify the child who may need help in an area, use two different colored pencils. A black or blue pencil is used to write "P" for "pass" and a red pencil to mark "N" for "needs help or refer." Inter- and intra-individual strengths and weaknesses are identified in this manner. Post measures are obtained by checking the same areas in the spring. Teacher accountability is inherent in this procedure.

SUMMARY

For more precise measurement of the areas covered in this paper, the following formal instruments are useful: The Detroit Tests of

TABLE I. Profile of abilities.

Grade: _____ Reading Expectancy Grade Date: _____ Name	Mary	Jim	George
Visual Discrimination			
Visual Memory			
Auditory Discrimination			
Auditory Memory			
Letter Identification			
Writing the Alphabet			
Phonetic Knowledge			
Haptic Ability			
Reversals and Rotations			
Verbal Skills (Oral)			
Copying: Far Point			
Copying: Near Point			
Reading Levels			
Self-Concept			
Eye-Hand Coordination			
Written Language			
Following Directions			
Directionality Concepts			
Gross Motor Skills			

Learning Aptitude, the Slingerland Screening Tests, the Illinois Test of Psycholinguistic Abilities, the Boehm Test of Basic Concepts, the Wepman Auditory Discrimination Test, the Wagner Reversal Test, the Gilmore Oral Reading Paragraphs and the Wide Range Achievement Test. These are only a few of the many standardized tests which are available.

The informal measures recommended here are adequate for rough assessment of particularly critical areas. Some norms from standardized tests were given but were not intended as inclusive.

In some instances, several different procedures are stated which involve the same area. Thus, the teacher will select the procedure she finds most appropriate for her pupils. Needless to say, informal diagnostic procedures do not yield age and grade scores which are provided when formal measures are used.

This paper is not to be interpreted as recommending a band-aid approach when major surgery is indicated. For many children, however, extensive formal testing is not necessary.

FOCUS   *Matrix of IEP Role Responsibililty

IEP COMPONENT / COMMITTEE MEMBER	Assessment of Present Levels of Child's Performance	Yearly Goals	Short Term Objectives for Each Yearly Goal	Recommendations for Specific Special Education Services	Statement of Planned Activities with Non-handicapped Children
School Administrator					
Special Education Administrator					
Special Education Teacher					
Parent					
Psychologist					
Guidance Counselor					
Social Worker					
Support Service Personnel (speech path., P.T., O.T., etc.)					
Medical Personnel (physicians, school nurse)					
Others					

	Evaluative Criteria for Each Goal and Objective	List of Support Services Needed to Meet Each Objective	List of Persons Responsible for Implementing Each Objective	Beginning and End Date for Each Listed Service	Placement Recommendations and Justification

*This matrix was developed by Robert Piazza and Irving Newman for use by LEAs to ascertain the perceptions of child study team members toward their responsibility for various IEP components. The information gained can be used as the basis for inservice workshops to clarify role responsibility and/or a decision model to be used by those responsible for choosing members and maintaining committee checks and balances.

USE THIS KEY TO FILL IN BOXES

1 = usually responsible
2 = sometimes responsible
3 = seldom responsible

The Diagnostic/Prescriptive Teacher: An Elementary School Mainstream Model

Robert W. Prouty and Barbara Aiello

Contemporary theory in special education emphasizes the desirability of educating all children in the "least restrictive alternative" learning environment. This growing national thrust toward minimizing and, where possible, preventing the negative categorization and segregation of children in need of differentiated learning environments and experiences derives from (1) the general failure of repeated research efforts to demonstrate the efficacy of categorical, self contained special education service programs, (2) an increasing body of legal decisions (e.g., Mills, PARC) defining regular classroom placement as the preferred educational environment, and (3) the improving capabilities of regular class settings to provide for divergent learning and behavior styles of children through diversified and individualized experiences.

While recognition is given to the continuing need for specialized environments for those children whose complexity or severity of handicaps require more individualization than may be possible within regular class settings, there is a growing awareness that large numbers of children perceived as posing learning and/or behavior problems can experience success within the regular class if appropriate modifications responsive to their needs are made.

Such changes in regular class organization, techniques, materials, attitudes, and expectations often require a relatively new role for special educators whose function now becomes that of consultant to regular classroom teachers, assisting in the assessment of needs and the design and implementation of appropriate educational responses within the regular class setting.

THE DIAGNOSTIC/PRESCRIPTIVE TEACHING MODEL

One such model for the delivery of special education services is that of the diagnostic/prescriptive teacher (DPT). The DPT is a specially trained experienced teacher who serves as a school-based, non-categorical special education consultant to classroom teachers. Working with the classroom teacher, the DPT determines the needs of children referred and develops a specific,

"The Diagnostic/Prescriptive Teacher: An Elementary School Mainstream Model," Robert W. Prouty and Barbara Aiello, *Making It Work*, Council for Exceptional Children, 1975. U.S. Government Public Grant to the Council for Exceptional Children.

practical, written education program for implementation by the classroom teacher. In this role, the DPT does not directly remediate children but rather functions to assist the referring teacher in modifying existing regular class practices to provide a more responsive learning environment for a greater diversity of learning and behavior styles in children. Thus, the DPT joins the classroom teacher in a partnership as change agents and child advocates.

The diagnostic/prescriptive teacher provides service to all teachers and any children referred. Referral is made directly to the DPT by the classroom teacher and, with the referral, the DPT begins the following ten step sequence of activities.

Referral

The referral is the first step in the diagnostic and prescriptive teaching model. On the referral form the classroom teacher writes a behavioral description of the child for whom she wishes diagnostic/prescriptive service. The DPT encourages classroom teachers to write descriptions of the specific behaviors which prompted the referral, the academic or social settings in which the behavior occurred, and any methods she has employed to alleviate the problem. The DPT receives the written referral and provides the principal with a copy.

Classroom Observation

Following the referral, the DPT begins step two, a series of classroom observations. Observations are necessary in order that the DPT can develop a preliminary view of the classroom environment and the referred child's response to it. In addition, the DPT observes to gain insight into the ways in which the child perceives himself within his learning environment and to assess the referring teacher's particular teaching strengths within her classroom setting. The DPT asks herself, "What classroom experiences appear to be especially positive ones for the referred child and his teacher?" And, "How can I begin to build upon the strengths of the regular classroom teacher's particular teaching style so that she might better facilitate the progress and the development of the child she has referred?"

Conference

Step three involves the DPT and the referring teacher in a conference. Here the referring teacher and the DPT determine an appropriate time for the child to come to the DPT's resource setting or "Activity Room." With the help of the classroom teacher the DPT also selects other children from the regular classroom who have not been referred. These children are chosen to come to the Activity Room to comprise a cooperative, working group of children which replicates the regular class structure as closely as possible. With a cross section of children—some with definite academic or behavioral difficulties, some without—the DPT has the opportunity to experience some of the same problems that the classroom teacher must face; specifically, the management of an exceptional child within a group of "normal" students. Additionally, the inclusion of "normal" children avoids labels on the Activity Room, such as "the special class" or "the place where the problem kids go. "

Diagnostic Sessions

During this conference the DPT and the classroom teacher agree on a schedule for diagnostic and prescriptive teaching sessions and determine the days and times that the group will go to the DPT's Activity Room. Diagnostic sessions, step four, generally last from two to three weeks. The DPT works with the children for approximately one hour a day in order that peer and teacher contact can be maintained for the child within his regular classroom. These sessions include planned activities and learning experiences from which the DPT makes an educational diagnosis concerning the specific learning needs of the child. Experimental or prescriptive teaching occurs during these sessions as the DPT plans new and interesting learning activities which the teacher can use in her classroom to meet the referred child's needs.

Educational Prescription

Following these diagnostic and prescriptive sessions, the child is returned to his classroom. The educational prescription, step five, is then written for the referring teacher. In the prescription the DPT describes her perceptions of the child, discusses the child's personal, social, academic, and behavioral needs, and prescribes specific methods and materials found to be successful in meeting those needs and which complement his individual learning style. The prescription also includes a plan of action that specifies the how, when, and where of the classroom teacher's implementation of the prescriptive suggestions.

A Second Conference

After the classroom teacher has read the prescription she and the DPT confer once again (step six). They discuss each prescriptive item and the DPT shows the classroom teacher each material that has been used successfully in alleviating the child's particular problem.

Classroom Demonstration

Step seven, classroom demonstration, occurs when the DPT, with the referring teacher observing, demonstrates the major components of the prescription in the classroom of the referring teacher.

Follow-Up Activities

Intensive follow-up activities, step eight, include frequent DPT observations and consultations as the referring teacher implements the education plan with the classroom on her own.

Evaluation

A thirty day evaluation (step nine) follows the consultation phase. Thirty school days following the prescription conference, the referring teacher completes a written evaluation of progress to date and, with comments by the DPT, forwards it to the principal.

Long Term Follow-Up

Long term follow-up, step ten, concludes the diagnostic and prescriptive process. The DPT continues to observe and to consult with the referring teacher until such time as both teachers agree that the child's difficulty has been overcome or that alternative services or placements are required.

For the DPT the name of the game is success and the method as well as the material is of vital importance as the DPT looks for ways to build on the strengths of both referred child and referring teacher.

The diagnostic and prescriptive program differs from many other special and mainstream programs in that its primary focus is that of educational change that is specific to the setting, rather than child specific. Change must be made in classroom structure and teacher perception, rather than changing the child to fit a preconceived mold or an arbitrary expectancy level.

The DPT initiates this change process as the child enters the activity room. When he leaves, it is his classroom teacher who capitalizes on, continues, and develops the strengths of her individual teaching style and, with the consistent help of the DPT, permits the child to grow as his own person, successfully, adequately, and positively within her classroom.

The Diagnostic and Prescriptive Teaching program is
a one year intensive educational experience which leads
to a Master of Arts in Special Education from the
George Washington University, Washington, D.C.

Comprehensive Assessment for Educational Planning

JEAN NAZZARO

□ I don't know that much about fishing, especially fishing with a net, but it seems to be an appropriate, if somewhat homely, analogy with the process of finding children who need special educational services.

In order to catch fish with a net it is necessary to use an appropriate mesh so that fish too small do not get caught. It is also necessary to have a net strong enough to withstand strain.

When a group of fishermen set out to do their work, they must consider several things. First of all, there have to be enough people to man the net, for if one part of the edge is not held, some fish will spill out. Then each person has to be able to handle his part of the job, for if one lets go, the fish will escape. Once the fish are pulled in and a decision has been made as to what to do with the catch, the fishermen turn their attention to the maintenance of their net. They examine each strand checking for weak spots which may need repair or replacement.

If one constructs an analogy between fishing and the delivery of special education services, one can see that the net is like the policies which determine who will be identified for special help and how that determination will take place. The size of the mesh can be compared to the adequacy and comprehensiveness of the screening process which identifies children who can best be served through special education programs. Since the screening process acts as a filter it is important that children referred for evaluation are not caught in an unnecessarily restrictive placement if their needs can be more appropriately met in a less restrictive setting. The quality of the net is like the eligibility identification procedures, which depend on the integrity and commitment of the professionals responsible for supplying direct services. Each fisherman, in this analogy, is represented by a different group of individuals: parents, educators, psychologists, lawyers, and legislators.

For years special educators and parents of exceptional children have been struggling with the enormous task of obtaining public education services; meanwhile, many children have escaped notice while others have been caught in a system where they do not belong. During the late 1960's and early 1970's, parents of children from racial and cultural minority groups demanded appropriate screening and placement procedures for their children. These demands were taken to the courts (*Larry P. v. Riles*, 1972; *Diana v. State Board of Education*, 1970, 1973), thereby involving legal advocates. Decisions in these cases have strongly influenced current state and federal legislation regarding the education of exceptional children.

These same groups were concerned that inappropriate screening and procedures were being used in order to place youngsters in "tracks." It was argued that this kind of programing can permanently affect the student's options for career expectations. In the case of *Hobson v. Hansen* (1967) the issues involved the "tracking system" used in the Washington, D.C. public schools. In his article, "The courts look at standardized testing," Walden, 1975, summarizes the *Hobson v. Hansen* controversy:

> The school district argued that the system based on standardized tests administered to students, was designed to provide each youngster with educational opportunity suitable to his needs and abilities. This argument was rejected by the court, which looked carefully at the operational effects of the tracking system. The court found, for example, that there was a positive correlation between tracks and socioeconomic status and race. Poor Blacks predominated in the lower tracks, while middle class white children were disproportionately represented in the higher tracks. The court concluded that this situation resulted

"Comprehensive Assessment for Educational Planning," Jean Nazzaro, *Public Policy and the Education of Exceptional Children*, Council for Exceptional Children 1976. ©1976 Council for Exceptional Children.

from tests that were culturally biased. The tests were not measuring children's ability but rather their racial and socioeconomic backgrounds. The court said, "Because these tests are standardized primarily on, and are relevant to, a white middle class group of students, they produce inaccurate and misleading test scores when given to lower class and Negro students. As a result, rather than being classified according to ability to learn, these students are in reality being classified according to their socio-economic status or—more precisely—according to environmental and psychological factors which have nothing to do with innate ability."

Perhaps even more damning to the school district's case was the closed nature of the tracking system. The court found that children were placed in tracks as early as the fourth grade and were rarely able to move from a low track to a higher one. Since the curriculum in the lower tracks was designed for youngsters who generally did not aspire to a college degree, those assigned to lower tracks had virtually no chance to acquire the background necessary to enter college. The rigid operation of the system, together with the lack of equal educational opportunity implied in the differentiated curricula, caused the court to rule that the tracking system resulted in an inferior educational system for the poor and for Blacks. Such a system, said the court, is unconstitutional and must be abolished.

One response to these lawsuits and the issues being litigated was the passage by the U.S. Congress in August, 1974, of P.L. 93-380, the Education Amendments of 1974. Part of that act requires that states requesting federal money for the education of handicapped children submit a plan to HEW's Office of Education, Bureau of Education for the Handicapped (BEH) which (a) makes a commitment to provide full educational opportunities to all handicapped children, (b) provides due process guarantees, (c) insures that placements will be made in the least restrictive alternative environment, and (d) insures the use of nondiscriminatory testing and evaluation procedures. Government agencies then, especially the Bureau of Education for the Handicapped and the Office of Civil Rights, may be compared to the fishermen in charge of maintenance, repair, and strengthening of the policy network.

· To help the states write or revise their state plans mentioned earlier the Bureau of Education for the Handicapped (BEH) drafted a set of suggested guidelines and principles which are frequently called advisories (BEH, 1974). This chapter will review those guidelines as they refer to selection and placement of children, and discuss some of the implications for continuous maintenance of a quality system of services.

Before leaving the subject, one additional part of the fishing analogy needs elaboration. Fishing with a net is an unpredictable business; there is no telling what will be pulled up. Yet, it is fairly certain that a variety of sea life will be collected; the fisherman must decide how to sort out the catch quickly and appropriately.

Screening children for special services also turns up individuals with a variety of problems. The system must be general enough to encompass all exceptionalities and flexible enough to provide an appropriate program and placement for each individual. Laws and guidelines provide the basis for the operation of the system, but each school district will face different combinations of children and thus must devise different service patterns.

Section 613(a) P.L. 93-380 requires each state to guarantee the following:

Safeguards in decisions regarding identification, evaluation, and education placement of handicapped children including but not limited to (c) procedures to insure that testing and evaluation materials and procedures utilized for the purpose of classification and placement of handicapped children will be selected and administered so as not to be socially or culturally discriminatory.

Many times, the terms used to describe procedures for examining a child to determine his/her need for special services are varied and somewhat confusing. In this chapter the terms "assessment" and "evaluation" will be used interchangeably to mean a comprehensive examination of several dimensions of a child's behavior and adjustment which may include but is not limited to testing. "Testing" refers specifically to the use of instruments, both group tests and individual tests. "Screening," which usually precedes assessment and evaluation, refers to activities performed for the initial identification of children with suspected special needs. "Placement," which follows assessment, means the assignment of a child into a program. The purpose of the assessment is to determine the specific program that is needed by the child with the expectation that the assigned placement is the setting in which the needed program can be provided. Placement assignment of a child to a special education program does not necessarily mean a physical move into another classroom; rather it is, or can be, placement in a variety of settings, or modified educational strategies.

PARENT INVOLVEMENT

Part of the BEH advisories addressing nondiscriminatory testing and placements sets forth principles concerning parental involvement and approval. It is recommended that "written parental permission should be obtained before any individual evaluation procedures are carried out on a child" and that "clear procedures regarding evaluation should be set out in each local education association (LEA) and made known to parents e.g. the kinds of tests, how long the evaluation of a child usually takes, etc."

3. ASSESSMENT AND EVALUATION

(BEH,1974, p.26).

For many years the schools assumed sole position of authority in making decisions about testing and placing children; parents were not accorded much status in the decision making process. Typically, a teacher would refer a child for testing and a school psychologist would come and test. It was not until a placement decision had been made that the parents would be consulted. School administrators generally knew which parents should be consulted and which would be too intimidated to make demands or to voice complaints. It has only been recently that LEA's are being required to treat parents as equal and knowledgeable partners in the educational decision making process. Although the BEH guidelines refer specifically to written permission for individual evaluations, some attention should also be given to informing parents when standardized group tests are to be given and how the results will be used. Parents should be given the option of refusing to permit the child to be tested if they feel that the test would inaccurately reflect the child's level of functioning. If a child is not fluent in English, for example, his performance on an English language group test would not reflect his knowledge accurately. Or, if a child has a learning disability which involves visual perception problems his ability to handle printed material may be limited. Testing children with instruments to which they cannot respond to for reasons other than their knowledge of the material is meaningless.

For both group tests and individual assessments, school districts should consider providing the following information to parents and children before a test is given:

1. A description of the test with some sample items.
2. A statement concerning the purpose of the test.
3. An explanation of how the results will be used.
4. A statement as to whether or not the results will become a part of the student's permanent record.
5. A list of the rights of parents (Abeson, Bolick, & Hass, 1975) which includes the right (a) to review all records related to referrals for evaluation (individual assessment); (b) to review the procedures and instruments to be used in the evaluation; (c) to refuse to permit the evaluation (in which case the local education agency can request a hearing to try to overrule the parent; (d) to be fully informed of the results of the evaluation; and (e) to get outside evaluation for their child from a public agency, at public expense if necessary.

Recognition of the necessity for increased parental involvement and increased sharing of information with parents was one theme of a November, 1975, meeting on standardized testing, attended by representatives from 35 education organizations. Among the major items agreed to by all participants at the meeting (sponsored by the National Association of Elementary School Principals and the North Dakota study group on evaluation) were the following:

1. Parents and teachers need to be more actively involved in the planning and processes of assessment.
2. Any results of assessment reported must include explanatory material that details the limitations inherent in these measures.
3. Standardized tests used in school should be made available to educators, parents and the public to give these groups a better opportunity to understand and review the tests in use.

INITIATION OF EVALUATION REQUESTS

In the past, only referrals originating within the system, i.e., coming from a teacher or other professional, resulted in individual evaluations. Occasionally a referral would be made upon the request of a parent, but it was not obligatory for the principal to do so. Gorham, Des Jardins, Page, Pettis, and Scheiber (1975) declared:

> Thus, the parent who seeks special services for a handicapped child may have to "take on" the public school hierarchy for the sake of his child. He faces several problems: the problem of proving the need for a look and then a second look at a child's placement. (p.170)
> A parent who feels that there is something wrong and that his child should have a diagnosis to pinpoint the problem usually must wait a long time—sometimes a year or more.(p.177)

Now the BEH advisories provide that "Parents should have the power to 'trigger' the evaluation procedure i.e., to request the LEA to conduct an evaluation on their child when they feel he/she is in need of a special education program." (BEH, 1974, p.26) Consequently, states are now being advised to expand their delivery systems to serve children who are referred by their parents. Once parents know they can obtain this service, there may be a surge of referrals resulting in increased staffloads and/or the purchase of outside evaluations. On the other hand, no one is more sensitive to a child's development than his parents, for they after all, are the ones who are ultimately responsible for monitoring their child's progress. They are the only people who, without interruption, observe the developing child.

INVOLVEMENT IN PLACEMENT DECISIONS

Besides the option of granting or refusing permission prior to testing and an explanation of procedures, parents should be assured of a full report of results and given notice of any proposed change in placement. The BEH guidelines provide the following suggestions:

> Parent should be given a full report of the results of the evaluation. Prior notice must be given to parents whenever decisions are to be made which will affect the educational status of their child—including decisions based on both the initial evaluation and all subsequent reviews; and permission must be obtained from the parents before such decisions are implemented (BEH,1974,p.26)

Suggested procedures on such a report are quite specific in *A Primer on Due Process* (Abeson, Bolick, & Hass, 1975). "Within 15 days after completion of the evaluation, the parent shall be given, in writing in the primary language of the home and in English, and orally in the primary language of the home, the results of the evaluation, the educational implications, and a written individualized educational plan." Such a written report also allows the parents to keep records. In the past parents were usually not given written reports with the results of an evaluation. One parent writes, "What happens to the reports? They are collected in manila folders that follow the child from clinic to clinic and school to school. This would be fine if one master folder containing copies of all the information were in the hands of the parents."(Gorham,1975). In today's mobile society, it is good sense to allow parents to carry the child's records to new locations, for it sometimes takes weeks and even months for children's records to catch up to them.

Where the BEH advisories stipulate "that prior notice must be given . . .," they refer to a written announcement to the parents that the evaluation placement committee is going to review the educational status of the child. The BEH guidelines define "notice" as "written statements in English and in the primary language of the parents' home, and oral communications in the primary language of the home" (BEH,1974,p.7). It should be noted that this directive does not say anything about the parent being invited to the committee meeting. In reviewing the situation in California, which was among the first states to use the placement team concept for educable mentally retarded (EMR) and educationally handicapped (EH) children, the following condition was reported (Kirp, Kuriloff, and Buss, 1975).

> Special educators, while expressing their willingness to meet with a parent or representative at the admissions committee meeting, fear that the presence of an outsider might force bargaining further underground. The committee's handling of children, one program supervisor remarked, is "just too impersonal for the average person to understand . . .It would appear cruel." The presence of such an outsider might also pose a threat to the committee's usual style of operation and, more basically, to the credibility of its decisions. (p.374)

> Sometimes—to save time—permission for placement is obtained during the same visit as permission for testing, even though the school does not know into what special program (if any) the student should be placed.(p.372)

> The permission-before-decision approach gives the committee a blank check to place a student wherever it wishes, and negates any significant parental role. (p.375)

If parents are dissatisfied with the recommendations of the committee they are entitled to a due process hearing. Parents should be apprised of this recourse at the time they are notified that a placement decision is scheduled.

MUTIFACTORED ASSESSMENT

Awareness of the need for comprehensive assessment was triggered by the court cases of the early 1970's which dealt in part with the placement of minority children in EMR classes on the basis of single IQ scores. (*Larry P. v. Riles*, 1972; *Diana v. State Board of Education*, 1970). In 1971 the California legislature pioneered changes in assessment practices when they amended the education code to provide a legal framework for pluralistic assessment:

> No minor may be placed in a special education program for the mentally retarded unless a complete psychological examination by a credentialed school psychologist investigating such factors as developmental history, cultural background, and school achievement substantiates the retarded intellectual development indicated by the individual test scores. This examination shall include estimates of adaptive behavior . . .Such adaptability testing shall include but is not limited to a visit, with the consent of the parent or guardian, to the minor's home by the school psychologist or a person designated by the chief administrator of the district.(California Education Code; Sec.6102.08)

Although the initial reaction was in response to the use of tests judged to be inappropriate for certain minority group children, the need for comprehensive assessment has been generalized to all children.

The BEH guidelines request that assessment be viewed from two reference points, the school and the home. They stress the need for a multifactor and multisource assessment. This means that many kinds of behavior should be examined using a variety of techniques such as observations, interviews, and classroom performance as well as more formal tests. Specifically, the advisories provide that "an assessment should be made on the child's educational functioning in relation to the academic program of the school; and the results of this assessment should be expressed in terms of both the

3. ASSESSMENT AND EVALUATION

child's strengths and weaknesses. The assessment should be comprehensive, using a full range of available instrumentation and observations, including diagnostic tests and other appropriate formal and informal measurements" (BEH,1974,p.27).

Concern about the use of standardized tests for assessing the general school population was evidenced in 1972 when more than 8,000 delegates of the National Education Association (NEA) passed several resolutions calling for a total testing moratorium (Bosma, 1973). The key policy statement was submitted by the Michigan delegation: "The National Education Association strongly encourages the elimination of group standardized intelligence, aptitude, and achievement tests to assess student potential or achievement until completion of a critical appraisal, review, and revision of current testing programs."

Following that convention, a task force on testing was formed and a final report was presented to the 54th representative assembly of NEA in July 1975. Of note is the statement that "both the content and the use of the typical group intelligence test are biased against those who are economically disadvantaged and culturally and linguistically different. In fact, group intelligence tests are potentially harmful to all students," (NEA, 1975). "Whenever intelligence tests are adminstered, steps should be taken to assure that the IQ score, per se, will not be used in making inferences about the child's level of intelligence or learning potential; instead the full test (including protocols, content, subtests, etc.) should be interpreted by the qualified examiner who administered the test." (BEH,1974,p.28). The BEH advisories direct that "any 'classification' of students for educational purposes should consist of a description of the types of educational programs and services needed by each child to learn to the fullest extent possible in the school setting, rather than categorizing the child by some diagnostic label which is unrelated to educational programing" (BEH,1974,p.28). While norm referenced achievement tests are frequently used in the assessment process, their mode of construction may fail to reflect the academic program of the school. In constructing an instrument to measure learning as an outcome of instruction, test items should be selected which most students fail before instruction but pass after instruction.

It is Popham's opinion (1975) that in norm referenced achievement tests these very items are eliminated because they do not produce variance, and variance is an absolute requisite for comparing individuals. Items answered correctly by 50% of the examinees maximize a test's response variance. But items which are answered correctly by a larger proportion of examinees have to be modified or eliminated since they do not contribute sufficiently to the production of response variance. In general,

the items on which most students perform well reflect the concepts which teachers believe to be important and on which they have spent the most time teaching. But, on oft revised achievement tests, items measuring important concepts are systematically excised from the tests. What you have therefore, over time, is an achievement test which functions exactly like an intelligence test because it has been the untaught information that has been retained while the things actually taught in school have been eliminated.

On the other hand, by using criterion referenced tests which measure the child's knowledge against a set criterion, one gets a much clearer picture of what the child knows and what he has yet to learn. Criterion referenced assessment leads naturally to an educational plan that addresses the gaps in the child's knowledge base. Thus the results of the assessment can be expressed in terms of both the child's strengths and weaknesses.

Measures of Psychomotor and Sensory Development

A second aspect of school related assessment reflects psychomotor and sensory development. BEH's advisories specify that "an assessment also should be made of the child's psychomotor and sensory development, through the use of developmental scales (e.g., the Denver Developmental Scale, informal checklists, etc.), and audiological ophthalmological or optometric examinations" (BEH,1974,p.28).

The language of this advisory subtly focuses on possible problem areas rather than on strengths. Although it is essential to discover a child's limitations, it is also valuable to know a child's personal learning style. The emphasis in assessment should be on a child's strengths rather than on his weaknesses. Traditionally responsibility for learning has been placed on the child, but few choices or alternatives regarding ways to learn new things have been provided for him. (Aiello, 1975) People learn through their visual, auditory, and tactile senses. Some learn better by listening while others prefer reading, and most people prefer to manipulate materials physically while they are learning about them. Informal diagnostic techniques can be used by the teacher to determine how a child learns best. Consideration of such a learning style in developing his individual educational plan should greatly strengthen the total program.

Measures of Adaptive Behavior

The final area of assessment is adaptive behavior as reflected in both school and community settings. The advisories provide that

An assessment also should be made of the child's adaptive behavior in the school setting based on observations and records, and, where appropriate, the use of adaptive behavior scales. Information from the home should include (1) the child's adaptive behavior in the home, community and neighborhood, as perceived by his parents or guardians or principal caretakers, (2) the sociocultural background of the family, and (3) the child's health and developmental history. (BEH,1974,p.28)

California studies to determine the racial and ethnic composition of classes for the mentally retarded, showed that previous assessments clearly lacked measures of adaptability. Mercer (1975) reported:

Although official definitions of mental retardation require "that an individual manifest deficiencies in both adaptive behavior and intellectual functioning," . . .we found that most community agencies, especially the public schools, were relying mainly on measures of 'intelligence' in 'diagnosing' mental retardation. Ninety-nine percent of the labeled retardates nominated by the public schools had been given an intelligence test, but only 13 percent had received a medical diagnosis. The only measure of 'adaptability' was implicit. If a child's behavior violated the norms of the teacher and he was referred for psychological evaluation, he was judged to be maladapted. . . .No community agency systematically assessed the child's ability to perform complex nonacademic tasks in his home, neighborhood, and community. Assessment procedures were unidimensional. They focused only on the narrow band of behavior sampled in the psychometric situation. . . .(p. 143)

Traditional assessment procedures evaluate whether the child is meeting the expectations of one social system—the school. If he is referred by his teacher for psychological assessment, we know that he has somehow been identified as a "problem" and is not meeting educational norms. Standardized achievement tests and intelligence tests are formal assessments of competence in terms of the norms of the school. There is a high correlation among all these assessment procedures because they all represent the expectations of a single social system which is the culture bearer of the dominant society. To secure a multidimensional view of the child, we need an assessment in terms of the norms of social systems other than those represented by the clinician, psychologist, teacher, and school.

In assessing a child's adaptive behavior, we wish to secure information about his social role performance in the family, neighborhood, and community as perceived by significant others in those social systems . . . The construct of adaptive behavior includes both the development of skill in interpersonal relations and the emerging ability to play ever more complex roles in an expanding range of social systems. The sociological concept of the social role is the unifying focus. (p. 154)

Culturally and Linguistically Appropriate Assessment

Another aspect of assessment addresses adaptive procedures for children with linguistic or cultural differences. This is probably the most critical area of nondiscriminatory testing as it is implicitly stated in P.L. 93-380. The BEH guidelines recommend:

A procedure also should be included in terms of a move toward the development of diagnostic-prescriptive techniques to be utilized when for reasons of language differences or deficiencies, non-adaptive behavior, or extreme cultural differences a child cannot be evaluated by the instrumentation of tests. Such procedures should insure that no assessment will be attempted when a child is unable to respond to the tasks or behavior required by a test because of linguistic or cultural differences unless culturally and linguistically appropriate measures are administered by qualified persons. In those cases in which appropriate measures and/or qualified persons are not available, diagnostic-prescriptive educational programs should be used until the child has acquired sufficient familiarity with the language and culture of the school for more formal assessment. These evaluation procedures should also assure that persons interpreting assessment information and making educational decisions are qualified to administer the various measures and qualified to take cultural differences into account in interpreting the meaning of multiple sets of data from both the home and the school. (BEH,1974,p. 29)

The first step that should be taken in testing children who may have problems coping with assessment instruments is to sensitize the examiner and those who will be using the test results to the potential biases inherent in the protocols. Examiners and teachers who have themselves taken sample tests developed to demonstrate biases have a much better idea of what the child faces.(Nazzaro, 1975)

There has been some hope that culture free, or culture fair tests would be the answer to assessment problems, but little success is discernible in developing such instruments. According to Henry C. Dyer of Educational Testing Services, "There are only two conditions under which a test can be culture fair: (1) either the learning required to perform acceptably on the test is commonly and equally available to all people of all cultures, or (2) the stimulus material on the test is completely novel to all people of all cultures. Neither of these conditions is obtainable." (Purvin, 1975)

Podilla and Garza (1975) note that "efforts to develop culture-free tests were doomed to failure from the beginning. All human experience is modulated by human society, and no test can be experience free. The materials used in the test, the language of the test, the manner of getting the testee to respond, the criteria for

3. ASSESSMENT AND EVALUATION

choosing which responses to record, the categories into which responses are classified, the test's validity criterion—all are culture bound." Translated tests are also rife with problems because of the number of dialects, the scarcity of normative data, and the lack of experienced examiners.

The most valuable phrase in the BEH directive regarding adaptive procedures for children with linguistic or cultural differences is "In those cases in which appropriate measures and/or qualified persons are not available, diagnostic-prescriptive educational programs should be used . . ." Implementation of this directive will result in less use and dependence upon the IQ number and perhaps a diminishing of the self fulfilling prophecy phenomenon, that a child was expected to achieve only to the degree that was suggested by the IQ number.

Reasonable Evaluation Procedures and Instruments

Although no specific tests are recommended by the BEH guidelines, there is a statement concerning the selection of evaluation materials that meet the test of reasonableness.

> The various evaluation materials and procedures used for purposes of classification and placement of handicapped children should meet a test of reasonableness in the eyes of competent professional persons and informed laymen; and such procedures should be administered by qualified persons under conditions which are conducive to the best performance of the child. (BEH,1974,p. 26)

Meeting a test of reasonableness is open to broad interpretation, but surely one dimension of reasonableness would be to insure that the assessment procedures used are appropriate for the individual child. If a child is unable to respond correctly to a test item because of circumstances unrelated to the test, then the test is unreasonable or unfair. There are three types of problems a child may have: problems of reception or perception, problems of expression, and problems of conceptualization.

Blind children, deaf children, some learning disabled children, and children who do not understand English would be examples of youngsters with receptive or perceptive problems. Children who have physical limitations such as cerebral palsy, those who have speech problems and youngsters who speak a language other than English as a primary language, or who speak a dialect, have expressive problems. Finally, there are those children who cannot conceptualize or process the questions being asked because of some central nervous system dysfunction or because of a different conceptual, cultural, or racial frame of reference. (Nazza-

ro, 1975)

Most psychologists who do assessment in the schools do not have a broad knowledge of alternative instruments specifically designed for children with special needs. One can look at a "psychological" almost anywhere in the country and find the results of a WISC or Binet, a Wide Range Achievement Test, a Bender Gestalt, and perhaps some type of psycholinguistic test. The narrative will probably state that the results of certain subtests or items are not valid because of the child's specific handicap, but the scores are nonetheless recorded. In the case of group tests, children with hearing handicaps are unable to receive the instructions, children with visual perceptual handicaps are unable to read the test material, children with different conceptual frames of reference (which may include gifted children) do not always select the "best" multiple choice answers. One way to meet the test of reasonableness, then, is to make sure that professional persons, informed laymen, and qualified examiners are thoroughly acquainted with potential mismatches between particular assessment instruments and an individual's limitations.

Development of an Individual Educational Plan

One of the most revealing exercises in which a school psychologist can engage is to present a teacher with a cumulative record and pre-1975 psychological evaluation of a child and ask that teacher to develop educational plans from the information. Generally, it can't be done; perhaps, it can't be approached. The kind of information collected through testing has generally been of little use in terms of helping a teacher plan a program. The BEH guidelines address this problem and focus on the intent of evaluation: "The intent or effect of the evaluation should be the development of an educational plan for the child, based on a description of his/her strengths and weaknesses. Whenever possible, parents should participate in the development of the educational plan for the child" (BEH,1974,p. 27).

This advisory is no longer simply a recommendation. The long debated Senate Bill 6, now P.L. 94-142 requires each local educational agency in the state to maintain an individualized written education program for each handicapped child, review it at least annually, and revise its provisions when appropriate with the agreement of the parents or guardian of the handicapped child.

P.L. 94-142 defines "individualized education program" as follows:

> A written statement for each handicapped child developed in any meeting by a representative of

the local educational agency or an intermediate educational unit who shall be qualified to provide, or supervise the provision of, specially designed instruction to meet the unique needs of handicapped children, the teacher, the parents or guardian of such child, and, whenever appropriate, such child, which statement shall include (A) a statement of the present levels of educational performance of such child, (B) a statement of annual goals, including short-term instructional objectives, (C) a statement of the specific educational services to be provided to such child, and the extent to which such child will be able to participate in regular educational programs, (D) the projected date for initiation and anticipated duration of such services, and (E) appropriate objective criteria and evaluation procedures and schedules for determining, on at least an annual basis, whether instructional objectives are being achieved.

When an evaluation is undertaken with the intention of developing an educational plan, the approach to the total assessment process changes from one of identification to one of determination of what the child knows and does. This can provide a baseline from which to project what the child should be able to do and how long it will take to learn how to do it. The CORE Evaluation Manual developed by the Department of Education in Massachusetts presents some useful guidelines. (Audette, 1974) No one should be asked to describe what the student does not do or cannot do; such descriptions are of limited usefulness. The entire emphasis of this process should be positive—what the student does. Such information can be derived from information about performance observed under special conditions and further tested by team members. Constraints imposed upon the student's performance should be derived from information provided by a physician. Based on this information, objectives which are very specific and readily observable can be prepared in detail for the student.

The heart of the educational plan is the specification of objectives which will result in the provision of a quality education for that student. Three criteria must be met in outlining these objectives:

1. They must be developmentally rational: that is, if the student is using two word sentences, the objective should indicate that the student will be using three, four, and five word sentences. The long term goal will be that the student will use compound/complex sentences, but the most immediate objective should indicate gradual increments toward that ultimate goal.
2. They must be sensitive to parental priorities. If the student is demonstrating acting out behaviors, such as hitting people or destroying property, objectives should be set to eliminate this behavior so that the student can function in an increased number of envi-

ronments, thereby increasing the student's options.
3. Most important, all objectives must relate to the student's movement toward a less restrictive setting. Therefore, if a student is in a substantially separate program, objectives should be established so that, when met, the student is placed in more normal education programs for at least part of the day.

There is no doubt that some kind of assessment is necessary and desirable in order to let the child, the teacher, the parents, and others involved in the educational process know whether or not there has been a change in the desired direction as a result of instruction. The most promising kinds of assessment for this purpose may well be a combination of criterion referenced tests to find a beginning point, and then continuous measurement techniques to determine how learning is progressing.

All evaluation procedures have potential biases and any "one shot" sample of behavior, whether it be a test, an observation, or any other technique, tells little about a person's ability to learn. Only by sampling over time can one gain a fairly accurate picture of a child's potential.

REFERENCES

Abeson, A. Legal forces and pressures. In Jones, R. (Ed.) Mainstreaming and the minority child. Minneapolis: Leadership Training Institute for Special Education, 1976 (in press).

Abeson, A., & Bolick, N. A continuing summary of pending and completed litigation regarding the education of handicapped children, No. 8. Reston VA: The Council for Exceptional Children, 1974.

Abeson, A., Bolick, N., & Hass, J. A primer on due process. Reston VA: The Council for Exceptional Children, 1975.

Aiello, B. Mainstreaming: Teacher training workshops. Reston VA: The Council for Exceptional Children, 1975.

Audett, R. H. CORE Evaluation Manual. Bedford MA: Institute for Educational Services, Inc., 1974.

Bosma, B. The NEA testing moratorium. Journal of School Psychology, 1973,11 (4), 304-306.

Bureau of Education for the Handicapped, U. S. Department of Health, Education, and Welfare, Office of Education. State plan amendment for fiscal year 1975 under part B, Education of the Handicapped Act, as amended by Section 614 of P.L. 93-380: Basic content areas required by the act and suggested guidelines and principles for inclusion under each area. Washington DC: Author, 1974 (draft).

California State Legislature, Senate Bill 33. Approved by governor, May 18, 1971.

Diana v. State Board of Education. Civil Action No. C-70 37RFP (N.D. Cal. Jan 7, 1970 and June 18, 1973).

Gorham, K. A. A lost generation of parents. Exceptional Children, 1975, 41,521.

Gorham, K. A., Des Jardins, C., Page, R., Pettis, E., & Scheiber, B. Effect on parents. In N. Hobbs (Ed.), Issues in the classification of children (Vol.2).San Francisco: Jossey-Bass, 1975.

The Assessment of Children with Developmental Problems

MARK N. OZER

MARK N. OZER *is Associate Professor Child Health and Development, George Washington School of Medicine, Washington, D.C.*

Assessment of the child with learning or behavioral difficulties is considered an ongoing effort involving collaboration between the parents and teacher. Recent federal legislation has mandated parental involvement in planning (Public Law 74–103). The specified planning procedure described here has been designed as a vehicle for such collaborative planning. The goal of this planning system is not only a series of operational plans. The questions asked in this format emphasize the development of a more problem solving approach. Focus is not only on the concerns of any particular time but on what the child is now able to do successfully in the area of concern and more importantly on how such successes were brought about. The goal is, rather, the development of increasing awareness of what has worked and increasing collaboration of those involved in the various components of the planning procedures. The writing of plans to deal with changing concerns is merely the context for such to go on.

It is important to recognize that the asking of questions has an impact on those being asked. How can the questions asked lead toward a greater sense of problem solving and the sharing of ideas? How can such ideas be considered as part of the personal experience of those involved and therefore compatible with future commitments?

Collaborative Planning

The procedures to be described have been carried out by special education teachers of all the various categories of handicapping conditions. Formats have also been designed for the involvement of the child as well as the adults (Ozer, 1975). A consultant provides initial training for the teacher in the planning process. The professional background of the consultant and the time spent in the training of the teacher would vary with the resources available. Such training generally goes on in relation to the teacher's use of these procedures in practice with children and their parents.

Each step in the planning process is represented by the questions on a printed planning form with copies available for each participant. The training consultant initially meets with the teacher and parents separately prior to their joint meeting. Each is asked in the first question to explore their concerns at the present time prior to selection of a specific one. In the context of the selected area of concern, the second question asks what had gone on successfully in the recent past before again selecting one such successful situation that particularly stands out. At least three instances are sought during the exploration step. In the context of those successes, the third question asks for an exploration of what worked. The fourth question asks for an exploration of possible goals. The process has

"The Assessment of Children with Developmental Problems," Mark N. Ozer, *Exceptional Children*, Vol. 44, No. 1, September 1977. © 1977 Council for Exceptional Children.

been to start in the present and consider the recent past before proceeding to the future. The child has been considered in terms of opportunities rather than problems. Each has had an opportunity to think through possible goals and means by which they might be accomplished before the joint meeting in which a specific plan is written.

Goals

The stated goal of this planning process is to establish a basis of commonality between the parent and teacher. Each step has sought at least three examples in the process of exploration. The more options generated, the more likely that some may be in common. Commonalities frequently exist but are stated in terms of varying experience. For example, the teacher is concerned about number facts, the mother about the child's ability to get the correct change at the store. The consultant helps the two recognize their mutual interests. Collaboration is also enhanced by the fact that both are prepared to share what the child has accomplished successfully. A common ground is based upon what both like about the child even in the area in which there has been greatest concern.

Another goal of increasing awareness of the individual's own competence is also supported by the requirement of at least three successful instances. The recital of something three times seems to be confirmatory of its validity. Furthermore, the situation in which the ideas are to be generated is one within the recent memory of the person. Attempts are made for that memory to be as vivid as possible in terms of details. The feeling tone of that situation is evoked as well as the ideas generated. For example, the mother recalls

that the child stayed in the yard yesterday after school as an instance when he listened to her. What worked was asking him to repeat what he was to do, showing him the boundaries of the yard, and promising him an ice cream cone. It is not suggested that these ideas are unusual. It is their simplicity and relation to the person's own experience that would make them compatible with future use. It is the reception of these ideas by the teacher as the mother is helped to verbalize them that increases awareness.

At future meetings, the plan that had been made will be reviewed in terms of what had been accomplished and what worked. The number of ideas to be shared might increase as well as the clarity with which they are stated. The degree of agreement would increase between the participants. The specific objectives of any such collaborative planning system would vary with the types of participants and the degree of training support available.

Conclusion

The goal of this planning process has been to enlist the ideas of both the parent and teacher toward the solution of problems. The past has been evoked not as a source of blame but as a context for planning for the future. A genuine social situation is developed in which each person can pursue his or her own goals while sharing in the concerns of the other.

Reference

Ozer, M. N. Introduction to the collaborative service system. Washington DC: Program for Learning Studies, 1975.

Placement and Services in the Least Restrictive Educational Environment

With the advent of the Massachusetts State Law and P.L. 94-142, providing services in the least restrictive environment and all it includes has become an issue for everyone in education – administrators, regular education teachers, special education teachers, parents, support personnel and unions alike. The term least restrictive environment most simply means that handicapped students should be served in the "most normal education program possible." Although P.L. 94-142 does not specifically define this term some state statutes have an adequate description. The Tenessee State Statute, which was formulated prior to P.L. 94-142 in 1972 states:

> To the maximum extend practicable handicapped children shall be educated along with children who do not have handicaps and attend regular classes. Impediments to learning and to normal functioning of handicapped children in the regular school environment shall be overcome by the provision of special aids and services rather than special schooling for the handicapped. Special classes, separate schooling, or other removal of handicapped children from the regular school environment shall occur only when and to the extent that education in the regular classroom, even with the use of supplemental aids and services, cannot be accomplished satisfactorily.

The concept of least restrictive environment is based on the existence of a continuum of placements for handicapped children. Thus, each child should be considered individually and be placed along the continuum on the basis of his/her needs. To be effective the continuum must be flexible, taking into account that the child's needs change over time. Some of the steps along this continuum from least restrictive to most restrictive are the following:

1) Regular class placement with consultation from special education personnel to the regular class teacher.
2) Regular class placement plus itinerant services by a special educator two or three times a week.
3) Regular class placement with daily remedial instruction in a resource room by special education teachers.
4) A cooperative plan in which a student is enrolled in a special education class but attends a regular classroom for part of the day.
5) Special class placement under which a student is assigned to the special class and receives instruction from the special education teacher, but may attend specific non-academic subjects such as art, music, physical education, industrial arts or home economics with his peers.
6) Special class placement in a regular school with no possiblities for integration with normal children.
7) A special day school where children need comprehensive special education services for the entire school day, but can return home at the end of the day.
8) Students with chronic illnesses or other handicaps that require long-term treatment in a hospital or home may receive homebound tutoring from a special education teacher.
9) Residential or boarding schools and institutions which provide for the educational needs of the children as well as what is needed for a twenty-four hour service by children who are severely and/or profoundly handicapped.

The following selections discuss the least restrictive environment with specific emphasis on mainstreaming handicapped children into regular classrooms. Suggestions for improved programs and related services are made.

ESSENTIALS OF SPECIAL EDUCATION FOR REGULAR EDUCATORS

Colleen S. Blankenship

and

M. Stephen Lilly

The mainstreaming movement has resulted in the need to re-evaluate and restructure special education teacher education programs. The former practice of training special education graduates to assume the role of teachers in self-contained special classrooms for the "mildy handicapped" is outmoded. The practice of integrating "mildy handicapped" students into regular education programs, and the emphasis upon non-categorical teacher training, demands a very different sort of teacher preparation program.

In the last ten years, an increasing number of special educators have spoken of a cooperative relationship between special and regular education, with regular educators assuming a greater responsibility for the education of students with learning and behavior problems, assisted by special educators who can function in a supportive and consultive role (Lilly, 1975; McKenzie, Egner, Perelman, Schneider, & Garvin, 1970; Reynolds, 1975). The need to prepare both regular and special educators to assume these new roles is of paramount importance if mainstreaming is to result in quality educational experiences for children.

The focus of this article will be on the preparation of regular educators to teach children with mild learning and behavior problems. The issues to be addressed include: the present level of training offered regular educators, the need to provide regular educators with pre- and inservice training in special education, and considerations in planning preservice programs. A preservice program for undergraduate education majors will be presented, and delivery systems for providing inservice training to regular educators will be discussed. Finally, conclusions will be drawn concerning pre- and inservice training for regular educators.

Present Level of Training

One of the first concerns expressed by many special educators relative to mainstreaming is, "Are regular classroom teachers equal to the task of educating the mildly handicapped?" (Brooks & Bransford, 1971, p. 259). The consensus has been that few regular educators have received training which would

"Essentials of Special Education for Regular Educators," Colleen S. Blankenship and M. Stephen Lilly, *Teacher Education and Special Education*, Vol. 1, No. 1, Fall 1977. © 1977 Journal of the Teacher Education Division, Council for Exceptional Children.

equip them to teach children with mild learning and behavior problems (Brooks & Bransford, Gearheart & Weishahn, 1976). It can be expected that, at most, regular educators may have listened to one introductory lecture on exceptional children.

The certification requirements for teachers and other educational personnel are only now beginning to include coursework in special education. At this time, only five states require regular classroom teachers to take even one course in special education. While this is a step in the right direction, there is a danger that this practice may delude us into thinking that one course will somehow be sufficient. The question is not one of the number of courses which should be required, but rather one of content of the courses to be offered. Of the states passing new certification requirements, only the legislation from Missouri specifies that the course should include information on teaching techniques. None of the remaining four states requiring a course in special education has set any restrictions on the type of course to be taken. In those states, a teacher could satisfy the certification requirement by enrolling in a single survey course on exceptional children. While we might expect teachers enrolling in such a course to increase their knowledge of handicapping conditions, it is unrealistic to expect that a survey course would contain the more practical and skill-oriented information which would be of assistance to teachers in regular classrooms.

It is safe to assume that the present level of training afforded regular educators is not equal to the demands which will be placed upon them in instructing children with mild learning and behavior problems. It is incumbent upon special education teacher education institutions to work cooperatively with general educators to assure that all regular teachers will receive sufficient training in teaching children with mild learning and behavior problems.

Need for Preservice and Inservice Training

In the past ten years an increasing number of "mildy handicapped" students have been returned or allowed to remain in the mainstream of education. The continued emphasis which will be placed upon special education in the regular classroom is evident in the passage of PL 94-142, which requires placement of children in the least restrictive environment. For the majority of children with mild learning and behavior problems, the least restrictive environment will be a regular classroom.

The need to provide preservice and inservice education to regular classroom teachers has a wide base of support. The training of regular educators has been identified as an area of concern by the Bureau of Education for the Handicapped. BEH funding, which was nonexistent in 1974-1975, has increased to over 3 million dollars for preservice education of regular educators. Similarily, funding for inservice training over the last three years has increased from 1 1/2 million to over 4 million dollars (Comptroller General, 1976).

Numerous special educators have voiced support for training regular educators, as have state, local, and university special education administrators (Comptroller General, 1976). As Gearheart & Weishahn (1976) aptly pointed out, "The question is no longer one of 'should all teachers learn how to deal with handicapped children?' but rather, 'what should they learn?' " (p. vi).

Planning Preservice Programs

There are a few difficulties which must be overcome if we are to provide regular educators with preservice training in special education. First among them is the characteristic separation which exists among departments within colleges of education. In recent years, some special educators have come to realize that they share common interests with their colleagues in curriculum and instruction, particularly in the areas of remedial reading and arithmetic.

Several benefits could be derived from a closer association between regular and special education teacher educators at the college level, among them the opportunity to engage in cooperative research. One area which needs to be explored concerns the applicability of applied behavior analysis techniques in regular classroom settings. As Lovitt (1975) pointed out, logistics research concerning the application of measurement techniques to children in regular classrooms has been a neglected area of study. The results of research in this area could be of assistance in selecting and modifying the measurement skills to be included in preservice courses for regular educators.

It will take more than common interests, however, to get departments to work together. The impetus for change would most likely arise within departments of special education. What is needed is an organizational structure which encourages discussion and development of cooperative teacher education programs.

A second difficulty which may hamper the development of preservice programs concerns the manner in which training in special education can be incorporated into on-going teacher preparation programs. There are at least two solutions to this problem. The first would be to make the completion of a course(s) in special education a college requirement for regular educators. This approach has a number of pitfalls. First, it suggests little control over the training to be offered. Unless the course(s) are specified, students would be free to choose from among special education courses, some of which may be knowledge-based rather than skill-oriented. Second, if regular educators enroll in methods courses designed to prepare resource teachers, the course may not focus on the skills which are directly relevant to the regular classroom situation. Third, the requirement of a single course denies departments of special education the opportunity to systematically develop model training programs for regular educators.

A second option would be to offer a minor, or an area of concentration, in special education to regular educators; a minor which does not result in special education certification. This approach has much to recommend it. First, it implies a cooperative effort between different departments within a college of education. Second, it does not entail adding additional coursework to the regular education teacher preparation program. Third, it allows a greater degree of direction on the part of special educators over the training to be provided. Fourth, it encourages the development of courses which are specifically designed for regular educators and tailored to the demands of the regular classroom.

If training in special education is offered on an elective basis, then it stands to reason that some regular educators will receive appropriate training while others will not. There seems to be a trade off between the need to train all regular educators and offering comprehensive programs to a limited number of persons. In the initial stages of developing training experiences for regular educators, we would be wise to err on the side of quality training for a few, rather than mediocre training for the masses.

The second option for providing preservice training to regular educators was seen as the most attractive possibility by the Department of Special Education at the University of Illinois. Planning was begun in 1975 by the Department of Special Education in cooperation with the Department of Elementary and Early Childhood Education to develop an undergraduate program to provide future classroom teachers with the necessary skills to deal with children with mild learning and behavior problems in the regular classroom. The decision to offer preservice training to regular educators, the decreased demand for teachers in self-contained classrooms for the "mildy handicapped", and the increased demand for resource teachers, led to a restructuring of programs offered by the Department of Special Education.

At the time planning was initiated to develop the undergraduate area of concentration in special education, a decision was made to discontinue admittance to the undergraduate EMH program. At the present time, two on-going programs dealing with the education of children with mild learning and behavior problems are offered through the Department of Special Education. One is the Resource/Consulting Teacher program, a master's level program preparing experienced teachers to assume special education resource teaching positions; and the other is the Specialized Instruction (SI) program for undergraduate elementary and early childhood education majors. The SI program is described in the following section.

Specialized Instruction Program

The intent of the SI program at the University of Illinois is to provide regular educators with the necessary skills to deal with children with mild learning and behavior problems in the regular classroom. Program development was based on the following assumptions: graduates are expected to seek regular teaching positions in grades K-9 and it is anticipated that supportive help from a special educator, analagous to a Resource/Consulting Teacher, will be available.

Several parameters served to define the nature of the program. First, the emphasis was to be on a functional approach to behavior problems. Second, a list of hypothesized job skills were to form the basis for establishing performance objectives to be attained by students in the SI program. Third, practicum experience was to be provided to allow for the application of learned skills in a regular classroom setting.

Due to the desire to provide an intensive and well supervised practicum experience, enrollment was limited to approximately 20 undergraduate education majors. The students were selected on the following basis: sophomore standing, cummulative GPA of 3.5 (5 point scale), elementary or early childhood education major, and expressed interest in the SI program. Although enthusiasm was not included among the selection criteria, it has proved to be an unexpected bonus.

Students in the SI program begin their coursework in special education during Spring Semester of their sophomore year. The first course deals with trends and issues in special education. During the students' junior year, they enroll in one special education course per semester; the first focusing on assessment and remediation of social behaviors and the second dealing with assessment and remediation of academic behaviors. The practicum experience, which occurs during the senior year, is arranged so that half of the students enroll during the Fall Semester and the other half during the Spring Semester.

The SI program was conceptualized around the role that a regular classroom teacher would assume in education children with mild learning and behavior problems. Essentially, the role requires the teacher to act as a team member, a student and program advocate, an instructional planner and implementer, and a behavioral manager. Mastery of a set of skills is implied in each of the aforementioned functions ascribed to a classroom teacher. Each of these functions will now be addressed accompanied by a description of the major skills to be mastered.

Team member. The intent of the SI program is to prepare regular educators to assume a major responsibility in educating children with mild learning and behavior problems. It is not anticipated that they will be able to function as program planners and implementers without the supportive help of special educators, nor is it intended that they should. Rather, it is expected that regular educators will function as team members in planning and implementing educational programs for exceptional children.

The emphasis on involving regular educators in program planning is evident in the federal regulations for PL 94-142, which require the presence of a child's regular or special teacher, or both, at the placement and planning conference. It stands to reason that due to the number of students with learning and behavior problems who will be placed in regular classrooms, a significant number of regular educators will be involved in jointly planning and carrying out individualized education programs. Therefore, regular classroom teachers need to acquire those skills which will allow them to function as members of an educational team.

Some of the skills which are stressed in the SI program include: 1) identifying needed supportive services and making appropriate referrals, 2) participating in placement and planning conferences, 3) working cooperatively with other team members, and 4) communicating progress to a child's parents and to other team members. Students in the SI program are given the opportunity to act as team members via role playing exercises which are incorporated into their coursework. During the practicum experience, SI students meet with the parents of at least one child with whom they have been working, to discuss the child's progress.

Student and program advocate. A regular classroom teacher is in a rather unique position to advocate placement in the least restrictive environment. His/her very presence at a placement or planning conference for a child can signify a willingness to integrate the student into the mainstream of education. Who is in a better position to know the demands which will be placed upon a handicapped child than the teacher of the regular class in which the child will be placed? Based on the child's present level of performance and the demands of the setting, the regular educator is in a good position to request the provision of an appropriate level of special education services to allow the child to function in the regular classroom.

In order to serve as an advocate, SI students must have a knowledge of the literature pertaining to least restrictive placement, legislation, litigation, and the services of professional organizations. SI students are given the opportunity to demonstrate their advocacy skills via simulation exercises which are part of their coursework.

Instructional planner and implementer. As an instructional planner, a teacher must be able to accurately assess a student's present levels of educational performance. In all cases, a teacher will find it necessary to go beyond the results of standardized tests in order to precisely identify a student's strengths and weaknesses. Knowledge of and the ability to use criterion-referenced tests and curriculum-based assessment devices should be of great assistance to teachers in planning instructional programs. One of the major goals of assessment should be to identify skills in need of remediation and to describe them in measurable terms. Based on a child's performance during assesment, the teacher will need to sequence the skills which,when mastered, will result in the amelioration of identified academic deficits. Attention must also be given to the selection of instructional materials. A teacher must be prepared to adapt materials when possible and to create instructional materials when none exist.

Once a teacher has identified a starting place for instruction, it is necessary to select an instructional technique which can then be systematically applied. A thorough knowledge of a variety of instructional techniques and their uses will be needed if teachers are to select appropriate interventions. In order to precisely identify academic deficits and to determine the effectiveness of corrective techniques, a teacher must be familiar with measurement techniques and become proficient in their use.

The specific skills which students in the SI program are expected to master include the ability to: 1) conduct criterion-referenced and curriculum-based assessments, 2) describe instructional problems in behavioral terms, 3) construct and use task analyses, 4) write instructional objectives, 5) sequence instructional objectives, 6) generate and select teaching techniques, 7) observe and chart academic data, 8) make data-based decisions, and 9) adapt/create instructional materials. Students demonstrate their knowledge of these skills by completing a number of projects in their courses, and by planning and implementing instructional programs for children during the practicum experience.

Behavioral manager. A teacher can be expected to encounter a number of behavior problems with which he/she will have to deal in order to provide a proper learning environment. Being able to reduce the occurrence of socially inappropriate behaviors and to increase the occurrence of appropriate ones are critical skills for a teacher to possess.

An aspect of significant concern is improving the behavior of "mildy handicapped" children to the extent that they are able to successfully interact with their non-handicapped peers. A teacher is seen as being in a pivotal position as the facilitator of interaction to increase the social acceptance of "mildy handicapped" students by their classmates.

It is a wise teacher who can make use of natrual reinforcers in the classroom, arrange group contingencies, and use self-management techniques to improve the behavior of students. The teacher who can effectively employ behavioral management techniques will be in a good position to structure the learning experiences of students and assure success in the regular classroom for students experiencing problems.

In order to increase the ability of SI students to deal with social behavior problems, they are expected to be able to: 1) use a variety of observation techniques, 2) identify problem behaviors in measurable terms, 3) record and chart social behaviors, 4) select appropriate intervention techniques, 5) make use of behavioral management techniques, and 6) make data-based decisions. Coursework offers the opportunity for SI students to complete a number of projects requiring the application of behavioral techniques to classroom behavior problems. During the practicum experience, the students design and implement strategies for improving a child's study and social behaviors.

It should be stressed that the SI program confers no new teaching certificate. It does provide, however, an opportunity for regular educators to take a substantial block of coursework in special education and to gain experience in teaching children with mild learning and behavior problems in the regular classroom setting. It is anticipated that due to the nature of the program, graduates will have a distinct hiring advantage as they seek positions as regular classroom teachers. In order to help assure that this occurs, each graduate of the SI program will have a special set of materials included in his/her placement credentials describing the SI program and assessing the student's performance in the program.

Inservice Training

Recently, Ed Martin, Deputy Commissioner of Bureau of Handicapped, U. S. O. E., commented that "efforts to provide training and experience for regular classroom teachers are not keeping pace with the efforts to mainstream" (1976, p. 6). While this is not excusable, it is certainly understandable considering the number of regular educators (approximately 1.8 million) who require inservice training in special education.

If inservice training of regular educators is to be effective, it must overcome at least two obstacles. The first deals with teachers' attitudes and the second concerns the mystique which has surrounded special education. It is not so difficult to understand the reticence felt by some regular educators, such as those questioned by Hall & Findley (1971), concerning their willingness to teach low achieving pupils. Nor is it difficult to understand why some regular educators feel they cannot teach "mildy handicapped" youngsters without the aid of special equipment (Shotel, Iano, & McGettigan, 1972). These teachers have simply accepted the mystique which surrounds special education and which has been fostered by maintaining self-contained classrooms, thereby implying that regular classroom teachers were not capable of teaching children with mild learning and behavior problems.

Several special educators have placed a great deal of stress on changing teachers' attitudes (Brooks & Bransford, 1971; Shotel et al., 1972) and some researchers have been successful in bringing about desirable attitude changes (Brooks & Bransford, Glass & Meckler, 1972). An undue emphasis upon changing attitudes to the neglect of providing teachers with the skills necessary to teach problem students should not be encouraged. Changing attitudes is a tricky business; sometimes attitude shifts are accompanied by concomitant changes in behavior and sometimes not. A more direct approach is to focus on improving the skills of classroom teachers. It seems unlikely that a teacher could maintain a "poor attitude" toward a child if he/she possessed the skills to individualize instruction and to demonstrate that the child was making progress as the result of his/her teaching efforts.

The skills approach to inservice training has the support of a number of school district administrators, who when asked for suggestions concerning inservice training responded that it should be "practical and specific", include "both observing special educators and working with the handicapped," and provide "follow-up" to assist participants in their regular classes (Comptroller General, 1976, p. 11).

If everyone agrees that inservice training of regular educators is necessary, the question then becomes, "How is inservice to be provided?" There are at least three options: 1) onsite training conducted by special education personnel who are employees of the school district, 2) onsite instruction provided by specialists under contract as consultants to the school district, and 3) stipends for short-term study at colleges or universities. When school district administrators were asked to indicate their preference of the above mentioned options, they rated onsite training by contracted specialists as the most desirable and stipends for short-term campus study as the least desirable alternative (Comptroller General, 1976). The preferences of school district administrators seem to suggest a rather cautious view concerning the capabilities of school district special education personnel to conduct inservice training. This may be due to the fact that insufficient numbers of special educators have been trained to serve in a role analogous to that of a Resource/Consulting teacher. If sufficient numbers of special educators were trained in that capacity, it would seem logical that they would be in the best position to provide the kind of "practical" information and "follow-up" which school district administrators indicated they desired for inservice training. In recognition of this reality, trainees in the master's level Resource/Consulting Teacher program at the University of Illinois are taught to plan and implement inservice workshops as a part of their preparation for that role in the public schools.

Conclusion

Based on the discussion thus far, the following recommendations concerning pre-and inservice training of regular educators seem warranted:

1. A single survey course in special education is not sufficient to prepare regular educators to assume the responsibility of educating children with mild learning and behavior problems. What is needed is a program which stresses skills and includes practicum experience in a regular classroom setting. While the clear implication of this statement is that training of regular educators will be a task of greater duration than many special educators would like, the alternative is likely to be mass training, almost sure to result in sparcity and mediocrity of application.

2. Training of regular educators should focus on increasing direct teaching skills, on the assumption that successful experiences in teaching children will result in positive attitudes toward the children being taught. If programs are initiated which focus on change of attitudes of regular educators, assessment of concomitant changes in teacher behavior should be an integral part of such endeavors.

3. Departments of special education, elementary education, secondary education, vocational-technical education, etc. should engage in cooperative planning to develop quality preservice programs in special education for regular education students.

4. College and University Departments of Special Education should consider reallocation of scarce financial and human resources from undergraduate preparation of special educators for self-contained teaching situations to training of regular educators to deal constructively with learning and behavior problems in the regular classroom. This is not to say that continued preparation of special educators is not needed, as is implied in the Comptroller General's report (1976) on the federal role in special education teacher preparation. Rather, it is suggested that the majority of special education teacher training should be done at the master's level, and an increasing amount of our capability for undergraduate education should be focused on regular educators.

5. Inservice training should be skill-oriented and be conducted onsite, preferably by special educators who work in the schools as Resource/Consulting teachers and who can provide follow-up assistance to regular educators.

As mentioned earlier, the question is no longer whether regular educators should be trained to deal with learning and behavior problems in the classroom, but rather, how such training should be provided. It is the opinion of these authors that the monumental task of providing such training to regular educators must be approached with patience, and with constant attention to quality as well as quantity of effort. We must remain constantly aware of ill-advised and often ineffective efforts to prepare large numbers of special educators during the 1950's and early 1960's, and insist that new undertakings be systematically planned and executed. Undoubtedly, the need for training of regular educators will outstrip our capability to deliver such training in the forseeable future, for the change process in education is political in nature and does not follow a logical, developmental pattern. Even if change in education tends to be chaotic, however, we must be systematic in our response to it. The current demand for special education training for regular educators offers a unique opportunity for improving the educational experience of countless children, and our response to the challenge must be nothing short of the best we have to offer.

Mainstreaming: One Step Forward, Two Steps Back

By JOYCE G. ASHLEY

Joyce Ashley is a Learning Disabilities Specialist with the Nassau County Board of Cooperative Educational Services, Cerebral Palsy School; Roosevelt, New York. She is also a second-term member of the New York State United Teachers Standing Committee for Special Education.

Passage of the Education for All Handicapped Children Act has added a new word to the teacher's lexicon: mainstreaming. The regulations for the new law require that the handicapped student be placed in a program that provides the least restrictive environment "harmonious with the child's needs and free of stigma." Implicit in this requirement is the notion that the handicapped child will be accepted once he is placed into the regular classroom.

In a book entitled, *Public Law: Implications for Mainstreaming*, Robert Herman said:

. . . an active policy of mainstreaming means helping handicapped children participate as much as possible in our society. Not only do handicapped children benefit from exposure and involvement with their non-handicapped colleagues, but many educators believe that *all* children benefit from mainstreaming. The non-handicapped child who goes to school with handicapped children has an opportunity to show you his acceptance of individuals who have differences. This acceptance requires a cooperative and compassionate attitude.

But how is acceptance to be legislated? Where is the preparation for the non-handicapped population's compassionate attitude? The closest many of us have come to handicapped children is seeing them on telethons. Now, faced with a handicapped child in our classrooms, we experience fear and anxiety. What can we expect from this unknown person? What does he have to offer other than his handicap? And the most pressing question: Can the handicapped child be assured more than tolerance and pity, or will he face isolation and rejection?

Nearly everything written on the new education for the handicapped act refers to it as the civil rights bill for the handicapped. Like other civil rights legislation, it creates new problems as well as solving old ones. Its merits will be determined only by the test of time. However, it is not too soon to voice some concerns about shortcomings in the law.

Three areas of the act present special problems: (1) the difficulties inherent in developing individualized education programs for each handicapped child; (2) the mechanics entailed in providing due process to the handicapped child and his parents; and (3) the increased costs to the state of complying with the federal regulations.

Individualized Education Program
The term individualized education program (IEP), as required by the new law, means a written statement

for each handicapped child which includes: (a) a statement of the present educational levels; (b) a statement of annual goals, including short-term instructional objectives; (c) a statement of specific educational services to be provided, and the extent to which the child will be able to participate in regular educational programs; and (d) the projected date for initiation and anticipated duration of the services, and appropriate objective criteria and evaluation procedures and schedules for determining, on at least an annual basis, whether the instructional objectives are being achieved.

Nowhere in the federal regulations is there a safeguard for teachers against performance contracting. Nor is the teacher protected against malpractice litigation.

The teacher who executes the IEP may not know the handicapped child and may have had no part in writing the statement, yet that teacher may be responsible for the objectives in that statement. Parents of non-handicapped children in regular classes may begin to demand individualized education programs for their children as well.

Due Process
Parents of a handicapped child are afforded certain safeguards including due process in the evaluation, placement, and programming of their child. When the parents or guardians are unknown or unavailable, or when the child is a ward of the state, an individual must be assigned to act as a surrogate for the child in all proceedings. The individual assigned may not be an employee involved in the education of the child, however.

The question of whether or not children are being appropriately served by due process guarantees has yet to be resolved. Local school districts too frequently attempt to avoid due process as time consuming and costly. They adhere to the wishes of the parents in the hopes of avoiding demands for due process as soon as any conflict arises, regardless of the best needs of the child.

In an attempt to address himself to this issue, the New York State Commissioner of Education has amended the state's regulations to read:

Unless a surrogate parent shall have been previously assigned, the impartial hearing officer shall (prior to the hearing) determine whether the interests of the parent are opposed to or inconsistent with those of the child, or whether for any other reason, the interests of the child would best be protected by assignment of a surrogate parent, and where he so determines, the impartial hearing officer shall designate a surrogate parent to protect the interests of such child.

Increased Costs
Thomas Hobart, president of the New York State United Teachers, recently recommended that New York elect not to participate in federal funding of the Education for All Handicapped Children Act (P.L. 94-142). In testimony before the State Assembly, Hobart said:

New money required to meet the newly mandated costs has been conservatively estimated by the New York State Education Department to be at least $1,000 per handicapped child in New York State. This means it will cost our state . . . an estimated $310,000,000.

In Florida, an appropriations committee of the Florida state legislature voted unanimously to refuse federal money under the act. In a policy statement following the decision, the committee said:

Although P.L. 94-142 is a laudable attempt to address the unmet educational needs of our nation's handicapped children, the current legislative and regulatory language forces those states with established on-going quality programs to either compromise state laws and existing programs or to refuse money which is badly needed.

The Goals of Mainstreaming
Robert Herman listed eight goals to be achieved through mainstreaming. Those goals provide a useful framework in which to examine whether the Education for All Handicapped Children Act as it is presently written will insure full educational opportunity for the handicapped.

1. *Remove the stigma associated with special class placement.*

It should be obvious that when a handicapped child is placed in a regular class, he comes with a label. Will his teacher be able to understand that disability? Does the teacher feel trapped, threatened, and inadequate? Will there be opportunities for in-service training? Does the teacher have a liaison person, someone who can be consulted regarding the child?

Is this a flexible teacher excited by new challenges, or will this child become an enemy in the classroom?

2. *Enhance the social status of handicapped children with their non-handicapped peers.*

In an article in the *New York Times Magazine,* David Milofsky described what took place in Massachusetts when mainstreaming was introduced. A high school student with cerebral palsy had a scholarship endowed in her name by her peers. In an art class, peers wiped drool from the mouth of a handicapped classmate and they cut his paper straight for him. In a local community in New York, a high school student's fallen books were kicked down the hall. A junior high student had his very own graduation. The audience applauded as he crossed the stage. That ceremony was followed by the virtually anonymous graduation for his non-handicapped peers. Peers, if they are friends, do not endow you. They find ways to share their lives with you. They push wheelchairs, they talk to you during free play, they join you for lunch, they accept crooked cutting, and they let you wipe your own drool.

3. *Provide a better learning environment.*

The implication is that the handicapped have been educationally short-changed in the special school. Yet special classes were intended to provide opportunities for personal independence to the fullest extent possible. They have helped students develop good self-images and self-acceptance, and special classes have provided a basis for dealing with reality. These accomplishments should not be minimized so readily.

4. *Provide a real world environment.*

Mainstreaming in education, however, will be meaningless unless it leads to full opportunity to jobs, to transportation, and to buildings without barriers. Only then can mainstreaming truly mean freedom from what Herman calls "restriction of fundamental liberties."

5. *Provide a flexible service delivery mechanism more adaptable to individual children.*

Federal regulations outline numerous supportive services not generally available in regular schools. These include transportation, speech pathology and audiology, psychological services, physical and occupational therapy, recreation, early identification and assessment of disabilities, counseling services, school social work services, parent counseling, and training in child development. The regulations further stipulate that the cost of mainstreaming must come from new money and may not stem from a reallocation of funds from old programs. Furthermore, the money must follow the child. All of these services require funds that school districts do not presently have.

6. *Enable more children to be served.*

Many school administrators regard mainstreaming as a money saving device. A teacher from Ohio related to me that her class size had doubled since mainstreaming was introduced. In addition to her normal caseload of fifteen, she was given an equal number of handicapped children. When I asked what she had done about it, she replied, "I prayed a lot." The handicapped child and his peers are penalized by so callous an attitude. The result of this kind of administrative conduct could be chaos in the classroom or an end to mainstreaming. Nowhere in the federal regulations have reasonable class sizes and teacher caseloads been safeguarded. This

translates at the state and local levels into more children to be served by fewer teachers. Everywhere special education teachers, who should be providing additional services to districts, find themselves instead in growing numbers on the unemployment lines.

7. *Provide decentralized services, avoiding costly transportation charges.*

Youngsters who are moderately to severely physically handicapped are transported to physical therapies, occupational and speech therapies, special medical services, and occupational education programs. In some instances, however, decentralized services translate into an increased caseload for the districts' school psychologists. Savings in transportation costs furthermore cannot be used to supplement the cost of appropriate services in the mainstream.

8. *Avoid legal services involved in segregated classes.*

On the contrary, two aspects of the new law which are sure to instigate numerous time consuming and costly court cases are the individualized education programs and the due process mechanisms.

* * *

The Education for All Handicapped Children Act is a mammoth undertaking. Some argue that the law goes too far by usurping the pol-

icy making function of state education departments. Others claim that it doesn't go far enough by excluding the most severely handicapped children from the benefits of mainstreaming. One thing is clear, however. Educators have had too little time to prepare to meet the requirements of the law.

As the deadline for states and local districts seeking to comply with the federal regulations approaches, let us hope that the handicapped child with his unique individual needs is not swept away and drowned in good intentions. Let us hope, in the words of Robert Herman, that mainstreaming will:

. . . enrich the lives of all our children and society. It can be the cutting edge of a more realistic educational experience for all children, handicapped and non-handicapped alike. If we look at the school settings as a place where humane and compassionate values are transferred to each child, if we prepare ourselves for the mainstreamed classroom, if we understand the reason behind the trend to mainstreamings, and if we can deal with the broad spectrum of variations that make up the delivery of equal educational services to all handicapped children, then we shall enter a new era.

If not, mainstreaming may have taken us one step forward and two steps back in our efforts to achieve equal educational opportunity for the handicapped.

Some Thoughts on Mainstreaming

EDWIN W. MARTIN

Edwin W. Martin is the Deputy Commissioner for Education of the Handicapped. His role as a major advocate of rights of handicapped children was recognized on June 2, 1974, when Emerson College in Boston awarded him an honorary Doctorate of Humane Letters. Before joining the Office of Education, Dr. Martin was Associate Professor and Codirector of the Speech and Hearing Clinic at the University of Alabama. He also served as the Director of a special House of Representatives subcommittee studying the educational needs of handicapped children. For the last seven years, Dr. Martin has worked closely on the development and design of the growing federal program for education of handicapped children. This article is based on his remarks at The Council for Exceptional Children's April 1974 convention.

"... they [the handicapped] trouble us in deep, unexplainable, irrational ways, and we would like them ... out of sight and mind."

Several weeks ago, our CLOSER LOOK program, which provides information to parents and others about education for handicapped children, received a letter from a young girl, a seventh or eighth grader, asking if we could help find a special school for a retarded girl in her class. The letter went on to express her grievances that the retarded girl was given too much of the teacher's attention and that she received good grades for work that the others would have received poorer grades for. In all, the writer felt this retarded youngster should be put somewhere else, a suitable place.

Her letter, while clearly understandable from a young, maturing person, summarizes in one short page the major historical response of our schools and our culture to the needs of handicapped people. They are different, they trouble us in deep, unexplainable, irrational ways, and we would like them somewhere else, not cruelly treated, of course, but out of sight and mind.

If in advocating mainstreaming, we don't plan today for these societal patterns of response to the handicapped we will be painfully naive, and I fear we will subject many children to a painful and frustrating educational experience in the name of progress.

The Reasoning Behind Mainstreaming

Let's focus attention for a minute on why so many of us favor increasing the positive interactions between handicapped and nonhandicapped learners, which is the essence of mainstreaming.

"Some Thoughts on Mainstreaming," Edwin W. Martin, *Exceptional Children*, Vol. 41, No. 3, November 1974. © 1974 Council for Exceptional Children.

Our experience with segregated societal institutions has shown them to be among our most cruel and dehumanizing activities. I recently heard former Attorney General Ramsey Clark make this point very well. Think for a moment about the conditions within Indian reservations, about the internment of Japanese-Americans in World War II, about the Willowbrooks, about the jails, about the racially segregated schools. In each instance we have created these institutions, supposedly for the good of those to be incarcerated, or at least to provide them humane treatment, and in each, there has been a classic pattern of neglect, isolation, rejection and ultimate dehumanization of the persons on whose behalf society was supposedly acting. This has been true (fortunately in some lesser degree) of our approach to handicapped children within public education. Yet we all know of the insufficient budgets, the unqualified teachers, the condemned buildings, the lack of materials, the failure to provide effective identification, and the out of sight/out of mind syndrome.

> "... we have created ... institutions, supposedly for the good of those to be incarcerated ... [but] there has been a classic pattern of neglect. ..."

On this basis alone, *the human concern for human beings,* we must attempt to have handicapped children, in sight, in mind, and in settings where they will receive the fullest measure of our educational resources. If we also believe their actual achievement in educational terms will also prosper—so much the better.

> "On this basis alone, *the human concern for human beings,* we must attempt to have handicapped children in sight [and] in mind. ..."

I am concerned today, however, about the pell-mell, and I fear naive, mad dash to mainstream children, based on our hopes of better things for them. I fear we are failing to develop our approach to mainstreaming with a full recognition of the barriers which must be overcome.

Barriers in Our Way

First, is the question of the attitudes, fears, anxieties, and possibly overt rejection, which may face handicapped children, not just from their schoolmates but from the adults in the schools. Principals, teachers, and teacher

"Principals, teachers, and teacher aides, after all, are only human . . . and most have had no formal training or experience with the handicapped child."

aides, after all, are only human. Their attitudes are created by their experiences and most have had no formal training or experience with the handicapped child. In fact, as any of you who have worked on revision of college curricula know, efforts to include such training for regular educators have been fiercely resisted for the most part.

If the majority of handicapped children—the mildly and moderately retarded, the children with behavioral disorders, the children with language and learning problems, the children with orthopedic difficulties—are to be spending most or much of their time in regular classrooms, there

". . . there must be massive efforts . . . not to just 'instruct them' . . . but to share in the feelings, to understand their fears . . . ."

must be massive efforts to work with their regular teachers, not to just "instruct them" in the pedagogy of special education but to share in the feelings, to understand their fears, to provide them with assistance and materials, and in short, to assure their success.

Can you imagine what the educational experience for handicapped children will be if they and their teachers are left to sink or swim by one sudden impulsive administrative judgment?

Some Other Problems

While no one wants such a condition to occur, my discussions with people suggest we need to be aware of some of the problems we face.

First, efforts to provide training and experiences for regular classroom teachers are not keeping pace with the efforts to mainstream. We can predict that much of this training will be rationalistic and skill oriented and fail to respond to the feeling and attitude issues. It may also be that the practical involvement which should be part of the training will be relatively laissez-faire and not carefully or intensively supervised. This is all too true of much current training.

". . . efforts to provide training . . . are not keeping pace with the efforts to mainstream."

Second, there are a range of logistical problems. Children come and go from class at inappropriate times. Special education resource teachers use different sets of materials from the regular classroom teachers, and the fact that the teachers are parts of separate administrative budgets may mean that they can't get together on materials.

One major ingredient in mainstreaming, frequently cited as essential, is the development of educational prescriptions or programs for each child. Reports reach me that we need to look carefully at this process. In some instances, there is not enough material effort in developing the programs. The special education or school psychology people are drawing up plans for the teachers to follow. My prediction is that this approach will fail, that it will be seen as too externally oriented a device. Further, in some instances the manpower shortages mean that such plans can only be drawn annually or perhaps semiannually. These

". . . manpower shortages mean that such plans . . . drawn annually . . . are likely to be quickly obsolete and relegated to the desk drawer. . . ."

plans are likely to be quickly obsolete and relegated to the desk drawer, with psychologists' reports and other educational artifacts.

Finally, there is all too frequently a failure to evaluate carefully the child's progress toward specific educational objectives so that we will have to rely, as in the past, on our subjective judgments as to whether or not the child is, in fact, better off in mainstreamed settings. I would like to add, parenthetically, that our observations on the effectiveness of programs must include the emotional and social aspects of the children's lives, for much of our hope for mainstreaming lies in this realm.

"... our observations on the effectiveness of programs must include the emotional and social aspects of the children's lives. ..."

Concluding Comments

I have used this discussion to speak to several major issues or concerns, societal attitudes, mainstreaming itself, new demands for teacher education, new demands for effective educational planning and programing and finally the need for a more effective evaluation of our work.

"... my concern is that we do not deceive ourselves because we so earnestly seek to rectify the ills of segregation."

There is a mythical quality to our approach to mainstreaming. It has faddish properties, and my concern is that we do not deceive ourselves because we so earnestly seek to rectify the ills of segregation. We must seek the truth and we must tolerate and welcome the pain that such a careful search will bring to us. It will not be easy in developing mainstreaming, but we cannot sweep the problems under the rug.

Alexander Solzhenitsyn in the last letter he circulated among his friends in the Soviet Union called on them to renounce the lies in that society and its governance. He spoke not only of the lies that the intellectuals and writers were called upon to write or speak under government pressure but also of the lies which others spoke and about which they had chosen to remain silent. He predicted that if that small brave band of dissidents would refuse to lie, the pattern would spread from 100 to 1,000 to many thousands and the weaknesses in their system would be forced to change, quickly.

There are many messages for Americans in Solzhenitsyn's words and especially for us in special education. We cannot keep silent about some of the lies in our present system—the failure to provide services, the poor facilities, the failure to identify learning problems, the failure to move children out of institutions or out of special programs into regular settings.

"We cannot keep silent about some of the lies in our present system. ... But we must also avoid ... well intentioned lies. ..."

But we must also avoid those well intentioned lies that ignore the weaknesses in a well intentioned system, because we are afraid that exposure will hurt our cause. We should not allow our belief in the promises of mainstreaming to cause us to be silent if we see faults in its application. With the newly recognized *rights* of children to the education we offer, there must be an equal *responsibility* to see that those rights are truly fulfilled.

Mainstreaming: Some Natural Limitations

Wyatt E. Stephens

Author: WYATT E. STEPHENS, Ph. D., Professor and Chairman of the Department of Special Education at Southern Illinois University, Carbondale, Illinois.

The matter of "mainstream" education for the mildly retarded is one of the most controversial issues facing special education. On one hand its advocates claim that segregated placement has actually perpetuated maladaptive cognitive, behavioral, academic and vocational skills in this group (Christoplos & Renz, 1969; Dunn, 1968; Johnson, 1962; Lilly, 1970, 1971; Reger, Schroeder & Uschold, 1968). On the other hand, its critics (most recently Kolstoe, 1972) claim that most criticisms of the special class philosophy are not substantiated by research findings, and suggest that the situation is not as bad as it is claimed to be.

Reflection on what is known about mild mental retardation suggests that in fact some mildly retarded children could be expected to profit from mainstreaming, while others would not. The specific factors involved are available through examination of the causes of mild retardation.

It would seem to be a foregone conclusion that there are numerous reasons for a child to exhibit an intelligence test score in the mildly retarded range. He may be a child of average mental ability who was tested badly, a child to whom an unsuitable test was administered, an emotionally disturbed child who was not capable of dealing with the test situation, or he may be a child with mild generalized dysfunction of the brain or central nervous system. He may have inherited genetic characteristics from the lower end of the normal distribution of genetic traits that underlie intelligence, or he may have developed inadequate cognitive skills because of severely disrupted early environmental experiences.

Since all of these possibilities occur as real events in the actual world, it is speculated that although the theoretical distribution of potential intellectual function in the population at large is perfectly symmetrical, the actual distribution obtained when real people are tested is considerably lower on the average than the theoretical distribution, since all persons have been subjected to physiological and/or environmental factors that have an adverse effect on their overall development. Moreover, it is speculated that actual function is further below potential function for persons in the lower half than in the upper half of the distribution, because adverse factors that decrease intellect occur more frequently and with greater strength among this group. Specifically, less adequate genetic endowment, at least in our society, is associated with lower socio-economic level and its attendant problems of inadequate prenatal care, malnutrition, unstimulating child rearing practices and increased incidence of emotional instability. Furthermore, even children with higher genetic endowment who grow up in deprived socio-economic circumstances are subject to most of these same adverse factors, and with similar results. The net result is that all human beings exhibit intellectual levels less than their original potential, since all have been subjected to adverse factors; but the exhibited intellectual levels of the subnormal are further below their initial (theoretical) potential than are those of persons who had higher potential to begin with.

Based on this point of view, it is possible to make some realistic predictions about the outcome of mainstreaming mildly retarded children in the educational process. The critical variables to be considered are (a) the upper limits of the child's potential (determined by the causes of his reduced function), and (b) the effectiveness of special educational programs in helping him to attain his level of potential. The issue at stake is that of providing experiences for the mildly retarded which result in their becoming successfully integrated into the population by the time they have attained adulthood. The question is whether mainstreaming accomplishes this objective better than other approaches.

This question may be approached by posing a hypothetical situation: Given a maximum effectiveness of special education programs (whatever form this might take), what are reasonable predictions for children who are mildly retarded, that is, whose IQ scores are in the 60 to 90 range? The answer is that some of this group would rapidly exhibit performance in the range of normal intellect because their initial scores were spurious as a consequence of inaccurate or inappropriate psychological tests. Children in whom the cause(s) of reduced intellective function were more serious and more persistent should also show substantial gains, but only up to the limits imposed by physiological factors, including genetic endowment. Some of this group would come to function within the existing "average" range because the upper limit of their potential was as high as the exhibited levels of function of nonretarded children who were not operating at the upper levels of their potential. Other mildly retarded children, who began with lower levels of function and/or who had lower upper limits, would also show gains but these gains would place them at a higher level in the mildly retarded range and not in the average range.

"Mainstreaming: Some Natural Limitations," Wyatt E. Stephens, *Mental Retardation*, Vol. 13, No. 3, June, 1975. © 1975 American Association on Mental Deficiency.

Since these predictions are made on the basis of a hypothetical situation in which maximum effectiveness of special education programs exists, the corrolary question must now be posed: Is there any particular pattern of delivery services, such as mainstreaming, that insures maximum program effectiveness? If realistic expectations for the gains possible for children in the mildly retarded range are taken into account, then there may be no single pattern for delivery of services that demonstrates a clear superiority above all others. For example, mildly retarded children with higher maximum potential would probably profit substantially from mainstreaming, but those with less potential would still be "retarded" in mainstream settings even if they attained their maximum gains. The fact that they are numerically fewer than mildly retarded children with higher ultimate potential is a factor to be considered but nevertheless this would be a substantial group for whom mainstreaming might interfere with the overall objective more than it would contribute to it.

While no claim is made that the point of view described is original, it does seem to have some merit as a basis for establishing and evaluating a number of important criteria which will determine whether or not mainstreaming of mildly retarded children holds the promise of success, and if so, for whom. Examination of the idea of mainstreaming from this point of view seems quite desirable, since many of the strongest advocates of the practice seem to overlook the likelihood that even extremely powerful educational techniques and forms of program organization may still be unable to bring the intellective and cognitive skills of all mildly retarded persons to a level where they will be tolerated in, much less integrated into, even the most enlightened regular education classroom.

References

Christoplos, F. & Renz, P. A critical examination of special education programs. *The Journal of Special Education*, 1969, 3, 371-379.

Dunn, L. M. Special education for the mildly retarded — Is much of it justifiable? *Exceptional Children*, 1968, 35, 5-22.

Johnson, G. O. Special Education for the mentally retarded — A paradox. *Exceptional Children*, 1962, 29, 62-69.

Kolstoe, O. D. Programs for the mildly retarded: A reply to the critics. *Exceptional Children*, 1972, 39, 51-56.

Lilly, M. S. A training based model for special education. *Exceptional Children*, 1971, 37, 745-749.

Lilly, M. S. Special education: A teapot in a tempest. *Exceptional Children*, 1970, 37, 43-49.

Reger, R., Schroeder, W., & Uschold, D. *Special education: Children with learning problems.* New York: Oxford University Press, 1968.

ARRANGING SPECIFIC EDUCATIONAL SERVICES TO BE PROVIDED

Jeptha Greer
Scottie Torres

Jeptha Greer is the Assistant Superintendent of Instructional Programs for the DeKalb County (Georgia) Board of Education. He was formerly a classroom teacher for the educable mentally retarded, a supervisor for the educable mentally retarded, and a director of special education.

Scottie Torres is the Director of the Special Education Administrative Policy (SEAP) Project at The Council for Exceptional Children.

DURING the meeting(s) to develop the child's written individualized education program, two main issues emerge. First, a clear understanding of what the child presently can do, with a projection based on the child's performance to indicate annual goals and short term objectives, is developed. Second, a list of the type(s) of services the child will need is established. This chapter will present some items for schools and parents to consider when determining the educational services to be provided to the student. Public Law 94-142 makes a distinction between educational services that a child needs and the actual type of placement the child will have.

DEVELOPING EDUCATION SERVICES

The language set forth in the law and amplified in the proposed rules (December 1976) requires that each individualized education program contain a statement of specific educational services needed by the child. The language states:

(d) A statement of specific educational services needed by the child (determined without regard to the availability of those services) including a description of:
(1) All special education and related services which are needed to meet the unique needs of the child, including the type of physical education program in which the child will participate, and
(2) Any special instructional media and materials which are needed. (Section 121a.225)

It is important to note that the proposed rules require documentation of the specific services a child needs, as determined without regard to the availability of those services. Developing this statement will be difficult for both the parents and the school personnel. What services does the child minimally need and what ser-

"Arranging Specific Educational Services to be Provided," Jeptha Greer and Scottie Torres, *A Primer on Individualized Programs for Handicapped Children*, 1977. Foundation for Exceptional Children, Reston, Va.

vices will provide for all the educational needs of the child? Frequently, professionals are hesitant to recommend services that currently do not exist within the local education agency. Sometimes, services required for a child are available from other human service agencies such as the departments of mental or public health. How does one begin to document those service needs?

The proposed rules do provide a skeletal framework on how to proceed. Subsection 1 under section d requires specification of all special education and related services needed to meet the unique needs of the child. The reader is encouraged to review the legal definitions presented in chapter 1 and remember key phrases such as "specially designed instruction to meet unique needs" in the definition of special education and "as required to assist a handicapped child to benefit from special education" in the definition of related services.

It seems logical then that the law is requiring a documentation of that specially designed instruction and an indication of how any related services will support the child's special education. No longer will it be sufficient to say that a child "needs to be placed in a junior high program for educable mentally retarded students and see the psychologist weekly." Rather, it will be necessary to describe any specially designed instruction and describe the related services. This process will be a natural "next step" once the annual goals and short term objectives have been developed. Based on the annual goals and short term objectives, a statement of educational services in the example above might read:

A work-study program will be established to work on the prevocational skill sequence. The student will need to spend at least two weekly half hour sessions with the work-study coordinator to continue the link between on the job training and the classroom skill sequences for this training.

It is critical that the related services correspond directly to the child's needs. Specifying the relationship that the supportive services are to have to the rest of the child's program minimally accomplishes two tasks. First, it makes it possible to go beyond the general level of the services—speech pathology, for example—and begin to describe the necessary services within the area of speech pathology that will be delivered. Perhaps this will be a step toward unveiling the "mystery" behind the "therapy." Second, everyone, including parents, school personnel, and the related service people, will have a clearer understanding of what services everyone expects will be provided to the child.

Included in the statement of educational services is the proposed requirement that a list be included of "any special instructional media and materials which are needed." A word of caution must be offered: The key to the specificity with which media and materials should be listed in the child's education program has to come from the term "special." In other words, what *special* material or media is required to implement the individualized education program? Otherwise, professionals would be required to list all instructional materials and media that they will use with the child. Common sense and the intent of Public Law 94-142 should prevail. The intent clearly seems to require documentation only of those highly "specialized" pieces of material or media that are necessary.

The issue of time becomes important when determining the educational services to be provided. The law requires that the statement include "(e) The date when those services will begin and length of time the services will be given" (section 121a.225).

There are several points to consider. First, when does the child need the services and how soon are they available? For instance, if the child needs the services from a source other than a local agency, some time delay may occur. It is the responsibility of the school to document the estimated time the service will begin (e.g., in two weeks, pending acceptance to a private school or availability of the physical therapist from the department of human resources). If it is apparent that there will be more than a two week delay, however, documentation must include the services the child will receive while waiting for the appropriate designated service(s).

The length of the service is an area that few professionals have experience in predicting. It is relatively easy to estimate that a child needs the service for at least one month, one semester, or even one year. But when the time sequences are more discrete, some difficulties arise. Why does the child need to see the speech clinician two times a week for 30 minutes? Why not once a week for 60 minutes? Or, what is so "special" about 60 minutes? This time analysis becomes important whenever time is scheduled away from the regular program. For instance, if the child needs some "resource" help, it is necessary to ask: How much, when, and for how long? There are no clear-cut answers to these questions. Rather, those persons responsible for determining the educational services must begin with each child's needs and then work toward estimating the degree of time necessary to implement the individualized education program.

DETERMINING APPROPRIATE PLACEMENT

Historically, schools have based placement recommendations either on the type of handicap-

4. PROGRAMS AND SERVICES

ping condition or the currently existing available programs. Either a child was handicapped enough to go to a special class or the child was not handicapped enough and so might not get the appropriate support services. Through the years and particularly over the past 10 years, schools have realized the inadequacies of this placement procedure. Today, many more program options are available in the schools. Local and intermediate education agencies have an option to contract with other public or private agencies or personnel to provide services that they may not offer—but these services as well must be provided in the least restrictive environment.

Translating needed educational services into the most appropriate placement for the child requires one basic change in thought. The concept of least restrictive environment, as set forth in Public Law 94-142, provides the framework to build the bridge between needed services and where those services will be delivered. Any time the child's individual needs require that the child be removed from the regular program for special education or the provision of related services, that removal must be documented. As indicated in the law, documentation of the educational services must include:

(f) A description of the extent to which the child will participate in regular education programs;

(g) A justification for the type of educational placement which the child will have. (Section 121a.225)

Following the intent of the law, the justification for the type of placement must correspond to the specific educational needs of the child. The appropriate placement is the placement option that will meet those needs.

When an individualized education program is being developed, it is important that the justification specify the type of placement rather than name the placement. For example, if a child needs a residential type of program, the individualized education program must delineate the types of services required rather than state a recommendation for a specific residential school. Too often, recommendations have been in the nature of, "The child shall be placed in the Oscar Private Schools." Trouble and delay result when it is determined that the school does not have room for the child, that the same services could better be provided at a different school, or that a more appropriate residential program can be established through collaboration with other local or intermediate agencies. Caution must be exercised most frequently when a placement recommendation is out of district to insure that promises and commitments made on behalf of the child can be fulfilled and monitored.

In some education agencies, based on either state or local policy, it is the responsibility of the team members developing the individualized education program to delineate the type of placement appropriate for the child. The administrator of special education then has the responsibility to locate the exact program and notify the parents of the actual recommended placement. This distinction might help schools and parents to make better educational decisions for the child. Once the actual placement has been agreed to by the parents, "(h) a list of the individuals who are responsible for implementation of the individualized education program" will be included in the child's program (section 121a.225).

It is important to remember what is happening to the child throughout all phases of the development of the individualized education program. The child shall remain in the regular school program where he or she was when deliberation began. If the child is not in a public school program, he or she has the right to be enrolled in one until placement procedures are completed. Agreement by the parent or guardian and the appropriate administrator is necessary. It may also be necessary to obtain a written agreement from the administrator and the teacher(s) at the receiving school where the pupil will receive his or her education pending completion of the individualized education program.

IDENTIFYING DISTRICT RESOURCES

The administrator of special education should be responsible for uniform procedures regarding the development and implementation of each individualized education program. Factors to consider minimally include establishing procedures for communication with parent(s) or guardian; observation at home, school, center, or other environment when appropriate; a staffing process that includes interpretation of services available, alternatives, and interventions; parent consent; and the hearing process when required. Due to the importance of each of these aspects in the development and implementation of the individualized education program, it is important that districtwide procedures be established.

Existing resources within the school district that are traditionally outside the realm of special education can add to the district's capacity to meet the child's individual education needs. Often the school library or media center supplies special instructional materials, equipment, media, and other resources. Recommendations for the use of support services such as remedial reading or math instruction should be incorporated in the district's procedures. The district may already have in effect such concepts as differentiated staffing, individually prescribed

Figure 1
A Sample Resource Inventory

Program type	Staff	Material resources	Instructional interventions	Interagency services
Regular classroom	Teachers	Regular curriculum guides	Diagnosis	Human resources Physical health Mental health Vocational rehabilitation Family and child services
Regular classroom with direct or indirect assistance (provide definition)	Consulting teachers	Special curriculum guides	Intervention	
Itinerant	Itinerant teachers	Special equipment	Treatment	Natural resources Recreation Lifetime sports
Crisis intervention	Methods and materials and curriculum specialists	Special instructional materials	Therapy	
Resource room	Resource room teachers	Diagnostic material	Training	Intermediate school district Direct services Indirect services
Self contained	Special therapists Audiologists Speech therapists Physical therapists Occupational therapists Recreation therapists Music therapists Medical consultants Other		Programing	
Multisystem unit			Regular education	
Special center			Special education	State department of education Instruction Special education Vocational rehabilitation Federal programs Other
Private center, school			Reevaluation	
Homebound/hospital			Followup	
Residential	Support teachers Reading Math Other	Other resources Curriculum modification Intraschool differentiated staffing	Staff development	Other Special hospitals Special clinics Community service organizations
	Paraprofessionals			
	Counselors			
	Visiting teachers			
	School social workers			
	School psychologists			

4. PROGRAMS AND SERVICES

instruction, informal learning, instructional television, micro-teaching, modular scheduling, continuous progress, open classroom, performance contracting, programed instruction, and open education. These concepts should be used when applicable.

It will become increasingly difficult for administrators to keep track of all special education and related services that are required and specified in each individualized education program unless some mechanism is established to identify and follow the available resources within the local or intermediate education agency. Administrators of special education will want to make good use of this information in order to better plan for the resources that are or will be required as part of the child's individual-

ized education program.

As existing district resources are identified, it is possible to compile a resource inventory for planning purposes. The essential areas to identify include the types of programs, existing personnel, materials available, present instructional interventions, and current interagency services. Figure 1 is a partial listing of the components of a sample resource inventory. Each district will be able to identify its own existing resources. Once the district's resources have been identified, this information should be widely circulated so that professional staff and parents can view what is and what needs to be included to provide the necessary resources to implement the educational services component of the individualized education program.

What Does "Mainstreaming" Mean?

Roger Reger, M.A.

The application of the mainstreaming concept does not mean that all handicapped children have to be placed in classes with nonhandicapped students. A realistic and flexible application of the concept is discussed.

Today we are witnessing a major overhaul in thinking about programming for children with various problems. In many places thinking has led to action — or, in some instances, action sometimes has taken place in the absence of thinking.

In former days much was made over the "integration" of children in self-contained special classes into "regular" classes — still today a common form of programming. A few children are assigned to other classes for periods of instruction in reading or social studies, or more typically, the special class children are placed with other children in music, art, physical education, home economics, library, industrial arts, and in the lunchroom.

Today we are becoming familiar with such words as "normalization" (Wolfensberger 1972), "mainstreaming" (Birch 1974), and "de-labeling" (Forness 1974). Resource-room programs have gained popularity in part because of the link with mainstreaming (Hammill and Wiederholt 1972, Reger 1973, Sabatino 1972). Courts and legislatures are becoming increasingly unsympathetic toward traditional classification practices (Kirp 1974).

Mainstreaming means different things to different people. To some, the concept is similar to what we have called integration, where children who were housed in isolated facilities are moved into regular school buildings and placed in special self-contained classes alongside classes of nonhandicapped children. At the other extreme, to some people the concept means the total elimination of any semblance of specialized grouping on the basis of *type* of disability. In this way, children are assigned to grades on the basis of age, as is done with most other children.

Between the two extremes are varying efforts to assign handicapped children into the same programs as nonhandicapped students, but with special assistance provided to help maintain progress and prevent failure. The special assistance may be provided by resource-room teachers, itinerant teachers, diagnostic teams or diagnostic classes, teacher aides, consultant personnel with various titles and functions, after-school tutors, or, in some cases even older children.

Frequently missing when schools move toward mainstreaming is an appreciation of what really is involved. While some people delight in seeing self-contained classes eliminated, it is forgotten that unless basic changes are made in programming, the children are put back into the very failure situations which originally led to their specialized placements. While this may be a purifying experience for the souls of some, it is a devastating experience for many of the children.

Also missing in some cases is an understanding of the nature of stigma and its effects upon teachers and other children. Classifying children in traditional, medical-model categories only highlights their differences rather than minimizing them. The fourth-grade teacher faced only with knowing there is a new pupil in the class who is "mentally retarded" or "emotionally disturbed" is more than likely to be at a loss as to what this means in specific instructional terms. In a real effort toward mainstreaming, children are not classified and labeled in traditional ways. For example, a child is not called "mentally retarded" and then placed into a fourth grade. Instead, children are classified according to specific and objectively defined needs, and services are designed to meet those needs. If this fourth-grade teacher is given a description of the child's specific strengths and deficits, there *is* a basis for planning a program around these needs. Instructional strategies and materials can be organized and applied around a meaningful plan, with needed supportive services similarly oriented around the plan.

Still another missing ingredient in mainstreaming plans is the recognition that not all children can, in fact, be mainstreamed. Wholesale elimination of special education programs in the name of mainstreaming is an extreme and unworkable form of action. A five-year-old child with no speech, who is not toilet-trained, who may have a severe sensory loss, and who may be extremely difficult to manage, is simply not going to be accommodated and provided with a beneficial instructional program in a class with 20 to 30 other children. In actual practice, this child is more than likely to be excluded from school. He or she then must seek private school placement, or do without a school program at all. While the school can boast of its mainstreaming efforts, this type of child is a personal casualty to the system. And what about the 15-year-old child who is so severely limited that he cannot even find his way around the school building? Is he going to be enrolled in algebra, social studies, and English literature?

The application of the mainstreaming concept *does not* mean that *all* handicapped children have to be placed in classes with nonhandicapped children. To apply the concept in its extreme form, strictly and rigidly along such lines, only would put many handicapped children back where they were before the advent of special education. On the other hand, a realistic and flexible application of the mainstreaming concept would allow more handicapped children to attend public schools than ever before.

By way of a listing of principles, following is a compilation of what is involved in mainstreaming:

(1) No child should be categorized with a label reflecting a gross diagnostic category.

(2) Children should be evaluated with relevant instruments to determine those areas of strength and weakness that relate directly to specific, objective instructional actions. ("Instructional actions" means more than "academic skills." It also means changing inappropriate behavior, providing training in occupational skills, etc.)

(3) All children should be housed in the regular school building complex, or wherever other (nonhandicapped) children are housed.

(4) Groupings of all children in the school should be based on defined needs. For children with special needs, as much as possible in the way of additional support services should be provided both directly to the children and to their teachers.

(5) Diagnostic and prescriptive services for children with special needs are not enough. Such services should be directly tied to implementation services, and whenever possible the same personnel who provide diagnostic and prescriptive services also should implement the instructional program, in cooperation with other teachers.

(6) Consultation services to teaching personnel should have direct application to the instructional program, providing materials to use, techniques to try and management strategies. Consultant personnel whose major offering is high status, with limited or no recommendations that can be translated directly into useful action, should not be used. Whenever possible, consultants should offer direct instructional service to children combined with service to other teachers; it should be remembered that a fancy title does not necessarily mean superior knowledge and skills.

(7) Some children with severe disabilities will have to be grouped together for at least part of their day, if for no other reason than they cannot be placed to their advantage with nonhandicapped children. Such groupings should be based on individual performance criteria, not on gross and irrelevant noneducational diagnostic categories.

(8) The leadership of the school, from the superintendent to the building principal and president of the teachers' union, should work together on total program implementation. Needs for teacher inservice training should evolve out of the perceptions and experiences of the teachers themselves, not poured in, uninvited, from "experts."

A final plea: Special education always has been plagued with a variety of experts whose services in the educational realm, when boiled to the bone, may be of questionable value. For example, while a physician can give certain useful kinds of advice about children, it is seriously doubtful that his medical training has had any connection with what is involved in educational programming. It is unknown for a teacher to be consulted by a committee of physicians about whether a hospital patient should receive an operation for a disease; but it has been common for a physician to have a strong voice in determining whether a child should be offered a certain kind of instructional program. Advice from persons with little or no qualification for giving the advice cannot reasonably assist in the school's efforts. Schools should be careful that money spent for services goes for personnel who can offer concrete educational assistance to children and their teachers. The pie, after all, has only so many pieces. — *BOCES Service Center, Special Educational Services, 455 Cayuga Rd., Buffalo, N.Y. 14225.*

REFERENCES

Birch, J. W.: Retarded Pupils in the Mainstream: The Special Education of Educable Mentally Retarded Pupils in Regular Classes. Reston, Va.: Council for Exceptional Children, 1974.

Forness, S.: Implications of recent trends in educational labeling. J. Learn. Disabil., 1974, 7 (7), 445-449.

Hammill, D., and Wiederholdt, J. L.: The resource room: Its rationale and implementation. Philadelphia: The Journal of Special Education, 1972.

Kirp, D. L.: Student classification, public policy, and the courts. Harvard Educ. Rev., 1974, 44, 7-52.

Reger, R.: What is a resource-room program? J. Learn. Disabil., 1973, 6 (10), 609-614.

Sabatino, D. A.: Resource rooms: The renaissance in special education (Symposium No. 8). J. Special Educ., 6, 335-347.

Wolfensberger, W.: Normalization: The Principle of Normalization in Human Services. Toronto: National Inst. on Mental Retardation, 1972.

Integration of Young TMR Children into a Regular Elementary School

Suzanne Ziegler
Donald Hambleton

Two classes of young trainable mentally retarded (TMR) children were moved from a school for the retarded to a regular public school where they interacted with the school population daily, mainly in nonacademic (nonclassroom) situations. Their behavior at two time points during the year was compared to that of a matched group of TMR children in a school for the retarded.

Evaluation Design

The evaluation was designed to assess the effects of placing TMR children in a public school setting, primarily through direct observation and recording of the quantity and quality of interactions between retarded and nonretarded children.

As the two classes to be included in the regular school were selected prior to the initiation of evaluation, pretreatment equivalence of the experimental (integration) and contrast (segregation) groups through random assignment of children could not be achieved. Therefore, a matched group design was chosen. Variables on which children were matched included sex, chronological age, mental age, social age, etiology, language(s) spoken in the home, student's expressive and receptive language, number of siblings in the home and birth order, and socioeconomic background, based on the father's education and occupation.

As a check of the efficacy of the matching process, group means of several of the matching variables were computed (Campbell & Stanley, 1963). The experimental (integration) and contrast groups were found to be similar. For example, for IQ scores, the mean of the integrated group was 40.4; for the contrast group, the mean was 42.2. Group mean scores on sections of an adapted version of the Cain-Levine Social Competency Scale (Cain & Levine, 1963) filled out by the children's own teacher subsequent to the matching procedure, also supported group comparability.

Collection of Data

The tools developed included a behavior checklist to be used in play situations outside the classroom and an interaction analysis.

The Behavior Checklist

The checklist details the relative frequency of 13 kinds of interactions among retarded and nonretarded students. Scoring involved coding of occurrence, quality, and the source (initiator) of interactions involving the retarded children. These 13 categories, which ranged from solitary noninvolvement to cooperative interaction, were collapsed for analysis into three: *inadequate, adequate* and *extremely adequate* social behavior.

The data gathered during two time periods (December/January and April/May), showed no statistically significant differences between the experimental and contrast groups.

A comparison of total instances of aggressive, ignoring and hostile behavior by the nonretarded children in the integrated environment supports the findings of some previous studies (e.g. Hayes, 1969) that nonretarded children, contrary to commonly held beliefs, do not single out and deliberately victimize the retarded.

The Interaction Analysis

In addition to the behavior checklists, additional data was collected and subjected to an interaction analysis, to document not only frequencies of specific social behaviors, but also patterns or chains of such interactions. Tabulations of selected interaction patterns are presented in Table 1.

Interactions involving only retarded chil-

"Integration of Young TMR Children into a Regular Elementary School," Suzanne Ziegler and Donald Hambleton, *Exceptional Children*, Vol. 42, No. 8, May 1976. © 1976 Council for Exceptional Children.

TABLE 1

**Frequency of Selected Behavior Patterns
on the Playground Integration Site—35 Hours Observation**

Interactions	N[1]+E[2] female/female	N+E female/male	N+E male/female	N+E male/male	Total N+E
Positive					
Friendly conversation	87	44	18	51	200
Friendly physical contact	127	47	31	77	282
Game	17	5	1	2	25
Parallel play	9	8	0	6	23
Play	5	2	1	17	25
Instruct (verbal)	6	10	1	8	25
Teach skill	13	13	1	0	27
Intervene and correct	10	12	7	24	53
Reprimand	7	6	1	9	23
Comfort	10	3	1	7	21
Help	23	13	3	12	51
Total positive and/or teaching interaction	314	163	65	213	755
Negative					
Verbal aggression	1	0	1	0	2
Physical aggression (without distinction as to initiator)	11	2	1	13	27
Total aggressive interactions	12	2	2	13	29
Total interactions	326	165	67	226	784

[1] N = nonretarded children
[2] E = retarded children (experimental group)

dren observed at both schools were also predominantly positive in character, but included more provoked aggression and much less teaching, intervening and comforting/helping than interactions involing nonretarded and retarded children. It is important to note that retarded children not only play and converse together, but also that retarded children *help, intervene,* and *comfort,* although apparently less frequently and less effectively than nonretarded children in comparable situations.

As well as studying the interaction of retarded and nonretarded students on the playground, independent measures were used to assess how well known the retarded students were as individuals to the nonretarded children. A surprisingly large number of regular students knew the special class children, not only as a group, but individually and by name.

Conclusions

There can be little doubt that the placement of the special classes in a regular school was extremely effective in promoting interaction between the retarded and nonretarded students, and thus in providing a more normal environment for the retarded children.

References

Cain, L.F. & Levine, S. Effects of community and institutional programs on trainable mentally retarded children. *Research Monograph*, Washington DC: The Council for Exceptional Children, 1963.

Campbell, D.T. & Stanley, J.C. *Experimental and quasi-experimental designs for research.* Chicago: Rand McNally, 1963.

Hayes, G.A. The integration of the mentally retarded and non-retarded in a day camping program: A demonstration project. *Mental Retardation*, 1969, October, 14–16.

Mainstreaming in Massachusetts Under Law 766

By FREDERICK ANDELMAN
*Assistant Director of Professional Development,
Massachusetts Teachers Association.*

Massachusetts has a new comprehensive special education law known as Chapter 766. Passed in the summer of 1972 to take effect in September 1974, the law is similar in many ways to comprehensive special-education laws that exist in several states at this time and that will probably come into being in many more in the future.

The law consolidates all of the former separate statutes and processes with regard to special education and provides a single uniform process for identifying and evaluating special needs in children. It guarantees children with special needs an educational program responsive to those needs, with a major emphasis on mainstreaming.

The law includes parents, as well as teachers, in the process of designing individualized programs of instruction to meet childrens' special educational needs, and it establishes an elaborate review and appeal process in the event that the school and the parent disagree regarding the school's proposed programs to meet the needs of a given child.

Teachers are involved in many of the processes established by 766, and several aspects of the law are of great concern to them. Now that we are well into the second year of implementation, we have been able to identify specific problems that the law poses for teachers, and this article will examine some of them.

Chapter 766 is not only a very ambitious educational venture but it is also an extremely complex exercise in social policy. It has brought into focus a number of basic educational problems that Massachusetts faces at the present time. It also serves to highlight problems likely to be encountered in other states implementing similar educational mandates or in states seeking to bring them into being. Rather than being called a comprehensive special education act, the law might better be called a more responsive schools act, for it does nothing less than require of the schools something which most teachers have wanted for a long time: that the schools respond to the individual needs and uniqueness of every child.

A major set of concerns deals with the role of the teacher in implementing a mandate such as 766 and with how teachers feel about the increasing demands being placed upon them by the public to remedy, in a very short period of time, certain problems or defects in the system of public education which have been in existence for a very long period of time.

Generally speaking, most teachers in Massachusetts think that 766 is a good law. Their concerns relate to the unsatisfactory manner in which the law is being implemented. For example, they feel that the in-service education and training resources authorized in 766 are woefully inadequate to prepare them (especially regular education personnel) to work with youngsters with special needs.

Teachers are also concerned with the accountability factor in 766. The law stipulates that parents of a child with special needs must approve the educational program designed for the child before such a program is implemented. Once the parents approve and sign the plan, the local school committee is legally bound to its specifications and required to produce the educational outcomes specified for the child. Teachers believe that they will be held responsible for failing to produce in children certain desired educational outcomes, when in fact, it is the larger system of public education which has failed to provide adequate resources for such outcomes even to be approximated.

Teachers have been further concerned with the fact that while the law was passed in 1972, it was not until the spring of 1974 that the Massachusetts Department of Education issued regulations pertaining to the school processes required to implement the law in September of 1974. As a result, teachers spent almost two full school years uncertain as to what their responsibilities under Chapter 766 would be, unsure of how their instructional roles and duties might be changed, not knowing what kinds of training or reeducation would be both available and/or required, and unaware of how 766, in general, would affect their local employment situation.

During this two-year period of time, of course, collective bargaining continued to proceed, which brings us to a discussion of a whole other set of problems and concerns for teachers. Since 1965 Massachusetts has had a collective bargaining law for teachers, and this has had profound consequences for the implementation of Chapter 766.

I believe it was Secretary of State Kissinger who said that the most difficult public issues to deal with are those which involve the collision of two rights, not the collision of right and wrong. This principle can be applied to the collision in Massachusetts between Chapter 766 and collective bargaining rights for teachers.

For almost a decade teachers in our state have been negotiating their wages, hours, and conditions of employment. Hundreds of local collective bargaining agreements (a number of them negotiated on a multi-year basis) have established the structure of the teachers' work day and the nature of working conditions as they pertain to instructional assignments, preparation time and responsibilities, access to professional development resources, in-service education, participation in curriculum development, and many other issues.

Aware of the fact that there was bound to be some conflict between their present collective bargaining agreements and what the requirements of the new Chapter 766 might be, teachers hoped that regulations for the new law could be promulgated sometime during the school year of 1972-1973 so that the collective bargaining required for the 1974-1975 school year could take into account the shape and scope of the new mandate. However, regulations for Chapter 766 were not promulgated until the spring of 1974, and many of the provisions of those regulations did prove to be incompatible with many local collective bargaining agreements.

For example, Chapter 766 requires that meetings to plan special-needs programs for children are to be scheduled at the convenience of the child's parents. In an industrial state like Massachusetts, where both parents usually work, this means that many such school meetings have to be held after the school day and sometimes in the evening or on weekends. The requirements of a new state mandate that certain things may have to take place after the normal work day of the teacher are incompatible with collective bargaining agreements which define the structure and nature of the teacher's work day. After two years of

collective bargaining, the problem is still not resolved in many communities.

The issue of adequate staffing is another example of the conflict between mainstreaming and certain provisions in collective bargaining agreements. Adequate staffing provisions in local teacher contracts speak to two issues: first, the class size or pupil load factor; second, assignment procedures which link student needs with teacher abilities as determined by certification or some other factor. In many Massachusetts school districts, mainstreaming has produced increases in the size of regular education classes without a corresponding increase in various specialized support services necessary to assist regular classroom teachers in the mainstreaming effort.

Many of the problems connected with the implementation of 766 arise from the fact that Massachusetts is nearly broke. When Chapter 766 was passed in 1972, few if any could have predicted our state's current fiscal crisis. Today, however, there is a freeze on state jobs, many of which are jobs related in some way to the implementation, compliance, and monitoring functions called for by Chapter 766. There are also reductions in force in city and town school systems in Massachusetts which reflect the state's financial problems.

While 766 requires an increase in school spending and staffing, the state and local financial situations in which we find ourselves point to increasing scarcity of funds. This affects the implementation of 766, which is funded by local communities through a reimbursement formula from the state. (The fact that Massachusetts, like other states, is having a hard time paying its bills has made many school districts reluctant to fund those programs and services required by 766 in anticipation of reimbursement.)

In addition, it is almost impossible to get a reliable estimate on the actual costs of implementing Chapter 766 and what the impact of those costs has been on both state and local budgets. Initial estimates for first year implementation costs ranged from $25 to $150 million, although in 1972 the predicted cost was $15 to $20 million. Preliminary data released in December 1975 place first-year costs at about $61 million.

In November 1975, the Massachusetts Coalition for Special Education and the Massachusetts Advocacy Center released the findings of a statewide monitoring project designed to assess the performance of state and local education officials responsible for the implementation of 766 and to stimulate and support citizen advocacy at the community level to ensure proper implementation of the law. The report revealed the following major finding of special interest to teachers:

4. PROGRAMS AND SERVICES

On the whole, Chapter 766 seems to be working pretty well for the youngsters it serves.

Chapter 766 requires significant changes in the procedures by which schools identify, evaluate, and serve children with special needs. These changes affect the structure of the classroom and the techniques of teaching. The concept of maximum integration of handicapped youngsters, for example, requires that all school personnel be involved at some point in the education of handicapped children. Formal orientation and ongoing training for all school personnel are central to the implementation of the law.

Teachers and other school personnel must be trained to identify potential special-needs students, to teach in a diverse classroom environment, and to address the individual needs of students. Training efforts accordingly must include a broad range of activities and issues and should provide all school personnel with a thorough knowledge of the provisions and requirements of the law, the identification and evaluation process, procedures utilized in their own school systems, and their own responsibilities. . . . [However] ratings for individual school systems reflect a wide disparity in the quality of training in school systems. Statewide, the training of local school personnel has been very inadequate, as is reflected by the lack of formality and continuity of the training. Only 5 percent of the school systems of the state, for example, conducted training on a sustained basis 10 months or more during the period between 1972 when the law was enacted, and May 1975 when this survey was undertaken. . . .

Another measure of staff training is its formality and comprehensiveness. This is reflected by the number of training meetings and activities during the period of time in which training was conducted. Some school systems reported more than 100 planned activities to prepare their personnel. Yet the average number of such activities reported was 21.

Recently, a Governor's Commission was organized to advise him of the current status of Chapter 766 and to make appropriate recommendations. Representatives of the Massachusetts Teachers Association on that Commission proposed that a major priority be assigned to the training and professional development activities in which teachers must engage and for which public resources must be supplied in order to successfully implement Chapter 766. The Commission has accepted that recommendation.

The emphasis on early identification of special needs in 766 means that most of the day-to-day work in schools with regard to the law is being done at the elementary school level and most of the training and staff development programs and resources supplied for teachers are designed with elementary schools in mind. Moreover, a disproportionate number of the programs and resources available to help teachers in regular education understand handicapped children in general often refer only to children with particular learning disabilities and do not extend to the full range of special needs in children.

Although many teacher preparation programs continue to emphasize the needs of the elementary school child, some of the most difficult problems of an educational, emotional, behavorial, or psychological nature arise at the secondary school level. Educators at this level justifiably feel that youngsters at the middle, junior high, or high school are being shortchanged and must be helped.

The Massachusetts Teachers Association has called for full funding and full implementation of Chapter 766. We believe that many of the problems highlighted here stem largely from inadequate and inappropriate implementation and insufficient funding. On the whole, Chapter 766 seems to be working pretty well for the youngsters it serves. It does not require the mandatory integration of special-needs youngsters in regular classrooms but rather seeks to provide regular school programs responsive to the needs of youngsters in a manner which will produce the maximum possible mainstreaming. Our main concern as a teacher association is that thousands of youngsters (many of them at the secondary level) who are entitled to services and programs under 766 are not being reached at the present time.

If one major lesson has been learned from the 766 experience in Massachusetts, it is that legislative mandates in themselves are insufficient guarantors of the services or programs which they bring into being. Mainstreaming is a good and appropriate idea, but we owe it to our students and to ourselves as professionals to see that when it is put into practice it is done right and that special-needs children are assigned to educational settings which are prepared to meet and respond to their needs.

Clinical Evaluation and Coordination of Services: An Ecological Model

ELLIDEE D. THOMAS
MELODY J. MARSHALL

ELLIDEE D. THOMAS *is Professor, Department of Pediatrics, University of Oklahoma Health Sciences Center and Director, Child Study Center, Oklahoma Children's Memorial Hospital, Department of Institutions, Social and Rehabilitative Services, State of Oklahoma, Oklahoma City, and* MELODY J. MARSHALL *is Assistant Professor, Department of Family Practice and Community Medicine and Dentistry, University of Oklahoma College of Medicine, Oklahoma City.*

Abstract: A four phase ecological working model for the clinical evaluation and coordination of services for the child with a handicap is presented. This model, based on the experience of a medically based multidisciplinary program, stresses the importance of coordinated services in order that the family can view the interrelationship of each component (medical, educational, and family) of the child's habilitation program. In order for this to take place, interdisciplinary and intradisciplinary communication must occur.

THE environment seldom adapts, and never completely, to the specific needs of an individual with a handicap. Therefore, the ultimate purpose of any special education program is to assist that individual in adapting to the environment to his maximum capacity. How well he is able to do this depends upon how effectively medical, psychological, and social services; educational training programs; the family; and the community have acted together as facilitators to his specific adaptation needs. Sometimes it may be difficult for individuals in various disciplines to recognize their role within a total program, thus making interdisciplinary communications difficult.

The model presented here is based on the Child Study Center at Oklahoma Children's Memorial Hospital. Our experience at the Center demonstrates that an interdisciplinary approach can be effective if the program is based on a model in which roles are understood and communication is good.

The Ecological Process

Human ecology, or the interrelationship of man with his environment, involves a reciprocal association. An individual's actions affect his environment; conversely, changes in a person's habitats influence his self perceptions, his situation, and his behavior. The success with which a person meets life's challenges is dependent upon his ability to reach a desired functional balance between his physical and social habitats, and himself. Three concepts are fundamental to the maintenance of such a balance: adaptation, homeostasis, and ecosystem.

Operationally defined, adaptation is the means by which man copes with his environment. The process of adaptation, learned from birth, allows man to achieve increasing freedom from the limitation of his habitats. These habitats are dynamic, necessitating periodic alterations in adaptive mechanisms (Cohen, 1968). The individual adapts not only to his physical environment; he also adapts socially. One's ability to successfully interrelate with others provides the framework within which he copes with his physical environment.

Homeostasis is the ability of the human organism to maintain a sense of equilibrium within his environment and to make the necessary internal changes for adaptation. Homeostasis and adaptation, equally essential for the success of life, apply to social groups (e.g., community agencies) as well as to individuals.

Society's ecosystem is comprised of the various habitats within which people function. It is within this ecosystem that one accomplishes adaptation and homeostasis. The ecosystem of the child with a handicap includes his family and his educational, recreational, health, and vocational milieus. Coordination of the child's program should be accomplished by individuals in one of his habitats, excluding the family.

The system's habitats are connected with the child and each other so that modification in any one area causes a shift in the other spheres. For example, an increase in the frequency and/or severity of a child's seizures will require diversification of his medical regimen (perhaps further tests or medication change), his educational program (even if merely reduction of stress through a decrease in the length of time spent in his studies at any one period), his recreational program (perhaps a change in the types of activities), and his family (the child's mother may need to spend more time with him to accomplish the other modifications and less time with other family members).

Health, Illness, and Adaptation

Health is the individual's capacity to successfully meet the demands of homeostasis and adaptation; disease is the inability to do this (Dubose, 1967). While health and illness are culturally defined, the definition of health and illness for one individual will differ from that of another within the same culture. Further-

more, these states fluctuate along a continuum for any given individual. One's needs will vary, depending upon his state of health at a particular point in time.

If health and illness represent the success with which an individual adapts to his environment, and if the definition of health for one individual varies from that of another, agencies serving the child with a handicap must develop a flexible program that will meet the child's requirements at any given time. In addition, the program must be modified depending upon the results of periodic reassessment of his needs. Failing to do this, the agency's adaptive mechanism is faulty and may also be defined as ill.

Adaptation and the Child with a Handicap

In addition to those factors involved in basic adaptation, unique patterns of coping must be mobilized for the child with a handicap and his family. For example, the child with visual or hearing impairment runs a greater risk of environmental deprivation than does one not so deprived.

The ecological model facilitating successful adaptation for the child with a handicap and his family includes information gathering (phase I), data pooling (staffing) and initial program recommendation (phase II), initial programing (phase III), and periodic reassessment and program modification (phase IV). Figure 1 illustrates this four phase model.

How well the child adapts depends upon the following general component factors of programing: (a) the handicapping condition, (b) the family, (c) medical services, (d) training and educational services, and eventually, (e) the community as it relates singly to the individual, and the individual to the community. While technically much is understood about each of these, and appropriate services have been delivered, experience at the Child Study Center has been that families often report a feeling of confusion because they perceive services as isolated events. Services should be coordinated so the family perceives that each, though unique, is not an isolated event but that each forms part of the whole in the habilitation plan for the individual, both for the present and future. This is the art of delivery of services and is the principal key to the family's satisfaction and cooperation. Following is a discussion of these factors.

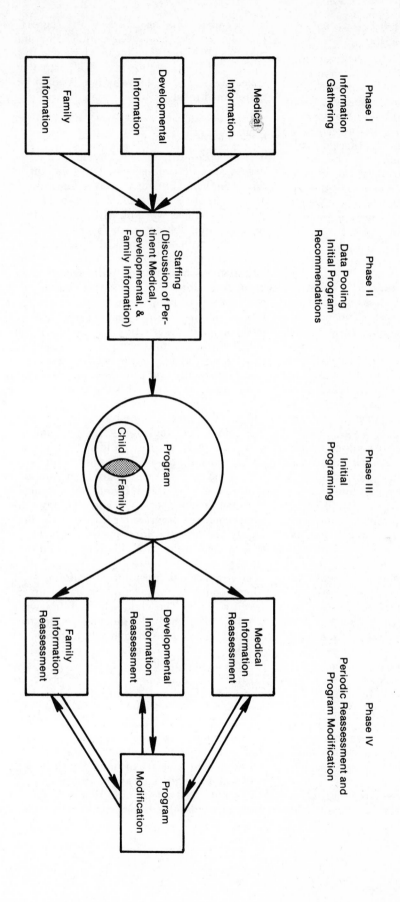

Figure 1. Ecological problem oriented model.

4. PROGRAMS AND SERVICES

General Component Factors of Programing

The Handicapping Condition

Each handicapping condition presents different considerations for training/education programs and for job and living. Many, if not most, of these can be anticipated early. It is important that the family and those directly concerned in the training and educational programs be aware of these anticipated effects as early as possible so the program can be planned in an anticipatory manner. It should, however, remain flexible to meet changing needs.

The Family

The family is probably ultimately the most important factor in the success or failure of the child's adaptation process. This does not imply that sole responsibility rests on the family or that they are to be blamed for failure of a program. It does imply that professionals must recognize that families need to be dealt with—not just told of the child's condition—from the beginning and must be prepared to help the family at whatever stage they may be at any given time.

Professionals' support of families in preparing for their key role should begin as soon as the problem is recognized. At this time it may be appropriate to express human sympathy and understanding in addition to providing specific information about the condition (Hare, Laurence, Paynes, Rawnsley, 1966). To be most effective, professionals must also recognize that parents of a child with a handicap have certain needs and must go through certain processes, both early and later. These may include modification of the initial maternal touching response if the problem is recognized at birth (Klaus, Kennell, Plumb, & Zuehlke, 1970); initial regression and disorganization (Goodman, 1964); and anger, depression, denial, marriage strains, and deterioration of religious beliefs (Stone, 1973; Drotar, Baskiewicz, Irvin, Kennell, & Klaus, 1975). A feeling of participation in their child's habilitation program is also a parental need while at the same time maintaining an identity of themselves (Hammer, 1972).

Our experience has been that at any given point the family must be met "where they're at" whether this be a stage of progress, plateau, or regression. The child's program may need to be modified (even if temporarily) because of the parental stage at a particular time. Close contact with the family must be maintained if this is to be done effectively.

Medical Services

The purpose of the medical evaluation is to assess specific problems and to treat them where indicated, using whatever disciplines are necessary. Information should be provided to those working with the child in a program that indicates, so far as possible, implications that the medical condition has for training and for the individual's life situation. For example, will the seizure disorder, per se, necessitate specific educational training techniques (probably not), or modify the job possibilities (probably), or living alternative (it may not)? In addition to such information being essential to program planning, our experience has been that both family and professionals are more comfortable working with the child if they have this kind of information.

Figures 2 and 3 illustrate the various disciplines involved in specific information gathering pertinent to a child with multiple problems and the staffing/information gathered and assimilated for initial programing. Coordination of the information obtained from the various specialists and planning of a comprehensive program for the child and his family are essential for a maximum level of adaptation for the child, his family, and the agency.

The individual prescriptive training and educational program should be based upon specific needs. The child who is blind will require a different evaluation and training for mobility and education than the child who is paraplegic. For example, the child with paraplegia may need an orthopedist, a physical therapist, and a brace maker in order to gain mobility skills. If paraplegia alone is the problem, no special educational techniques may be required. The child who is blind, on the other hand, may need a teacher (rather than an orthopedist, a physical therapist, and a brace maker) to learn his mobility skills, as well as for specific educational purposes.

It should be kept in mind that individual training needs at different times will vary,

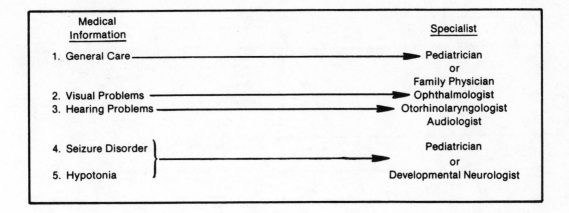

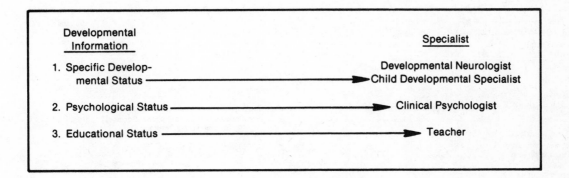

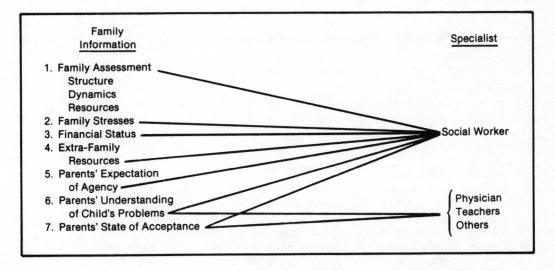

Figure 2. Information gathering.

4. PROGRAMS AND SERVICES

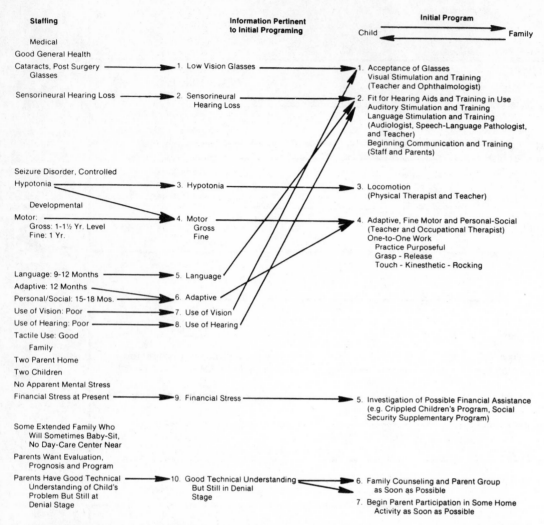

Figure 3. Interrelationship of staffing, information pertinent to initial programing, and initial program.

and current status information must be maintained in order that the training program may be periodically modified accordingly as shown in Figure 1, phases III and IV. This reassessment should be conducted both in a scheduled as well as an informal manner. Lines of communication between all professionals working with a child and his family should be such that an exchange of information pertinent to the child's program is facilitated as often as daily if needed.

The Community

The community, or ecosystem, is composed of the various habitats within which the child and his family function—home, medical, educational, social, recreational, vocational. Portions of these habitats come into play with the child and his family at different times depending upon their current needs and available resources within the community. This ecosystem can reach (or be reached) into a training/educational program early and need not wait until the more traditional community services (e.g., special education, vocational rehabilitation, sheltered workshops) begin. The agency in charge of the child's educational program can take the initiative in tapping community resources.

For example, the Child Study Center has called upon regular day care nurseries to take its children into their program part time, upon a local Girl Scout troop for assistance in its summer program, and upon a local cab company to provide transportation for children. There have been other instances when specific needs have dictated the community resource to which the Center turned, a resource perhaps not usually thought of in terms of a program for the handicapped. Examples of these include special equipment by woodworking students in a local high school, college engineering students, and senior citizens group. In each instance the group the Center has called upon has continued to show caring interest in the children and their programs. The authors believe that this type of interest and cooperation could be generated in almost any locality.

Summary

The primary goal of a program for the child with a handicap is successful adaptation—social as well as physical—for the child, and for his family as his main facilitator and in their own right. The exact process by which this adaptation occurs varies from individual to individual and family to family. There are, however, commonalities inherent in services for children with handicaps that may be identified in an ecological model. The components of this model have been identified as (a) information gathering, (b) data pooling, (c) initial programing, and (d) periodic reassessment and program modification.

The keys to the model's effectiveness are flexibility to meet individual needs; one central, coordinating agency/program; and effective interpersonal communication. Not only must the child with a handicap and his family adapt, but the agency must also be flexible so it can adapt the child's program to meet his specific needs. If this is not done, he is forced to function in a stereotyped program, thereby significantly restricting his level of adaptation.

The handicapping conditions that necessitate a special program for the individual child may persist into adulthood. However, if successful adaptation is achieved and maintained, the individual can have the chance to achieve at his maximum potential and become a participating member of the society within which he lives.

References

Cohen, Y. Culture as adaptation. In Y. Cohen (Ed.), *Man in adaptation: The cultural present.* Chicago: Aldine Publishing Co., 1968.

Drotar, D., Baskiewicz, A., Irvin, N., Kennell, J., & Klaus, M. The adaptation of parents to the birth of an infant with a congenital malformation: A hypothetical model. *Pediatrics,* 1975, *56,* 710-717.

Dubose, R. *Man adapting.* New Haven CT: Yale University Press, 1967.

Goodman, L. Continuing treatment of parents with congenitally defective infants. *Social Work,* 1964, *9,* 92-97.

Hammer, E. *Families of deaf-blind children: Case studies of stress.* Paper presented at the Regional American Orthopsychiatric Conference, Galveston, Texas, November 1972.

Hare, E. H., Laurence, K. M., Paynes, H., & Rawnsley, K. Spina bifida cystica and family stress. *British Medical Journal,* 1966, *2,* 757-760.

Klaus, M. H., Kennell, J. H., Plumb, N., & Zuehlke, S. Human maternal behavior at the first contact with her young. *Pediatrics,* 1970, *46,* 187-192.

Stone, H. The birth of a child with Down's syndrome: A medico-social study of thirty-one children and their families. *Scottish Medical Journal,* 1973, *18,* 182.

Communication Skills— Translating Theory into Practice

VILMA T. FALCK

An individualized education program (IEP), developed as the result of cooperative team planning, can help assure compliance with the mandate of Public Law 94-142—to provide a free appropriate education for every handicapped child. At the time an IEP is planned, a trajectory is established to serve as the basis for a tracking system to assure the appropriateness of long range goals, intermediate objectives, expected outcomes, and target behaviors. In this way, each child is provided with a plan that can be monitored to allow alterations to the projected program.

The key concept for assuring appropriateness of education is cooperative teamwork. Specific management plans, recommended regimens or educational procedures, and criteria for evaluation must all be part of a program that avoids fragmentation of services provided by different members of the educational team. Cooperative team management reflects more than the need to have input from a variety of human resources. It means integration and coordination of all services that are provided for the child within his or her environment, i.e., not only in the therapy room but in the classroom, playground, home, and community. This can occur only if special educators, regular classroom teachers, resource or support personnel, parents, and significant others within the total community reinforce each other's efforts to help the handicapped child.

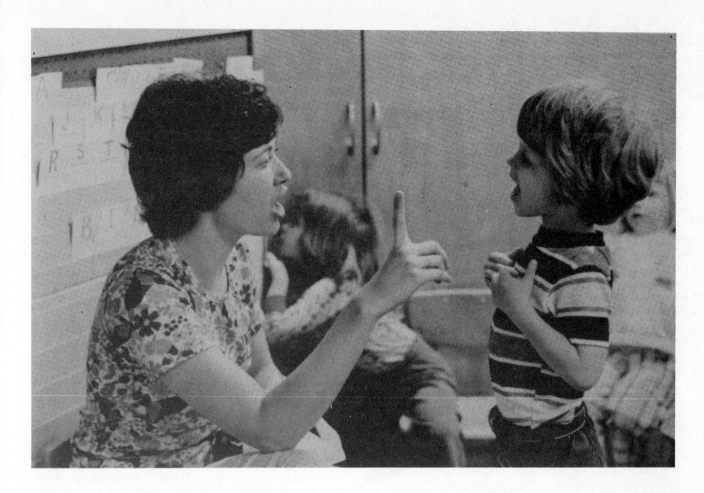

COORDINATION OF SPEECH AND LANGUAGE SERVICES

Speech and language services must be coordinated with other environmental influences that have a potential impact on the child's ability to learn and thrive within his or her environment. We have always recognized that it is impossible to separate the act of communication (reception, integration, or expression) from the educational program. Even so, all too often speech and language services in public schools continue to be offered as a part time activity, provided twice a week for 20 minutes each session, apart from the classroom, and sometimes out of touch with the 24 hour per day reality of the child's world.

There are many exceptions to this generalization. More and more innovative, creative programs are being initiated that do coordinate all services because they recognize the critical relationship between verbal language and educational achievement. The approach and trend is clearly away from the therapy room and into the regular classroom, a trend consistent with mainstreaming, normalization, and equal rights under the law.

ROLE AND RESPONSIBILITY OF THE SPEECH AND LANGUAGE SPECIALIST

Public school speech and language specialists are important members of the educational team. Their roles and responsibilities may vary depending on local situations, but their competency and professional acumen must reflect an ability to work with children, with other members of the team, with parents (who are considered members of the team), and with significant others within the community. Their contribution may be to provide:

1. Speech and language services to prevent deviations of communication.

2. Early intervention strategies in the regular classroom.

3. Direct services to children with mild to moderate communication disorders.

4. Support of intensive efforts on the part of many people who work to help a child overcome serious communication disorders.

5. Support services for team members to facilitate their communications.

The speech and language specialist in public schools may be labeled a speech-language pathologist (preferred by the American Speech and Hearing Association), speech clinician, speech therapist, speech teacher, or may have other similar titles. The specific title is significant only to the degree that it communicates function to others with whom the specialist in communicative disorders is working.

Educational objectives in the areas of speech and language must specify type of intervention (individual, group, or classroom techniques) as well as the target of intervention (the child, the parent, regular classroom teacher, and/or other personnel).

Integrating speech and language services into the total educational process mandates the need to build in objectives that specifically recognize the needs of the child to learn language patterns;

to improve articulation, voice quality, rhythm, syntax, semantic usage; and to develop alternative means of communication. The needs of the parents must also be recognized. These needs include understanding, making decisions, communicating with their child, and communicating with teachers.

Teachers' needs must also be considered when objectives are established. These needs include improving skills to communicate effectively (speaking, writing, listening), providing opportunities to practice speech and language skills in regular classrooms, knowing reinforcement techniques to use for children, and remembering individual objectives for each child.

EXPANDED CONCEPTUALIZATION OF THE SPEECH AND LANGUAGE SPECIALIST

Assuming responsibility to meet the speech and language needs of the child, the parent, and the regular classroom teacher as well as other members of the educational team requires an expanded conceptualization of the speech and language specialists who work in public schools. These specialists may need to demonstrate their new role of assisting children, parents, and/or teachers in implementing the IEP and integrating functions of communication. They may also need to develop new skills to work with parents and teachers as adult learners. Their motivation patterns, learning habits, life styles, and agendas are quite different from those of children who previously have been the primary target population.

New tools, new techniques, and new methods may well be required of all persons who contribute to individualized education programing for children who, as mandated by law, will tend to be those who were previously underserved and thus, often may be the most severely handicapped. Children with severe problems may require multivarious intervention programs that can become complicated because of the number of services which need cooperative coordination.

Speech and language specialists must recognize that each person who has contact with a child is a potential speech and language "teacher" and may be in an appropriate position to meet the speech and language needs of a child. They must be sensitive to the feelings of other members of the educational team who may have tremendous contributions to make in the areas of speech and language.

It is intriguing to consider that the problem for the speech and language specialist may not be to focus attention on the communicative needs of the child but to determine what skills it will take to solve the problems of communication, to identify the communicative needs of the planning and rehabilitative team, to determine what will facilitate the transfer of information to all appropriate professionals who may be working with a child, and to design ways to insure that people will use information provided for them to assist the child with speech and language disorders. Unless the needs for communication of all appropriate persons are considered, the best plan for an IEP may fail. Maximum impact for a child will require that all concerned understand, agree to, and support similar if not identical goals and objectives in order to reinforce the targeted behavior.

Thus, the role of speech and language specialists is to be professional partners working along with others who are significant to the child's environment. They must be willing to work with other special education personnel as well as the regular classroom teacher and the parent. The expanded role will require these specialists to provide or plan for speech and language services for the child as well as for those who are associated with that child. This will be necessary to an extent never before anticipated because there may be a need to overcome potential communication barriers that may occur due to interpersonal relations, traditional or obsolete points of view involving personal or professional attitudes, and role expectations.

CONSULTATION

Also necessary to an extent never before experienced will be the need for further development of consultative skills to assist regular classroom teachers to develop and implement the IEP. As a professional in the area of communication, the speech and language specialist can assist the entire IEP planning team to improve its interaction. Such specific techniques as suggesting constructive alternatives when feedback is negative, encouraging members to ask for clarification of points to insure common understanding, giving examples to defend points of view, justifying recommended procedures, and not giving commands (we must, you must, he must) can all be utilized, as well as suggested, by the speech and language specialist as the team members work cooperatively to consolidate group ideas into a workable plan.

The speech and language specialist will find many opportunities to demonstrate and encourage professional interaction skills, including:

- Smiling, being friendly, courteous, and cooperative.
- Giving feedback concerning a child's progress.
- Reinforcing positive statements made by members of the IEP planning team.
- Reporting the outcome of suggestions to the appropriate persons.
- Showing consideration to others.
- Seeking agreement.
- Resolving differences in points of view or agreeing to disagree.
- Assisting others to participate in the group process.
- Asking meaningful questions.

As part of the consultative process, it is important to develop a style acceptable to the person who is being provided the consultation. It is interesting to note that in industry, consultants are employed by a client who seeks help, assistance, advice, etc., whereas public school consultants are generally hired by the "establishment." The individual/classroom teacher for whom consultation is needed may not believe in the need for, may not need, or may not want, advice or help. For this reason the style or approach used in communicating with each classroom teacher or other person (parent or other educational personnel) may have to vary. Even traditional speech and language services may differ depending on committee or team constituency. For example, if psychological services exist, the specialist's role in parent involvement programs will be different than if no staff member is concerned with this important aspect of the total program.

ASSISTING TEACHERS AND PARENTS

Speech and language specialists have long been resources and consultants in public school programs; there has always been a need to help and work with others. The challenges presented by Public Law 94-142 do not markedly change this intent. However, there is a new focus on quality and on accountability as regulatory functions are built into the law. Thus, the need to be productive is mandated not only for the child, but for the regular classroom teacher and the parent as well.

Speech and language specialists will have to adapt their understanding of the therapeutic process, which is an inherent competency developed as part of their own training, to a plan that meets the needs of the classroom. They will have to assist the regular teacher to explore alternative procedures and techniques that can be used in teaching required skills to children and their parents. Encouraging parents to respond and contribute to the educational program to whatever extent possible is a significant part of the problem to be solved with the assistance of speech and language specialists. Parents who assume a role in extending or reinforcing speech and language patterns that are taught in school will greatly enhance their child's progress.

Many schools are now providing specific education programs to assist parents who have an awesome responsibility for their handicapped child. Communicating to the parents that they have an opportunity to take increased responsibility may or may not be the task of speech and language specialists, but they do have an important role in facilitating the communication process between parents and team members.

The speech and language specialist can alert team members and help them to overcome potential communicative barriers such as: (1) the tendency for a listener to agree with what is being said in order to please the professional, (2) the problem of mixed messages where parents (or educators) may be saying one thing but thinking another, (3) the tendency to stereotype, to judge others by one's own personal standards; seeing what is expected to be seen and hearing what is expected to be heard, (4) assuming that the listeners do not understand when they do not immediately respond

to information or instructions, (5) using too many words and/or providing more information than can comfortably be assimilated or remembered.

Since parents are the most important change agents in any child's life, excluding them wastes valuable and necessary resources. Thus, there is a general recognition of the need for parent involvement as:

1. Contributing members of the educational planning team.
2. Reinforcers of new language and learning skills.
3. Decision makers throughout their lifetimes (parents have a lifelong reponsibility for their handicapped child).
4. Formers of self concept (their role in assuring the self esteem of the child is acute).
5. Teachers of speech and language skills as they emphasize positive patterns of interaction, sensitive listening, and social reinforcement.

Parents are being asked to understand the status of our ability to determine the capability and potential of their child, communicate with educators about their child's progress, understand the law, participate in group process, understand the educational and health care system, participate in the decision making process, take a greater role in the management of their child, etc. To become so proficient and to be able to take action in positive ways requires an informed and socially competent parent. Public Law 94-142 can be regarded as a parents' rights as well as a child's rights law. Their right to understand educational plans and programs is implied. Parents must know their rights to a "free appropriate education" for their child. However, parents are being asked to assume weighty responsibilities and many will need assistance in assuming their appropriate role.

SUMMARY

The appropriate implementation of Public Law 94-142 will come about through the coordinated efforts of children, parents, educational professionals, health professionals, and decision makers in society. It will take no less than enthusiastic, sustained, and dedicated effort. In this new arena of educational opportunity, the speech and language specialist could be of invaluable assistance to insure effective communications that can provide the backbone to this effort.

BIBLIOGRAPHY

Dreikurs, R. *The challenge of parenthood.* New York: Meredith Press, 1958.

Falck, V. Communication and language barriers which may interfere with compliance. In *Health education and the Mexican American* (Report of project funded by the Center for Disease Control). Atlanta: May, 1977. (Contract No. 200-75-0568)

Freeman, G. *Speech and language services and the classroom teacher.* Reston VA: The Council for Exceptional Children, in press.

Gallagher, J. J. (Ed.). *The application of child development research.* Reston VA: The Council for Exceptional Children, 1975.

Shaw, M. E. Group dynamics. In *The Psychology of Small Group Behavior.* New York: McGraw-Hill, 1976.

PARENT INVOLVEMENT

Parental

Involvement

Historically, the bureaucratic skill that surrounds the public school has served to insulate the system from the outside world. In many instances, parents have literally been denied the chance of effectively participating in decisions having significant implications for the total life of their children. Perhaps this explains the leadership position parents have taken in securing due process safeguards in educational decisions effecting their children. Parents have also caused tremendous impact by successful legislation and litigation efforts.

With the passage of P.L. 94-142, parental participation during the development of an individualized educational plan has been mandated. Parents must be given the opportunity to participate as active members of the child study team. In a manual published by the National Association of State Directors of Special Education, direct participation of parents is said to be desirable for several reasons.

1. The information which they can bring to the Committee may greatly enrich the total Committee's understanding of the needs of the child and family;

2. Involvement will usually be associated with a greater chance of parent cooperation;
3. Cooperation is essential to the success of the child's program;
4. The parents' presence can help assure that they clearly understand the function of the committee;
5. The parents' informed consent is essential at several stages of the Committee's functioning.

Professionals must understand how parents perceive the IEP process and whether parents believe they are actually a part of decision making activities.

Increased parental involvement in determining the educational placement and programming of their child does not necessarily equate with a better educational model for the child. Many variables that effect parental involvement can not be mandated. Understanding the proceedings and the parents' due process rights within the proceedings are prerequisites for effective participation. Every effort must be expended to contact, motivate and involve all parents to understand and exercise their basic rights.

The following articles focus on the due process rights of parents and give recommendations for greater parental involvement in educational decision making.

The Rights of Children and Their Parents

State and federal courts have played an active role in the field of education in the past few years. The result has been a reshaping of the rules that teachers and administrators must live by as they make decisions on the educational future of children. Basically, the many court cases have defined further who is entitled to an education, and the due process to which every child and parent is entitled. Currently, the influence of the judiciary is seen in the modification of state and federal laws and procedures in education.

Basic Rights of Children and Their Parents

- All children are entitled to an appropriate education and an education in the least restrictive environment possible.
- Parents have the right to appeal a decision made to alter their child's educational program.
- Parents have the right to review and use in their appeal all information used by the school to make the decision.
- Parents have the right to have a neutral party decide on the most appropriate program for their child.
- Parents have the right to have the benefits of a special program specified and evaluated.

Implications for Educators

- Educational services must be available to all children regardless of severity of handicap.
- A variety of special education services must be available if children are to receive an education that is appropriate and as close to a program of normalization as possible.
- To promote understanding, parents should be informed early of difficulties experienced by their children. They should be involved in the planning and evaluation of the special services provided.
- Educational decision making must be based on the efforts of an educational team that collects and uses all appropriate information, not on a single test.
- Measurable objectives must be set for children receiving special services. The progress of these children must be reported to their parents.

The demands of courts and school laws should not frighten us. They are only saying that every child has the right to "fair play" and an appropriate education in the schools. This is no more than what we would wish for our children.

This material is provided as a service from The Council for Exceptional Children, 1920 Association Drive, Reston, Virginia 22091

A Model of Parental Participation in the Pupil Planning Process

Roland K. Yoshida
Jay Gottlieb

Authors: **ROLAND K. YOSHIDA**, Ph.D. (University of Southern California), Education Program Specialist, Intramural Research Program, Bureau of Education for the Handicapped, 1901 N. Moore St., #809, Roslyn, VA 22209; **JAY GOTTLIEB**, Ph.D. (Yeshiva University), Research Associate, Intramural Research Program, Bureau of Education for the Handicapped.

ABSTRACT. Most due process systems stress the formal hearing which occurs after special education placement has been recommended. However, it may become necessary to involve parents prior to this decision because of the passage of P. L. 94–142, which mandates parental participation during the development of an individualized education plan. A model is presented to enable school systems to classify their current practices vis a vis parental involvement during the pupil planning process and to serve as a guide for future activities that bear on the issue of parental involvement in school-related decision making.

The sequence of events that has occurred during the past few years has led to the inescapable conclusion that due process procedures have become an integral part of special education practices and are likely to become an even more firmly embedded aspect of special education in the future. Due process basically refers to the procedures which are intended to balance the interests of all concerned parties in decisions which affect them (Kirp, 1973). In the context of special education, the concerned parties are the student, his parents, and the school. The student's needs focus on receipt of educational opportunity to achieve his potential. The parents' needs center around their aspirations and expectations for their child, which the placement decision could affect. The school is concerned with equally legitimate but very different needs. It must consider the aggregate welfare of all students and the welfare of any individual child, as well as the problems of staff support for placement decisions. Due process procedures in theory enable these parties to air their concerns, and to have them fairly examined and weighed so that the result is an impartial and competent decision.

School systems were perceived to be abusing their exclusive power as educational sorters of children; as a result professionals and parents initiated the movement to establish a more equitable redistribution of that power. Professionals' and parents' concerns about the perceived abuses by the schools did not arise overnight. They resulted from a continuing dissatisfaction with the services that were being assigned to or withheld from a number of different groups. While there was considerable overlap in the overt expressions of professional and parental dissatisfaction, three distinct stages can be identified, each of which occurred in a particular time-frame and resulted in an identifiable extension of due process guarantees as originally set forth in the *Brown v. Board of Education* (1954) decision.

The first extension of the guarantees provided by the Brown decision emanated from professionals' judgments that many mildly retarded children were misclassified and provided with an inappropriate educational experience in special classes (e.g., Dunn, 1968). These professionals' judgments were buttressed by legal rulings which supported the view that special classes were stigmatizing to mildly handicapped children (e.g., *Diana v. State Board of Education*, 1970). Overlapping the concern for the inappropriate classification of mildly handicapped children was the second concern that the more seriously handicapped children were being excluded from receiving educational treatment. *The Pennsylvania Association for Retarded Children v. The Commonwealth of Pennsylvania* (1972) decision was a landmark in correcting this deficiency. Finally, the third extension emanated from recent federal legislation which mandated not only that all handicapped children, regardless of the severity of the handicap, are entitled to receive education, they are entitled to receive an appropriate education (P.L. 94–142). Each of the three stages in the evolution of due process procedures resulted in an increase in the rights of the child and his parents and concomitant eroding of the school's authority in making placement decisions.

5. PARENTAL INVOLVEMENT

Attempts by the courts and legislation to include parents in the decision-making apparatus has resulted in an erosion of the schools' authority as the sole arbiter of child placement decisions. However the schools' attempts to effect successful parental involvement have been hampered by several factors. The first factor results from the schools having had a long history of experience in placing children without parental involvement. Thus, they lack precedents for developing an appropriate role for parents. A second impediment to effective parental involvement has been the lack of clearly conceptualized models that provide alternatives for the schools. That is, there are a number of ways that parents could conceivably become involved in placement decisions, each of which entails different amounts of involvement. The scope of parental involvement has to be clearly articulated and schools have to decide the extent to which they actually want parents to be involved.

This paper is an attempt to provide a framework for the study of parental involvement procedures in the pupil planning process. Most due process systems stress the formal hearing which occurs after a decision has been made to change the child's education placement, but they do not stress the importance of parent and child involvement prior to this decision (Kotin, 1976). Given the new federal legislation (P.L.94–142) to include parents during the development of an individualized educational plan, it may become necessary for the schools to obtain information about a given child from the parents and to invite them to case conferences for this purpose, and others. It is our intent to provide a model to enable school systems to classify their current practices vis a vis parental involvement during the pupil planning process, as well as to serve as a guide for future activities that bear on the issue of parental involvement in school-relevant decision making.

In the absence of a functional model, school administrators may have a difficult time recognizing the many possible pitfalls that are inherent in any formal attempt to include parents in decision-making roles. An example of one of these possible difficulties is the considerable potential variability regarding the appropriate time for parents to be involved. Should parents be involved at the time of initial referral of the child for possible special class placement, or should they be involved after the school personnel have agreed that the child indeed belongs in the special class?

The model presented in this paper provides the summary stages at which parents may be involved in the appraisal process and, within those stages, classifies the degree of influence they have on the decisions made about their child. If we conceive of the appraisal process as a continuous sequence of events, its numerous functions may occur in the following three stages:

1. Input—School staff gathers psychometric, academic, social, familial, and medical information required to make a decision.
2. Process—The case conference(s) of the placement committee considers and evaluates this information.
3. Produce—A decision is made which provides an eligibility statement and educational plan for the student.

Within each of these stages, the degree of influence the parent has may vary considerably. By analyzing when parents are involved in the placement process and the extent of their influence, we can identify various roles parents may assume.

Input Phase

Permission-Giver. Most state laws presently prescribe that parents' written permission be obtained before any psychological or any related educational evaluation is performed on their child. As part of the permission-giver role, parents may wish to question school personnel regarding the series of events that are likely to occur during the proceedings which lead to a decision regarding the child's educational status. Without parental consent, further consideration of the child's education eligibility for handicapped status is precluded.

Information-Giver. There are several ways that the school can obtain information regarding the child's home life. One way is to review the child's school records. Depending on their completeness and recency, information could be obtained regarding the family structure, whether any serious medical problems existed prior to the child's enrollment in school, and the child's history of school attendance. The information that is obtained from school records probably supplies minimal, nondetailed information that will provide some insights into the child's functioning in the home. More detailed information about the child's home life is best obtained from direct interviews with the child's parents. Interviews can occur in the school or the parents' home. In either case, the parents function as information givers by providing data which will be applied to the final decision affecting their child. A possible danger of the parental interview to which the interviewer must be sensitive is the possibility that the parents may describe their child's home life inaccurately. Consequently, interviews conducted in the home by trained observers, e.g. social workers, may not only minimize the likelihood of biased reporting but would also serve as a basis to validate the parents' responses by providing observations of parent-child interactions as they occur in the home. Thus, although the school needs information from parents to complement the decision making process, they must ensure that the information is accurate and that the parents are operating with their child's welfare as the primary goal.

Preference-Giver. The preference-giver role represents the highest level of influence during the input phase. In this role, the school asks parents to give their preference for the educational program in which they want their child to participate. There are a number of degrees of specificity at which parents may express their preferences. For example, at the most global level, parents may simply indicate that they do or do not want their child to attend a segregated special class. At a more detailed level, the parents may express the desire that their child attend a particular class because they know the teacher and/or because they believe that a particular teacher has the right temperament and style. On the other hand, the parents may agree with the program options proposed by the school. In either case, the parents are given the opportunity to express their beliefs about the most appropriate education for their children.

Process Phase

Outsider. When parents give permission for the school to evaluate their child during the input phase of the placement process, they not only give permission for all necessary testing to be done, they also give permission for school personnel to conduct case conference(s) to evaluate the data that were collected and arrive at a placement decision. It is common practice in many states for parents to be invited to attend the case conference, even though it does not violate due process guarantees if the parents do not attend this meeting. When the parents choose not to attend or are not invited by the schools, they function in the role of an outsider. There are several reasons why parents may not attend the meeting, even when invited. They may be disinterested; there are system constraints such as when the case conferences are held during working hours; and perhaps most importantly, there is a lack of knowledge about the school system in general and the placement process in particular. It is probably good practice, however, for the schools to involve the parents during the case conference so they will not perceive that their wishes are being ignored or that their child's best interests are being violated. As a result, they may become more receptive to the placement procedure and decision and later appeals may be minimized.

Passive Participant. When the parents do attend the case conference, their role may involve minimal influence. This is demonstrated in two ways. First, the parents may be asked to provide information to the committee, to elaborate on previously collected data, and/or to resolve discrepancies in this information. For example, they may discuss the nature of their child's peer interactions at home, his study habits, temperament and so forth, which the committee may use when making decisions. On the other hand, parents could raise questions of the professionals in order to clarify some points for themselves, such as the meaning of test scores or the teacher's description of the child's behavior in the classroom. In either manner, the parents and case conference members have a clear understanding that the parents are not to offer suggestions for planning or programming or to serve as critics of the committee process or decision.

Active Participant. Participation in the group decision making process is not simply an aggregate of all interaction during a particular meeting, nor is it limited to the formal selection of a proposed course of action. Rather, it is conceptualized as a sequential process of three well-defined tasks in which members generate alternatives, evaluate those alternatives, and finally select a solution (Vroom, 1969; Wood, 1973). In our model, the active participant suggests placements for the child and, if appropriate, the corresponding instructional methods. Also, the parents may evaluate the proposed placement and programs by questioning their suitability for their child. Finally the parents have the power to help select the child's placement and program. Thus, the parents have a voice in the decision making apparatus equal to those of school personnel.

Product Phase

Legitimizer. The product phase of our model entails parental approval of the final placement decision made by the committee. The parental role becomes one of the legitimizer. That is, parents may accept or reject the recommendation of the committee. If they accept, then the child is placed into the recommended placement. However, when they reject the recommendation, detailed procedures for appeals to appropriate hearing officers and the courts, as specified in the PARC decision and in federal legislation, may be enacted if necessary. Thus, granting legitimacy to the decision rests with the parents.

Conclusion

The model suggested here can help identify variables related to parental participation, namely, the times at which they are allowed in the process and the degree of influence they exert at those times. The intersection of these variables defines roles for parents which are beyond the more familiar ones of giving permission for evaluation and judging the placement recommendation of the schools. The model may be used for at least two purposes. First, schools may use this model to help decide the extent to which they will allow parental involvement in the process. This use helps school personnel decide what parental role(s) is most appropriate for their system. For example, they may decide that the active participant is most desirable during the process phase. Once the role has been selected, they determine and implement the means by which parents can fulfill such roles. Second, the model may suggest variables for evaluating the effectiveness of including parents. This allows one to evaluate the magnitude of parental participation in any phase of the pupil planning process. To illustrate with the case of the active participant, such concerns as whether the parents do, in fact, suggest, evaluate and help decide the educational placement for their child can be examined. In either case, the model provides some useful guidelines for responding to those needs.

Assuming that greater parental participation in the decision making apparatus is associated with increased fulfillment of due process guarantees, what are some of the gains and losses that can be anticipated? On the positive side, parents may not reject school placement decisions as often, thereby reducing the number of due process hearings (Kirp & Kirp, 1975). Also, parents may become more receptive and less hostile to the school's demands, especially when they are involved in placing students in special classes. Finally, parents may be taught methods for dealing with the child in the home, thus fulfilling the "home-school" team effort so often advocated. This team relationship may become necessary as parents are required to be present during the development of the individualized educational plan as proposed in P.L. 94–142. However, there may be certain disadvantages that accompany parental involvement. Greater participation also means more opportunities for the parents to observe the system, and they may conclude that schools are not operating in the best interests of their child. Also, schools may have to adjust committee meeting times to accommodate working parents. More im-

5. PARENTAL INVOLVEMENT

portantly, the presence of parents may require major changes in the committee's handling of the case, which may affect the degree of openness with which members state opinions and suggest solutions. These costs and benefits must be weighed when defining the parental role.

These efforts to increase parental involvement in determining the educational placement and programming of their child focus on legal procedures which must necessarily be followed. However, fulfilling legal criteria should not be equated with remedying the fundamental problem which due process was intended to relieve. Do these procedures result in educationally sound practices which increase the student's achievement and adjustment? Until this question is answered positively, professionals and laymen alike should be cognizant that improvement in due process procedures does not necessarily imply a concomitant improvement in educational performance among those the litigation and legislation was designed to help most—the pupils.

References

Brown v. Board of Education, 347 U.S. 483 (1954).

Diana v. State Board of Education, No. C–70–37 (N.D. Cal., 1970).

Dunn, L. M. Special education for the mildly retarded—Is much of it justifiable? *Exceptional Children*, 1968, 35, 5–22.

Kirp, D. L. Schools as sorter: The constitutional and policy implications of student classification. *University of Pennsylvania Law Review*, 1973, 121, 705–797.

Kirp, D. L. & Kirp, L. M. The legislation of the school psychologists' world. *Journal of School Psychology*, 1976, 14, 83–89.

Kotin, L. Due process in special education: Legal perspectives. Unpublished paper, Center for Public Interest Law, Inc., 2 Park Square, Boston, Massachusetts, 1976.

Pennsylvania Association for Retarded Children v. Commonwealth of Pennsylvania. 343 F. Supp. 279 (E.D. Pa., 1972).

Public Law 94–142 (Education for All Handicapped Act of 1975).

Vroom, V. H. Industrial social psychology. In G. Lindzey and E. Aronson (Eds.). *The handbook of social psychology, Vol. 5* (2nd Ed.) Reading, Massachusetts: Addison-Wesley, 1969.

A Primer on Due Process: Education Decisions for Handicapped Children

ALAN ABESON
NANCY BOLICK
JAYNE HASS

Extensive litigation and legislation have resulted in mandates that state and local education agencies guarantee due process protection to handicapped children in all matters pertaining to their identification, evaluation and educational placement. This article presents excerpts from a new CEC publication which contains an approach to meeting those requirements. The background of due process, sequential procedures required, structure and operation of hearings, the surrogate parent and sample forms are all included in the full publication.

ALAN ABESON *is Assistant Director of State and Local Governmental Relations, The Council for Exceptional Children, Reston, Virginia;* NANCY BOLICK *is Information Associate, and* JAYNE HASS *is Research Associate, Special Education Administrative Policy Manuals Project, The Council for Exceptional Children, Reston, Virginia.*

The work performed herein was done pursuant to a grant from the Bureau of Education for the Handicapped, US Office of Education, Department of Health, Education and Welfare. The opinions expressed herein, however, do not necessarily reflect the position or policy of the US Office of Education, and no official endorsement by the US Office of Education should be inferred.

Children's rights cannot be secured until some particular institution has recognized them and assumed responsibility for enforcing them. In the past, adult institutions have not performed this function partly . . . because it was thought children had few rights to secure. Unfortunately, the institutions designed specifically for children also have failed to accomplish this aim, largely because they were established to safeguard interests, not to enforce rights, on the assumption that the former could be done without the latter. (Rodham, 1973, p. 506)

Exclusion and the Right to an Education

With the conflict between safeguarding interests and assuring individual rights as a backdrop, the rights of children in many areas of American life are being examined and clarified, often through judicial intervention. Nowhere is this examination more intense than in public education. In this decade, questions of "rights" for public school students have been raised in relation to freedom of expression, personal rights such as hair length and dress regulations, marriage and pregnancy, police intervention, corporal punishment, discipline, and confidentiality of records. While all of these have an impact on handicapped children, none is more pervasive than the right to due process which governs decisions regarding identification, evaluation, and educational placement.

5. PARENTAL INVOLVEMENT

Much litigation has been concerned with handicapped children seeking affirmation of their right to an education and the protection of due process of law. This wave of litigation is evidence of the way in which public schools in the past often ignored appropriate legal processes in denying these children their rights. The public schools often based such action upon law which was interpreted to give them the right to deny the opportunity of a public education to some children, either on a short term or permanent basis.

Today, it is a matter of public policy that the purpose of the public school is to provide every child with the opportunity for a free, public, and appropriate education. This policy makes it clear that to solve the problems a child is having in school by excluding him is not to solve the problems of the child, but of the school. It is unreasonable for the public schools to expel a child because of a behavioral problem (more popularly known as a discipline problem), an inability to learn, or any handicapping condition. Regardless of the types of exclusion that have been used and regardless of where they have occurred, the common denominator is that such practices have usually occurred with little or no regard for due process of law.

Placement in the Least Restrictive Alternative Educational Setting

Beyond the situation with excluded children is the requirement that handicapped children be placed for educational purposes in the least restrictive alternative setting. Public Law 93-380, the Education Amendment of 1974, focused specifically on this programing thrust by requiring that a state, in order to retain its eligibility to receive federal funds for the education of the handicapped, must develop a plan to be approved by the US Commissioner of Education, that will contain:

(B) procedures to insure that, to the maximum extent appropriate, handicapped children, including children in public or private institutions or other care facilities, are educated with children who are not handicapped, and that special classes, separate schooling, or other removal of handicapped children from the regular education environment occurs only when the nature or severity of the handicap is such that education in regular classes with the use of supplementary aids and services cannot be achieved satisfactorily. (Public Law 93-380, Title VIB, Sec. 612(d)(13B))

The relationship between due process and placement in the least restrictive alternative educational setting is extremely close. Due process establishes the procedures that require the schools to consider all program alternatives and to select that setting which is least restrictive. The basis of this entire concept is the existence of a variety of options or program settings that can be used to provide education to handicapped children depending on their individual needs.

Public Law 93-380 mandates the closeness by also requiring the states in their plans to:

(13) provide procedures for insuring that handicapped children and their parents or guardians are guaranteed procedural safeguards in decisions regarding identification, evaluation and educational placement of handicapped children including, but not limited to (A) (i) prior notice to parents or guardians of the child when the local or State

educational agency proposes to change the educational placement of the child, (ii) an opportunity for the parents or guardians to obtain an impartial due process hearing, examine all relevant records with respect to the classification or educational placement of the child, and obtain an independent educational evaluation of the child, (iii) procedures to protect the rights of the child when the parents or guardians are not known, unavailable, or the child is a ward of the State including the assignment of an individual (not to be an employee of the State or local educational agency involved in the education or care of children) to act as a surrogate for the parents or guardians, and (iv) provision to insure that the decisions rendered in the impartial due process hearing required by this paragraph shall be binding on all parties subject only to appropriate administrative or judicial appeal. (Public Law 93-380, Title VIB, Sec. 612(d)(13A))

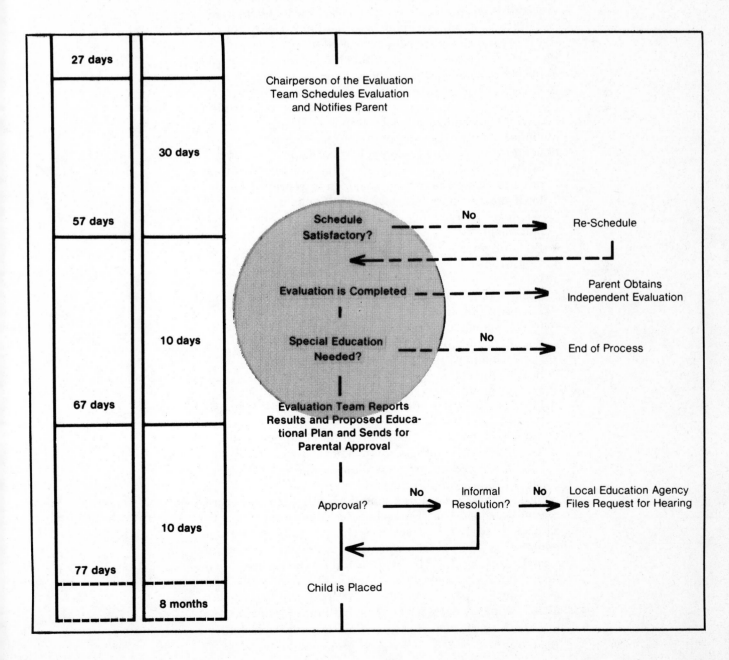

5. PARENTAL INVOLVEMENT

Providing a child with an appropriate education is of equal interest and importance to the child, the family, and the schools. To insure that education, it is imperative that, when initial educational evaluation and placement decisions or changes in existing placement are being considered, due process protections must be provided to the child, the family, and the schools. All of these parties will benefit from adherence to well developed educational practices and the elements of due process. When appropriate decisions about a child's education are made in a forthright manner, these parties will be in harmony and the challenges inherent in due process need not be involved. Under other less positive circumstances, however, conflict will emerge and require resolution. Hearings conducted by impartial officers serving as designees of the chief state school officer will be convened, not to place blame or determine right or wrong, but to achieve resolution of the conflict and define an appropriate education program for the child. While the procedures presented may appear complex and perhaps circuitous, it must be emphasized that none of the alternative routes to challenge need be used if all parties agree on the educational needs of the child and the appropriateness of the program proposed by the schools.

A review of judicial orders, existing state and federal legislation, and the work of legal analysts suggests that the following procedures must be provided in order to meet minimum due process standards in identification, evaluation, and educational placement of handicapped children:

1. Written notification before evaluation. In addition, parents always have the right to an interpreter/translator if their primary language is not English.
2. Written notification before change in educational placement.
3. Periodic review of educational placement.
4. Opportunity for an impartial hearing including the right to:
   Receive timely and specific notice of such hearing.
   Review all records.
   Obtain an independent evaluation.
   Be represented by counsel.
   Cross examine.
   Bring witnesses.
   Present evidence.
   Receive a complete and accurate record of proceedings.
   Appeal the decision.
5. Assignment of a surrogate parent for children when:
   The child's parent or guardian is not known.
   The child's parents are unavailable.
   The child is a ward of the state.

Typically, these procedures should be initiated when there is reason to believe that a preschool or school age child is in need of special education services and the child becomes a candidate for individual evaluation procedures including informal assessment or observation and formal testing. Then written permission must be obtained by the local education agency from the parents before the process can begin. This shall also apply when periodic reevaluation is planned.

Prior to the performance of an evaluation the parent shall be provided with both written and oral notices of intent to conduct an evaluation. The written notice shall be in the primary language of the home and in English and will be delivered to the parent during a conference or mailed by certified mail..Oral interpretation shall always be given in the primary language of the home. If the primary language of the home is other than English and a member of the household requests that English also be used, then a second oral interpretation shall be given in English. When necessary, arrangements shall be made to effectuate communication with hearing and visually handicapped parents.

The proposed procedures include a provision that no later than 8 calendar months after a child's educational status has been changed and during each calendar year thereafter, so long as the child continues to receive special services, the local education agency should conduct a review of the child's program to evaluate its effectiveness in meeting the educational needs of the child. At least 5 days prior to each review, the parent should be notified in writing, in the primary language of the home and in English, and orally in the primary language of the home, that the review is scheduled. The notice should also indicate the following information:

1. The date, time, and place of the review.
2. An invitation to the parents to participate in the review.
3. A description of the procedures to be used in the review.
4. A statement that the parents will receive the findings and recommendations of the review team within 10 days after completion of the review.
5. A reiteration of the procedures and rights first encountered at the initial evaluation.

Hearing Procedures and Officers

Public policymakers, whether legislators or judges at both the state and federal level, have made clear that decisions about identifying, evaluating, and placing exceptional children in education programs must be governed by due process safeguards. Implicit in that requirement is that whenever a decision is contested to the point that a hearing is to be convened, the hearing must be conducted in an impartial manner by an impartial hearing officer or a neutral review panel.

Specifying criteria which can be used for the selection of effective hearing officers in all settings is an impossible task. There are, however, a few general rules which can be made. Individuals selected should:

1. Not be involved in the decisions already made about a child regarding identification, evaluation, placement, or review.
2. Possess special knowledge, acquired through training and/or experience, about the nature and needs of exceptional children. An awareness and understanding of the types and quality of programs that are available at any time for exceptional children is essential.
3. Be sufficiently open minded so that they will not be predisposed toward any decisions that they must make or review. However, they must also be capable of making decisions.
4. Possess the ability to objectively, sensitively, and directly solicit and evaluate both oral and written information that needs to be considered in relation to decision making.

5. Have sufficient strength to effectively structure and operate hearings in conformity with standard requirements and limits and to encourage the participation of the principal parties and their representatives.

6. Be sufficiently free of other obligations to provide sufficient priority to their hearing officer responsibilities. They must be able to meet the required timelines for conducting hearings and reporting written decisions.

7. Be aware that the role of the hearing officer is unique and relatively new, requiring constant evaluation of the processes, their own behavior, and the behavior of all the principals involved for purposes of continuously trying to improve the effectiveness of the hearing process.

The Parent Surrogate

The specific due process procedures of Public Law 93-380 secure a child's right, through representation by his parents or guardian, to the opportunity for full participation in the total educational identification, evaluation, and placement process. The assumption is that the parents or guardians will be available and willing to participate in this decision making process, fully accepting the responsibility of representing the child's best interests.

There are, however, children who lack this kind of personal representation, protective legal doctrines notwithstanding. They are the children whose parents or guardians are unknown or unavailable, or children who are wards of the state. The rights of these children are not safeguarded if they are without an advocate to act for them. Recognizing this, Public Law 93-380 provides for the appointment of a "parent surrogate," i.e., an individual appointed to safeguard a child's rights in the specific instance of educational decision making-identification, evaluation and placement.

The task of locating individuals to act as surrogates could be done by a state level standing board or advisory committee established to advise and work with the state as it delivers services to handicapped children. Members of this type of board are concerned with quality education and generally include parents, teachers, professionals involved with the education and treatment of children with special needs, and other community members who are interested in the education of handicapped children. Such a group has channels of communication open to local professional organizations concerned with the handicapped (Association for Retarded Citizens for example) and to individuals such as parents of handicapped and nonhandicapped children, pediatricians, or attorneys sensitive to the needs of children. These are individuals who may be considered for selection as surrogates. It is recommended that any pool of surrogates not include state or local education employees. Because of their employment, they may be unable to act as impartially as desired. A surrogate must have the child's best interests constantly in mind, and if he is employed by a local or state system concerned with handicapped children, he is placed in the position of serving two masters.

Once the state board has identified persons it feels would be effective surrogates, it will send their names to the state education agency, which has the responsibility of assigning a surrogate to a specific child. Individuals should be located in all parts of the state so that every child will have easy access to his/her surrogate. The state agency should develop a training program, devise a system of compensation, determine the rules and regulations governing the employment of a surrogate, and develop plans to disseminate information about the program.

Implications for Public Education Agencies

It is important for public educators to understand that implementing due process may produce many positive benefits. The availability of due process procedures, particularly hearings, provides the parent with the opportunity for holding the professional accountable, a desire of many professionals. In this context, the procedures of due process that require parent-school communication create the opportunity for school personnel to be open and honest with the ultimate consumers of their services. These requirements will also enable educators to adopt an additional procedure that has long been a goal—the provision of individually designed education programs. Individual plans provide the basis for intelligent assessment of a child's progress in relation to the objectives initially established. The concept of periodic review, also a requirement of total due process protection, conforms with good educational programing as well.

Finally, educators must be aware that adherence to due process procedures will in no way reduce their professional responsibility or authority. It can provide them with the leverage to do that which must be their goal—to act openly and in the best interests of the children they serve.

Reference

Rodham, H. Children under the law. *Harvard Education Review*, 1973, *43*, 487-514.

A Primer on Due Process contains an appendix with forms designed to implement the procedures described above. 57 pages. Available from Publications Sales, CEC, 1920 Association Dr., Reston VA 22091, $4.95. Stock no. 104.

What Parents of the Learning Disabled Really Want from Professionals

Raymond J. Dembinski, EdD, and August J. Mauser, EdD

Teachers, psychologists, and physicians frequently discuss with parents the numerous concerns related to the learning disabled child. Seldom, however, are parents provided the opportunity to advise these professionals as to whether the information they receive is adequate. Consequently, the professionals seldom know what it is parents most want to know. This survey provides an answer for teachers, psychologists, and physicians as to what parents most want to know from each profession and includes suggestions for interacting more effectively with parents of learning disabled children. — G.M.S.

The major body of information on parent counseling is written by professionals. This study attempts to provide a vehicle by which parents of learning disabled children can express their concerns and recommendations to professionals. Parental recommendations are ranked in order of importance. Their implications for professional training and interaction with parents are discussed. The findings indicate that training programs for teachers, psychologists, and physicians must include specific skills on interacting with parents of learning disabled children.

A neglected area in preparing personnel in the childcare professions centers on the ability to relate to parents. One source of information for understanding these relationships can be found in literature related to the parent counseling process (Wolfensberger 1967, Noland 1970, 1971, Hewitt 1970, Schild 1971). Within this specific body of information, a series of recommendations has been

"What Parents of the Learning Disabled Really Want from Professionals," Raymond Dembinski and August Mauser, *Journal of Learning Disabilities*, Vol. 10, No. 9, November 1977. © 1977 The Professional Press Incorporated.

offered on how to relate to parents of educationally handicapped children. The information inevitably includes a discussion of deficits or inadequacies in the parents of handicapped children. The reader is given a series of strategies, techniques, or theoretical overviews on how parents may or may not respond to professional advice. These recommendations appear to be somewhat biased against parents. It is apparent that professional people have a channel by which to express their experiences and observations. Parents, on the other hand, have no such mechanism available to them, unless they themselves are in the child-care profession (Gorham 1975).

The purpose of this study is to provide parents of children with learning disabilities with an opportunity to react to and evaluate the diagnostic and counseling process they experience in relation to three distinct groups of professional people: physicians, psychologists, and educators.

DESCRIPTION OF THE QUESTIONNAIRE

The questionnaire consisted of four sections: Child Background Information, Parental Background Information, Professional Contact Information, and Recommendations to Professionals.

The Child Background Information section provided an overview of a particular child's characteristics, e.g., age, sex, disability, and treatment received. The Parental Background Information section yielded demographic and biographic information on the parents of the child. The Professional Contact Information section focused on the crucial elements of the study. In this section, parents had an opportunity: (1) to relate how long they have been aware of the child's disability; (2) to indicate their reaction to the diagnosis; (3) to indicate whether they returned to the professional who originally confirmed the diagnosis; (4) to cite any reasons for seeking additional opinions, if sought; and (5) to indicate their reactions to those opinions. Recommendations to Professionals is the critical section of the questionnaire. In this section, the parents had the opportunity to rank some traditional role behaviors ascribed to physicians, psychologists, and teachers in terms of their relevance to their child's disability. Parents were asked to rank the behaviors as important (I), not important (NI), or not applicable (NA). Opportunity was also provided for parents to list additional recommendations.

SUMMARY OF CHILD BACKGROUND INFORMATION

The questionnaires were distributed by state and local affiliates of ACLD to their membership. Response was voluntary. Approximately 10% of the respondents requested a questionnaire after learning of the project from other parents.

A total of 234 of the 500 questionnaires was returned from parents of children with learning disabilities. This figure represents a 46.8% rate of return on a national survey. This rate is considered an adequate rate of return on which to base generalizations (Kerlinger 1966). The 234 questionnaires included information on 168 males and 61 females, a ratio of approximately 2.5:1. This ratio is consistent with previously reported incidence figures. Sexual identification was not checked on five questionnaires. Of the 234 respondents, 213 represent natural children; 2 a step-child; 1 a foster child; and 17 represent adopt-

5. PARENTAL INVOLVEMENT

Service	N
Full-time public school special education classes	75
Regular class plus special help	17
Private residential service	8
Community clinic	8
Regular medical treatment	40
Counseling programs	4
Regular class but no extra assistance	16
No service	36

TABLE I. Services provided to respondents' children.

ed children with specific learning disabilities. One respondent did not provide background information.

Table I indicates that 22% of the families who responded were not receiving services for children already identified as learning disabled. It is hoped that implemented mandatory legislation and the work of concerned advocates will have had an impact on these children in the months since this study was completed.

SUMMARY OF PARENTAL BACKGROUND INFORMATION

Approximately 80% of the parents responding to this study ranged in age from 30 to 49 years old, and 95% were married. The responses appear to represent the views of intact, natural families. Over 73% of the respondents indicated they were living in a suburban or an inner-city area. Approximately one-fourth of the families are living in small towns or rural areas. The large representation from suburban and inner-city areas is significant. Services are typically available in metropolitan areas before they become available in small towns and rural areas. The large response from metropolitan areas may be interpreted as an indication of parents' reactions to the quality of services offered rather than a critical reaction to the scarcity of services.

SUMMARY OF PROFESSIONAL CONTACT INFORMATION

Confirmation of the parents' suspicions regarding their child's disability was obtained essentially from three major professional groups: physicians, psychologists and teachers. Interestingly, most of the parents indicated that when informed of the diagnosis of learning disabilities, they felt accepting, relieved, but yet frustrated. Approximately 14% of the parents indicated they felt shocked or guilty; 7% indicated that they were angry or disbelieving. Parents described the first professional consulted as understanding and knowledgeable. Very few parents described these professionals in negative terms, i.e., insulting, incompetent, cold, or nervous.

Of the 80% of the parents who sought the advice of another professional, the majority did so because they wanted another opinion regarding their child's problem. Over 27% sought a confirmation of the first diagnosis; 53% desired another opinion regarding the possibilities for treatment; and 47% sought another opinion for all of the above reasons. The second professional consulted was also described by parents as courteous, informative, helpful, and understanding. In general, parents described the second consultant more positively than the first consultant. This finding may be due to several factors, among which are increased familiarity with the child's problem and an under-

TABLE II. Parent's recommendations to teachers.

Recommendation	I N	I %	NI N	NI %	NA N	NA %	NR N	NR %
Tell us how our child gets along with others in class	220	94.0	1	.04	1	.04	12	5.1
Tell us if our child gets in trouble	210	89.7	2	0.9	4	1.7	18	7.7
Use terminology we can understand	207	88.5	2	0.9	6	2.6	19	8.1
Show us how to teach things to our child	205	87.6	7	3.0	7	3.0	15	6.4
Tell us what you expect our child to learn	203	86.8	8	3.4	5	2.1	18	7.7
Require us to attend parent conferences	191	81.6	11	4.7	8	3.4	24	10.3
Tell us if you feel our child has progressed as far as he possibly can	188	80.3	6	2.6	18	7.7	22	9.4
Be willing to discuss our child's problem with our doctor	184	78.6	19	8.1	10	4.3	21	9.0
Give us materials to read	183	78.2	20	8.5	9	3.8	22	9.4
Tell us what types of jobs our child could hold	158	67.5	16	6.8	36	15.4	24	10.3

I = Important
NI = Not Important
NA = Not Applicable
NR = No Response

TABLE III. Parent's recommendations to psychologists.

Recommendation	I N	I %	NI N	NI %	NA N	NA %	NR N	NR %
Use terminology we can understand	213	91.0			3	1.3	18	7.7
Give us materials to read	185	79.1	16	6.8	8	3.4	25	10.7
Require both parents to discuss their concerns with you	183	78.2	13	5.6	10	4.3	28	12.0
Give us copies of reports	177	75.6	25	10.7	7	3.0	25	10.7
Tell us how to discipline our child	160	68.4	24	10.3	22	9.4	28	12.0
Tell us what our other children might think about our handicapped child	138	59.0	29	12.4	30	12.8	37	15.8
Tell us what to do when our child throws a tantrum	134	57.3	21	9.0	48	20.5	31	13.2
Tell us our child's IQ	131	56.0	67	28.6	8	3.4	28	12.0
Tell us how to explain sex and drugs to our child	118	50.4	37	15.8	42	17.9	37	15.8
Suggest toys our child can play with	109	46.6	41	17.5	49	20.9	35	15.0
Tell us what to say to our neighbors	63	26.9	90	38.5	47	20.1	34	14.5
Do not explore our marital relationship	60	25.6	77	32.9	51	21.8	46	19.7
Tell us how to toilet train our child	44	18.8	29	12.4	117	50.0	44	18.8

standing of terminology used to describe the problem.

Significantly, one-third of the parents reported that they felt comfortable when interacting with a professional. The majority of the parents described themselves as feeling awkward, nervous, and to some extent, as if they were imposing on the professional when they questioned him. This finding seems to indicate that professionals must create an atmosphere in which parents are not only allowed to ask for specific information but are also encouraged to ask questions regarding their child. It is imperative that this supportive and en-

5. PARENTAL INVOLVEMENT

TABLE IV. Parent's recommendations to physicians.

Recommendation	I N	I %	NI N	NI %	NA N	NA %	NR N	NR %
Tell us diagnosis as soon as it is known	222	94.9	1	0.4			11	4.7
Allow us to ask questions	221	94.4	1	0.4			12	5.1
Use terminology we can understand	221	94.4			1	0.4	12	5.1
If you are not interested in treating our child, refer us to someone who may be	205	87.6	1	0.4	12	5.1	16	6.8
Be willing to discuss our child's problems with his teacher	198	84.6	11	4.7	10	4.3	15	6.4
Give us materials to read	196	83.8	19	8.1	3	1.3	16	6.8
Tell us about health problems our child may experience	181	77.4	10	4.3	29	12.4	14	6.0
Require both parents to discuss their concerns with you	180	76.9	18	7.7	11	4.7	25	10.7
Give us your opinion about how well our child will learn in school	172	73.5	19	8.1	26	11.1	17	7.3
Give the parents copies of reports	169	72.2	40	17.1	7	3.0	18	7.7
Give us the opportunity to call for advice — a hot line service	144	61.5	33	14.1	37	15.8	20	8.5
Give us more child rearing ideas (feeding, toilet training, etc.)	86	36.8	45	19.2	77	32.9	26	11.3
Tell us if we should place our child somewhere else outside the home	80	34.2	11	4.7	110	47.0	33	14.1
Do not tell us the diagnosis if you feel it will upset us	19	8.1	64	27.4	89	38.0	62	26.5

couraging attitude prevail in the initial contact with parents as well as throughout the relationship.

SUMMARY OF RESULTS

Analysis of the data on the parents recommendations to professionals indicates (see Tables II, III, and IV):

(1) Parents overwhelmingly disapprove of the use of professional jargon. The language used between professionals is not appropriate for communicating with the layman. The de-emphasis of jargon should facilitate the development of a comfortable, supporting atmosphere in which parents are free to ask questions and pursue topics or issues of concern to them.

(2) The inclusion of both parents at conferences is very important. Professionals have long encouraged joint parental participation in discussions affecting their child. Parents apparently recognize this need. Encouragement of joint parental responsibility for a child should reduce the possibility of family discord, distortion of information, and increase the understanding and acceptance of the child.

(3) Parents are seeking reading material or references on material they can consult in order to understand their child's problem. Clinics, schools, and private practitioners should have a library of lay-oriented material on various aspects of learning problems available for distribution to parents. The material could provide definitions of various terms, e.g., auditory perception and tactile-kinesthetic, pamphlets listing services available, position statements on

the definitions of hyperactivity, the use of medication with learning disabled children, or material describing a diagnostic process. The availability of this information should assist parents in their understanding of learning disabilities and thus reduce distortion of information between parents.

(4) Parents strongly encourage receiving copies of reports written about their children. Mandatory legislation has generally included a provision which realizes this particular parental need.

(5) Parents emphasize the need for interdisciplinary communication. Parents indicated that they had to deal with a number of different professionals in order to obtain either a diagnosis or service for their children. The initial stages of each experience were highly repetitive. School officials and physicians are encouraged to communicate particularly in those cases where children are on medication. Some types of systematic follow-up between physicians and teachers should be implemented so that teachers are aware of cognitive or behavioral changes anticipated when a child is medicated. Similarly, teachers should be able to report cognitive or behavioral changes directly to physicians rather than having physicians rely on parental reports of a teacher's observations.

(6) Parents emphasize the need of receiving immediate relevant advice, e.g., how to teach children to do certain things and how to manage tantrums, as opposed to offering long-term recommendations regarding future educational or vocational outcomes. Federal legislation (PL 94-142) stipulates the development of specific treatment plans for children (Aquilina 1976). This regulation should contribute to the realization of this recommendation. Educational objec-

tives and corresponding intervention techniques developed by school officials should be shared with parents, thus providing them with a source of direction.

(7) Parents request information on their child's social as well as academic behavior. This recommendation suggests that parents are becoming aware of the possible implications learning difficulties may have on a child's social adjustment. Professionals should consider not only the unique problems of a child but also the whole child.

(8) Parents agree more on their recommendations to teachers than they do on their recommendations to physicians and psychologists. Parents typically have more direct and consistent contact with teachers than with physicians and psychologists. Consequently, they would be expected to have clearer expectations of a teacher's role and responsibilities.

CONCLUSIONS

The degree to which the results of this study may be generalized to all families with learning disabled children is restricted to the following design limitations: (1) the age and degree of severity of the learning disabilities of the children in the study were not specified, and (2) there was no attempt to control for different developmental stages of parenting.

The results of this study indicate that parents are requesting an honest evaluation of their child's problem and capabilities. These parents express the point of view that they do want to confront their child's problem directly. If this is the case, then our findings have interesting implications for parent counseling programs.

5. PARENTAL INVOLVEMENT

The quality of existing and future program models is dependent upon clear communication and collaboration between the parents of learning disabled children and the professionals concerned with the learning disabled child's development. The findings indicate that training programs for teachers, psychologists, and physicians must include specific skills on interacting with parents of learning disabled children.

On the other hand, there are some implications for parents in this study. Parents can facilitate the interaction process with professionals by meeting the professional halfway. Also they can acquaint themselves with the professional jargon, share with professionals the inducements used to encourage fathers to attend conferences, develop a pool of materials on learning disabilities for distribution through local libraries, schools, and various childcare offices, help to arrange interdisciplinary professional appointments, and be aware of their rights. — *Department of Special Education, Northern Illinois University, DeKalb, Illinois 60115.*

REFERENCES

Aquilina, R. I.: *Revolutionary legislation for a bicentennial year. Education and Training of the Mentally Retarded, 1976, April, 189-196.*

Gorham, K. A.: *A lost generation of parents. Exceptional Children, 1975, 41, 521-525.*

Hewitt, S., Newson, E., and Newson, J.: *The Family and the Handicapped Child. Chicago: Aldine, 1970.*

Kerlinger, F. N.: *Foundations of Behavioral Research. New York: Holt, Rinehart, & Winston, 1966.*

Noland, R. L.: *Counseling Parents of the Ill and the Handicapped. Springfield: Charles C Thomas, 1971.*

Noland, R. L.: *Counseling Parents of the Mentally Retarded. Springfield: Charles C Thomas, 1970.*

Schild, S.: *The family of the retarded child. In Kock, R., and Dobson, J. C. (Eds.): The Mentally Retarded Child and His Family. New York: Brunner-Mazel, 1971.*

Wolfensberger, W.: *Counseling the parents of the retarded. In Baumeister, A. A. (Ed.): Mental Retardation. Chicago: Aldine, 1967.*

Matching Families and Services

MERLE B. KARNES
R. REID ZEHRBACH

Merle B. Karnes is Professor, and R. Reid Zehrbach is Associate Professor, Institute for Research on Exceptional Children, University of Illinois, Champaign-Urbana.

Family involvement has been recognized as a critical component of any educational program—from a legal, ethical, and educational point of view. Lawyers have focused on the legal aspects of family involvement. Teachers have tried to work with parents toward implementing educational goals. Social workers, guidance counselors, and psychologists have been preoccupied with social-emotional problems and/or different communication styles that interfere with parent-child relationships. However, little thought has been given to a *systematic* approach to this involvement.

This article attempts to provide such an approach to involving parents in programs. The basic assumptions reflected in the model include the following: (a) staff should adopt a positive developmental view of children and their families, (b) parents should be involved at the decision making level, (c) parents should have access to viable alternatives when they involve themselves, and (d) staff working with parents should view their role as consultative. Although the approach of this presentation is to concentrate on the parts of the system, the underlying assumption is that all of these parts are important only as they relate to the whole. The basic purpose is to "get the *system* working reasonably well, not perfectly" (Hobbs, 1975, p. 114).

Conceptualization of the Family Involvement Process

To cope with the multiplicity of problems and issues associated with the development and evaluation of a family involvement program, it seems most fruitful to describe a model process which highlights specific target activities and illustrates the interrelationships of all the parts. An 11 stage model is outlined here.

In stage 1, a careful total assessment is made of the child's actual functioning in critical areas—social-emotional, physical, cognitive-language, and intellectual. At stage 2, the assessment is continued by establishing specific goals and objectives for the child based on estimates of his potential. During stage 3, the discrepancies between where the child is and where he is capable of being are carefully scrutinized to determine his unmet needs. At stage 4, an attempt is made to determine what the home is capable of providing *without* the *intervention* of other than simple suggestions or recommendations. In stage 5, an assessment is made to determine the difference between the child's unmet needs and what the family is able to provide. Stage 6 is an entry level item designed to indicate that some person or agency must have a broad background of knowledge of alternative programs for involving parents. This knowledge is compared with the unmet needs of the child and parents during stage 7 to identify appropriate alternatives for meeting these needs. At stage 8, family members choose among the alternatives presented by the liaison worker —selecting the one(s) that they wish to follow to reach the child's unmet needs. In stage 9, the difference between the child's needs and what the family can provide must be determined. During stage 10, the agencies involved with the family assess their capabilities and responsibilities and decide whether or not they are willing and able to work with the parents toward the parents' selected goals. Also, they decide whether they will work with the child toward the same goal and/or provide the child with additional

5. PARENTAL INVOLVEMENT

services not available to or through the parents. At stage 11a, the chosen plans are implemented. At stage 11b, continuous evaluations and reassessments are conducted at preplanned intervals with new planned actions established when progress is made toward the needs that have been given prime attention. Concomitantly at stage 11c, records are maintained of the unplanned for, unmet needs. These records must be continually reviewed as progress is made toward the higher priority needs so that provisions for unmet needs can be added to the planning when resources and time permit.

Interpretation of the Model

An outline of a decision making process oriented family involvement process (FIP) model has been presented. How the model might work is illustrated here.

In stage 1, the functional level of the child has been briefly characterized in objective positive statements. For example, the statement that the child is able to hear 60 db sounds or louder presents a child's ability to hear in as positive a light as possible. On the other hand, it should be obvious to a knowledgeable individual that the child has a hearing problem and needs special attention, although no such implication is drawn at this stage. One criterion is that the items listed here have no age referent. For example, the child is not described as speaking like a 2 year old, but rather as speaking in one word sentences. A much longer list would obviously be needed to clearly explicate the abilities of the child but such a list would tend to follow the general categories of physical functioning, social-emotional functioning, intellectual functioning, cognitive-language functioning, interests, and special abilities.

In stage 2, staff members attempt to delineate the child's potential level of functioning in terms of both broad long range goals and short term objectives. For example, a goal might be to improve the child's ability to learn through the auditory channel. This might, or might not, be quickly enhanced through the provision of a hearing aid. Again, a fairly extensive list of long term goals and related immediate objectives might be developed for the child.

At stage 3, a comparison is made between the child's needs and functional level, and a list of unmet needs is developed which paral-

---

Application of the FIP model

1	**2**
Describe functional level of child	Define potential goals and objectives for child
a. Is able to hear 60 db sounds or louder	a. Improved hearing with aid
b. Speaks in one word sentences	b. Speaks in 2 word sentences
c. Responds to familiar faces	c. Play at parallel play level
d. Runs, walks	d. 1. Experience grocery store
	2. Experience bus ride
	e. Learn to swim

3	**4**
Determine difference between 1 and 2 (unmet needs)	Identify what family is able to provide without intervention
a. Hearing aid	a. Provide hearing aid
b. Language stimulation	b. Limited ability
c. Socialization in groups	c. Limited ability
d. Broadening travel experiences	d. Not able to provide
e. Train in swimming	e. Not now

5	**6**
Determine difference between child's unmet needs and what family is able to provide	Agency staff knowledgeable about wide variety of programs
a. (Met)	
b. Same as 3b	In preparation for selecting alternatives need list of all possible alternatives
c. Same as 3c	
d. Same as 3d	
e. Same as 3e	**(continued on next page)**

---

lels the lists developed at the first and second stages.

It can be seen in stage 4 that the family's abilities to resolve the unmet needs is minimal at this time. They are only able to provide a hearing aid. It does not, however, imply that they could not benefit from participation in an appropriate family program.

(FIP Model cont.)	
7	**8**
Agency/liaison worker develops list of alternative goals-programs	Family chooses alternatives to help unmet needs
a. (Met)	a. (Met)
b. 1. Parent training program (Karnes)	b. 1. Yes
	2. Yes
2. Language based preschool program	c. Yes
c. Preschool	d. 1. No
d. 1. Parent program "enhancing travel experience"	2. Yes
	3. Yes
2. Preschool	e. Later
3. Student volunteer	
e. Winter swimming program	**10**
	Agencies determine to:
9	a. work with parents toward their choices, and/or
Determine difference between child needs and what family agrees to provide	b. Choose to work with child in some other area(s)
All plans agreed to except d1: attend parent program on "enhancing travel experience" and to delay entrance into "swimming" program	a. (Met)
	b. 1. Agree to enroll in Karnes based parent training program
11a	2. Enroll in language based program
Continue action toward selected goals	c. Same as b2
a. (Met)	d. 1. No action—put on need list
b. 1. Parent started program March 1, 1974	2. Same as b2
2. Child started program April 1, 1974	3. No volunteer available—put on wait list
c. Same as b2	e. Put on wait list
d. 2. Same as b2	
	11c
11b	Unmet and unplanned for needs remain until resolved or added to plan
Reassess at stated intervals and replan adding unmet needs	d. 1. No action. Review need and possible re-schedule of parents into "enhancing travel" program in 3 months.
a. (Met)	3. Put on wait list for volunteers
b. 1. Review programs April 1, May 15, 6 week intervals	e. Schedule for summer swimming lessons
b. 2., c, d. 2. Internal evaluation and 9 week interim review and yearly total review	

At stage 5, it is clear that the family has essentially met the child's hearing aid needs but is unable to provide the language stimulation, socialization, broadening experience, and swimming opportunities that have been identified as desirable. Thus, intervention by an agency seems imperative to help the parents acquire the knowledge and skills essential for meeting the child's needs.

Stage 6 refers to the activities of agency staff required to help them become knowledgeable about the characteristics of various programs for family members. Later in this article, a procedure will be described for assessing family involvement programs in a systematic manner so that the development of the knowledge base needed to identify alternatives and make appropriate decisions can be facilitated.

During stage 7, the agency and/or liaison worker develops a list of alternative approaches designed to meet the specific unmet needs of this illustrative child. Participation in a program designed to teach parents how to stimulate and reinforce the language development of their child, as developed by Karnes (1968), has been identified as one alternative. Another is to enroll the child in a language based preschool program, which is consistent with the goals and procedures of the parent program. Similarly, a parent program has been identified which will provide the parents with assistance in using simple travel experiences to broaden their child's experiential background.

At stage 8, family members are presented with the list of alternatives and they decide which one(s) they would like to pursue. They chose to accept all the alternatives with the exception of participating in the family program on enhancing travel experiences. This was due to a lack of transportation. They also decided to postpone the swimming arrangement until summer.

At stage 9, the difference(s) between the child's needs and the alternatives agreed to by the parents are determined. In the example the parents agreed to all programs except "enhancing travel experiences" and the immediate swimming program.

At stage 10, the agency reviews the program and decides how and to what degree they are able to interact with the system. In the example, the agency was able to interact as planned, with the exception that it placed providing a volunteer on a waiting list.

5. PARENTAL INVOLVEMENT

At stage 11a the planned actions started on March and April, 1974, while at 11b the associated plans for evaluation and review were established. In 11c, the activities that have been established as appropriate for the child but for which no appropriate actions have been planned are listed.

The FIP model provides for the sequential planning of activities and alternatives and involves the family members both at the planning and action stages. On the other hand, analysis of the model reveals several critical points that have not been fully described in related literature.

Problem Areas of the Model

While information is widely available on some of the topic areas in the model, lack of information is judged to occur at stages 4, 6, 7, 8, and 10.

At stage 4, the basic problem is to identify the family's ability to meet needs with minimal intervention. In the example provided earlier, the child had a hearing loss that could be ameliorated with a hearing aid. A simple explanation of the problem to a family member of a higher income level who has no personal objection to the child's using the aid may be all that is required. They would make the necessary appointments and quickly obtain the aid. Another family, however, might lack the economic resources or resist the ideas of a young child wearing the aid. Thus, it would be judged that considerable effort would be required to meet the need; this would be listed at stage 5 as an unmet need.

One of the critical problems at stage 4 would seem to be the need to keep efforts to assess the family's abilities directed toward areas relevant to the child's needs. If the child needs a hearing aid, then the assessment procedures should focus on the economic, time, personal, social, and intellectual factors relevant to the provision of a hearing aid. Automatic digression to assessing the family's ability to stimulate the child intellectually is unwarranted. On the other hand, if, as a result of the hearing loss, the child has a need to develop language facility, then the family members' abilities to meet these needs should be assessed.

One of the benefits of the above procedure is that it reduces the amount of time and resources required to assess specific needs. Another is that it keeps the privacy of the family intact in those areas that do not directly impinge on the needs of the child. Such a procedure is obviously beneficial when the agency, such as a school, is concerned with meeting certain delimited needs of children. If the program is more broadly oriented as suggested by Hobbs (1975), then a broader perspective would need to be taken to define the needs of the child as a member of the system.

Some of the dimensions that need to be considered are (a) administrative considerations such as cost, time, space, and transportation; (b) parents' considerations such as cultural, intellectual, knowledge, skills, and attitudes; and (c) child considerations such as social, physical, motoric, intellectual, and cultural. It may not be necessary to consider all areas for every problem, but a checklist might be devised to insure that the possibility of need in each of these areas is at least explored.

The next problem area in the model is at stage 6, wherein agency and/or individuals need to develop the ability to implement a variety of programs rather than just one or two. The broad underlying philosophy is one of carefully planned eclecticism. Available programs can be analyzed and used as a reference when decisions need to be made about a specific family. One important aspect of this analysis should be to reveal those programs useful to the clients.

At stage 7, the agency and/or selected individuals are assigned the task of identifying multiple alternative programs which meet the needs of children through the training of family members. Development of the background information for the preceding step should reduce the time required to make decisions and, at the same time, insure a more relevant provision of programs and use of staff.

Stage 8 is concerned with the all important problem of providing for, and encouraging, family input into the decision making process. Too frequently families are left out or excluded until after all decisions are made. A social worker surveying the potential of a family will certainly include as a part of the assessment process determining if a family will agree to participate in certain types of suggested activities. In this way, parents' decisions will be anticipated early.

Focusing recommendations for alternative programs on the unmet needs of the child may help parents understand the specific decisions that they have to make. Further, it should be easier to make a decision among two or three alternatives rather than be forced to accept or reject only one. During the discussion, compromise solutions may develop to suggest additional alternatives.

Once the family has decided, the problem reverts to the agency to make certain that it can interact with the family. It may lack the trained personnel, the funds, or the time to complete the activities. Most frequently, these decisions will have been made before the family is approached so that false hopes are not raised by the alternatives presented to them. Action should begin as soon as possible. If some needs cannot be met, then most likely the list of the child's unmet needs would be expanded to include those areas the agency cannot serve.

References

Hobbs, N. *The futures of children.* San Fancisco: Jossey-Bass Publishers, 1975.

Karnes, M. B., Studley, W. M., Wright, W. R., & Hodgins, A. S. An approach for working with mothers of disadvantaged preschool children. *Merrill-Palmer Quarterly of Behavior and Development,* 1968, *14* (2), 174-184.

PARENT PARTICIPATION

Lynn Winslow

Lynn Winslow is the parent
of an exceptional child.
Having taught for seven
years, she is currently fin-
ishing her master's degree
in special education.

P REVIOUS chapters have dealt with the functions of the many professional educators
who are responsible for the planning and
implementation of a child's individualized education program. While reference has been
made to the roles and responsibilities of the parents, this chapter is designed to highlight some
specifics for the parents of a handicapped child.

ASSUMPTIONS ABOUT PARENTS

In attempting to determine what the role of parents is or ought to be in the development of an
individualized education program, it is necessary to start with the parent's responsibility.
Parents monitor, guide, and act as a resource for
a whole set of personal values that they want
and hope their children will incorporate into
their own life styles. While parents realize that
they do not have total control over their children's lives, they share a partnership with the
school in developing their child's individualized program.

Mistakes will be made, but there are two
important points to remember to avoid that pitfall as much as possible. First, the individualized
education program is not a contract. It is not
binding; it can be changed. Latitude exists for
flexibility and to make needed educational
changes when necessary. Second, parents of an
exceptional child have a wealth of valuable
information about their own child that others
may not have. They are a resource to the profes-

sionals, and it is their responsibility to share this
information as they continue to monitor their
child's education needs.

IDENTIFICATION OF A PROBLEM

Sooner or later, parents realize that their child
has some unique learning needs. The person
who confirms or identifies that there is a
problem (whether labeled specifically at this
point or not) can often vary. Depending on the
type of handicap and the severity, a doctor may
be the first to mention something. Or the parent
or a teacher may express concern. It is also possible that a child may ask for help. It is not
important who initiates concern, but it is important to try to understand why. What was
observed that led to this concern? It is advisable
for parents to start a notebook at this point. It is
easy to forget conversations that may be important later. A notebook can help organize
thoughts, keep everything in one place, and
serve as a reminder of what has been done for
the child.

When talking with professionals, parents
should not be afraid to question a word or
phrase they do not understand. Educational and
medical jargon can be confusing and they are
full of everyday words that are used differently.
Asking what is meant will not slow down any
meeting or conversation. Parents should be certain they understand what others are saying
about their own child.

TYPES OF INFORMATION

There are many kinds of information parents will discuss with professionals. The following four types of information might help parents organize a working notebook.

Informal Behavioral Observations

These will include parental observations as well as those of any professionals the parents may be in contact with. Frequently, children are observed as behaving and/or reacting very differently at home than they do at school. A parent's observations are important and should be recorded. They could be meaningful and well worth sharing at a later date.

Formal Observations

These observations are available to parents from the child's school as well as from doctors. Any medical, educational, or psychological test results should be entered into the notebook. Any questions about these reports should be listed, including terms used and the person who conducted the assessments. The answers should be noted so that they may be referred to at a later time.

Significant Differences

If at any point while collecting information parents note any significant difference, they should be sure to record it. Sometimes there is a difference between what a test says a child can do or what a parent knows a child can do and what the child is actually achieving.

Intervention Attempts to Date

Any attempts that have been made to change or intervene in a child's handicap should be noted, along with any approach that seemed to work.

COMMUNICATION

The importance of communication cannot be stressed enough. Much of the success of an individualized education program will depend on good communication. A parent notebook may help. During a phone conversation or any meeting about the child, the parent should take notes including the date, time, place, and name of the person spoken to. Taking notes often assures that the information will be more accurate.

The parents' communication with their child is very important. Obviously, the depth of this communication will depend on the age of the child and the severity of the handicap. Parents should be sure that their child understands their love and that they are trying to help.

One rule worth mentioning: At no time should parents make negative comments to their child about a professional who is involved with the child. Parents should receive and re-cord information, but they must not put the child in the difficult position of having to "take sides." Comments made about the child's handicap can be misinterpreted by the child *and* by his or her brothers and sisters.

REFERRAL FOR ASSESSMENT

Requesting assessment information does not mean that a child necessarily requires special education. Perhaps remedial help or tutoring will suffice. Parents should not prejudge the placement or service recommended for their child. Their first step should be to set up a contact person they can relate to, trust, and depend on to follow the case through. This person might be the child's current teacher, a special education teacher, a guidance counselor, a social worker, or the principal. Perhaps the family doctor is willing to help in this way.

Once a formal (written) referral for assessment has been made, the parent should be provided with both written and oral notice of intent to conduct the assessment(s) on their child. The following information should be provided to parents by the school (Abeson, Bolick, & Hass, 1975):

- The reasons the evaluation has been requested and the name of the person(s) who initiated the process.
- The evaluation procedures and instruments that will be used.
- A description of the scope of the procedures and the instruments that will be used.
- A statement of the right to review the procedures and instruments that will be used.
- A statement of the right to review and obtain copies of all records related to the request for the evaluation and to give this authority to a designee of the parent as indicated in writing.
- A description of how the findings of the evaluation are to be used, by whom, and under what circumstances.
- A statement of the right to refuse permission for the evaluation with the understanding that the local education agency can then request a hearing to present its reasons and try to obtain approval to conduct the evaluation.
- A statement of the right of the parent to obtain an independent educational evaluation, either from another public agency with the fee determined on a sliding scale, or privately at full cost to the parent.
- A declaration that the child's educational status will not be changed without the parent's knowledge and written approval or completion of the due process procedures described in the right to hearing section of these procedures.
- Identification of the education agency employee (chairperson of the evaluation team) to whom the parent response should

5. PARENTAL INVOLVEMENT

be sent and the deadline for response given in terms of the day, date, and time. In no case should the deadline be less than 10 school days nor more than 15 school days after receipt of the notice.

PREPARING FOR THE MEETING

Following the assessment, a meeting, which can be informal, should be scheduled to inform the parents of the outcomes. Parents should request copies of any test results that have been obtained on their child, making sure that they understand these results and adding them to their notebook.

In order to prepare for the meeting that will serve to develop their child's individualized education program, it is essential that parents review most of the information they have collected in their notebook and spend some time thinking about what they want to learn at the meeting. Questions such as the following may help parents organize their thoughts:

- Do I have any records from my child's doctor that will give additional information?
- Have I listed any home observations that either reinforce or disprove the possibility of a handicap?
- Have I recorded observations, past and present, from the school?
- Are test scores, past and present, recorded?
- What questions have I forgotten to ask at previous meetings or discussions?
- Is there any material, upon review, that I still don't understand?

Parents will be informed by the school as to a proposed date and time for the meeting. Although the law states that the meeting must be at a mutually convenient time, parents should be as flexible as possible. There are just two of them and there may be many school personnel involved. Regardless of when the meeting is held, once the parents agree to a meeting, they must be sure to be there on time. They should know ahead of time exactly who will be attending by name and what they do.

The professionals who attend will have had at least one staffing on the child, if not more. The school staff who has worked with, tested, or will work with the child often meet and exchange assessment information prior to meeting with parents. According to local district policy, parents may be invited to attend this meeting. If parents have the opportunity to attend a staffing, it is advisable that they go. At the meeting, parents will review relevant information regarding their child to develop the following components of the individualized education program:

- The child's unique educational needs.
- The child's present level(s) of educational functioning.
- The written annual goals and short term objectives the child is expected to achieve.

- The program services the child should receive.

When working with professionals to establish annual goals and short term objectives for their child, parents should keep in mind activities that can be done at home and ask what they can do to help. Perhaps they can listen to their child read or review arithmetic tables. If the child's annual goals include self help skills, teachers or therapists can demonstrate useful techniques for the home that will build on the skills the child is learning at school.

At the meeting, parents will be provided more information about their child's disability and any needed special education and related services. Parents should know the present level of educational functioning and be aware of annual goals and short term objectives. Where will the child be placed? Are there alternatives to this placement? Have provisions been made for the child to be with nonhandicapped children? Parents will also want to know when the effectiveness of this unique program will be evaluated and determine when the school will report the child's progress.

Whether or not parents have attended the meeting, they should receive a copy of the results of the meeting. They should not hesitate to call on the teacher for any necessary clarification.

INVOLVING THE CHILD

There can be no hard and fast rule for parents as to when and how to involve their child in the meeting to develop an individualized education program. This would depend on the age of the child, the severity of the handicap, and how well they feel the child can handle the situation. If a child is under the age of majority, the decision belongs to the parents. Should it be determined that, for one reason or another, the child is not ready to take part in a meeting such as this, an alternate arrangement should be considered. Perhaps the parent and child could sit down with the teacher and go over the results of the meeting. It is important that the child be aware of the annual goals whenever possible, and also realize that this is an effort that does not end at the close of a school day.

PROCEDURAL SAFEGUARDS

The system does not always work the way the law says it should. If along the way things do not work the way parents know they should—for instance, if they are not allowed to assess their child's files, are not included at some stage of program development, or reject the proposed education program—there are steps they can follow. If at any phase of the planning and programing for their child, parents feel that they are not getting cooperation, they should inform the administrator of special education they they are aware of their rights and are trying to accept the accompanying responsibility. Usually the key person to contact is the person in the school system designated as responsible for coordinating special education.

Once disputes or disagreements are spelled out between the parents and the school, the law sets forth procedures that parents can use to appeal the school's decision regarding the individualized education program for their child. The administrator of special education will be able to tell them how to request a hearing once they have rejected the program.

Specific procedures for an impartial hearing are set forth in Public Law 94-142. Naturally, it is preferable for parents not to have to go through a hearing. If they do, however, it is important that they be as organized as possible. This is another time when a notebook will help. Parents should remain as calm as possible. Although this can be an emotional experience, it is important they they try to control their frustrations and possible anger. Adversarial positions only cause bitter feelings between the parent and the school. It should be remembered that parents and the school are working together to provide the most appropriate program for the handicapped child.

ADDITIONAL RESOURCES

There are some resources that parents will want to have available. The following suggestions are offered to parents as the beginning of a resource list. Parents may want to add to the list and include it in their notebook.

- Obtain a copy of Public Law 94-142 from your member of Congress.
- Obtain a copy of your current state special education law and regulations from the special education division of your state department of education.
- Review your district's local education agency's special education application. It will tell you district procedures and how they work for you. This application is usually obtained from the director of special education.
- Identify active parent groups. Not only is it comforting to know you are not alone, but they can also provide "people resources" who can often identify other resources for you.
- Be informed: Obtain the most current literature.

All of these resources will assist parents to be informed of the rights that their handicapped child is extended so that he or she might receive a free, appropriate public education.

Parents have had great impact on the passage of legislation that affords basic rights and protection to the education of their handicapped child. Now it is up to parents to accept the responsibility of monitoring and involving themselves in their child's education.

REFERENCE

Abeson, A., Bolick, N., & Hass, J. *A primer on due process: Education decisions for handicapped children.* Reston VA: The Council for Exceptional Children, 1975.

INDEX

STAFF

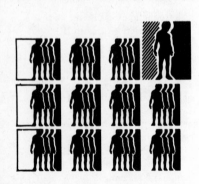

Publisher	John Quirk
Editor	Irving Newman
Editor	Robert Piazza
Director of Production	Richard Pawlikowski
Staff Consultant	Dona Chiappe
Permissions Editor	Audrey Weber
Customer Service	Cindy Finocchio
Administration	Linda Radomski

Cover Design   Donald Burns

Appendix: Agencies and Services for Exceptional Children

Alexander Graham Bell Association for the Deaf, Inc.
Volta Bureau for the Deaf
3417 Volta Place, NW
Washington, D.C. 20007

American Academy of Pediatrics
1801 Hinman Avenue
Evanston, Illinois 60204

American Association for Gifted Children
15 Gramercy Park
New York, N.Y. 10003

American Association on Mental Deficiency
5201 Connecticut Avenue, NW
Washington, D.C. 20015

American Association of Psychiatric Clinics for
   Children
250 West 57th Street
New York, N.Y.

American Bar Association
Commission on the Mentally Disabled
1800 M Street, NW
Washington, D.C. 20036

American Foundation for the Blind
15 W. 16th Street
New York, N.Y. 10011

American Medical Association
535 N. Dearborn Street
Chicago, Illinois 60610

American Speech and Hearing Association
9030 Old Georgetown Road
Washington, D.C. 20014

Association for the Aid of Crippled Children
345 E. 46th Street
New York, N.Y. 10017

Association for Children with Learning Disabilities
2200 Brownsville Road
Pittsburgh, Pennsylvania 15210

Association for Education of the Visually
   Handicapped
1604 Spruce Street
Philadelphia, Pennsylvania 19103

Association for the Help of Retarded Children
200 Park Avenue, South
New York, N.Y.

Association for the Visually Handicapped
1839 Frankfort Avenue
Louisville, Kentucky 40206

Center on Human Policy
Division of Special Education and Rehabilitation
Syracuse University
Syracuse, New York 13210

Child Fund
275 Windsor Street
Hartford, Connecticut 06120

Children's Defense Fund
520 New Hampshire Avenue NW
Washington, D.C. 20036

Closer Look
National Information Center for the Handicapped
1201 Sixteenth Street NW
Washington, D.C. 20036

Clifford W. Beers Guidance Clinic
432 Temple Street
New Haven, Connecticut 06510

Child Study Center
Yale University
333 Cedar Street
New Haven, Connecticut 06520

Child Welfare League of America, Inc.
44 East 23rd Street
New York, N.Y. 10010

Children's Bureau
United States Department of Health, Education
   and Welfare
Washington, D.C.

Council for Exceptional Children
1411 Jefferson Davis Highway
Arlington, Virginia 22202

Epilepsy Foundation of America
1828 "L" Street NW
Washington, D.C. 20036

Gifted Child Society, Inc.
59 Glen Gray Road
Oakland, New Jersey 07436

Institute for the Study of Mental Retardation
   and Related Disabilities
130 South First
University of Michigan
Ann Arbor, Michigan 48108

International Association for the Scientific Study
   of Mental Deficiency
Ellen Horn, AAMD
5201 Connecticut Avenue NW
Washington, D.C. 20015

International League of Societies for the Mentally
   Handicapped
Rue Forestiere 12
Brussels, Belgium

Joseph P. Kennedy, Jr. Foundation
1701 K Street NW
Washington, D.C. 20006

League for Emotionally Disturbed Children
171 Madison Avenue
New York, N.Y.

Muscular Dystrophy Associations of America
1790 Broadway
New York, N.Y. 10019

National Aid to the Visually Handicapped
3201 Balboa Street
San Francisco, California 94121

National Association of Coordinators of State
   Programs for the Mentally Retarded
2001 Jefferson Davis Highway
Arlington, Virginia 22202

National Association of Hearing and Speech
   Agencies
919 18th Street NW
Washington, D.C. 20006

National Association for Creative Children and
   Adults
8080 Springvalley Drive
Cincinnati, Ohio 45236
(Mrs. Ann F. Isaacs, Executive Director)

National Association for Retarded Children
420 Lexington Avenue
New York, N.Y.

National Association for Retarded Citizens
2709 Avenue E East
Arlington, Texas 76010

National Children's Rehabilitation Center
P.O. Box 1260
Leesburg, Virginia

National Association for the Visually Handicapped
3201 Balboa Street
San Francisco, California 94121

National Association of the Deaf
814 Thayer Avenue
Silver Spring, Maryland 20910

National Cystic Fibrosis Foundation
3379 Peachtree Road NE
Atlanta, Georgia 30326

National Easter Seal Society for Crippled Children
   and Adults
2023 W. Ogden Avenue
Chicago, Illinois 60612

National Federation of the Blind
218 Randolph Hotel
Des Moines, Iowa 50309

National Paraplegia Foundation
333 N. Michigan Avenue
Chicago, Illinois 60601

National Society for Autistic Children
621 Central Avenue
Albany, N.Y. 12206

National Society for Prevention of Blindness, Inc.
79 Madison Avenue
New York, N.Y. 10016

Orton Society, Inc.
8415 Bellona Lane
Baltimore, Maryland 21204

President's Committee on Mental Retardation
Regional Office Building #3
7th and D Streets SW
Room 2614
Washington, D.C. 20201

United Cerebral Palsy Associations
66 E 34th Street
New York, N.Y. 10016

SPECIAL EDUCATION SERIES

- ● Autism
- * ● Behavior Modification
- Biological Bases of Learning Disabilities
- Brain Impairments
- Career and Vocational Education
- Child Abuse
- Child Psychology
- Child Development
- Cognitive and Communication Skills
- Creative Arts
- Curriculum and Materials
- * ● Deaf Education
- Developmental Disabilities
- * ● Diagnosis and Placement
- Down's Syndrome
- ● Dyslexia
- Early Learning
- Educational Technology
- * ● Emotional and Behavioral Disorders
- Exceptional Parents
- * ● Gifted Education
- Hyperactivity

- ● Individualized Education Programs
- * ● Learning Disabilities
- Learning Theory
- ● Mainstreaming
- * ● Mental Retardation
- Multiple Handicapped Education
- Occupational Therapy
- * ● Physically Handicapped Education
- Pre-School and Day Care Education
- * ● Psychology of Exceptional Children
- Reading Skill Development
- Research and Development
- * ● Severely and Profoundly Handicapped Education
- Severe Mental Retardation
- Sex Education for the Retarded
- Slow Learner Education
- Social Learning
- * ● Special Education
- * ● Speech and Hearing
- * ● Visually Handicapped Education

● Published Titles   • Major Course Areas

Exceptional Children:
A Reference Book

An updated and welcome resource for educators and librarians.

COMMENTS PLEASE:

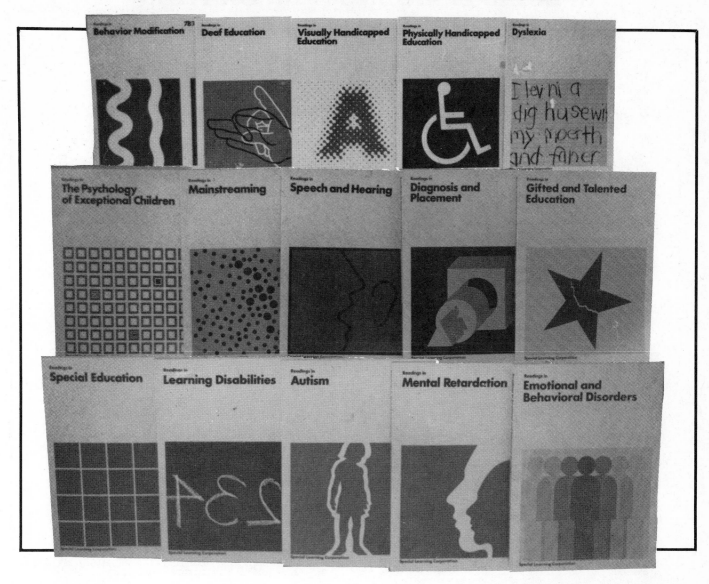

SPECIAL LEARNING CORPORATION

42 Boston Post Rd.

Guilford, Conn. 06437

SPECIAL LEARNING CORPORATION
COMMENTS PLEASE:

Does this book fit your course of study?

Why? (Why not?)

Is this book useable for other courses of study? Please list.

What other areas would you like us to publish in using this format?

What type of exceptional child are you interested in learning more about?

Would you use this as a basic text?

How many students are enrolled in these course areas?

_____Special Education _____Mental Retardation _____Psychology _____Emotional Disorders

_____Exceptional Children _____Learning Disabilities Other _____

Do you want to be sent a copy of our elementary student materials catalog?

Do you want a copy of our college catalog?

Would you like a copy of our next edition? ☐ yes ☐ no

Are you a ☐ student or an ☐ instructor?

Your name _____ school _____

Term used _____ Date _____

address _____

city _____ state _____ zip _____

telephone number _____

CUT HERE ● SEAL AND MAIL

I/E